100
Wei   Weiss, Paul

           First considera-
           tions

WITH COMMENTS BY

ABNER SHIMONY

RICHARD T. De GEORGE

RICHARD RORTY

ROBERT NEVILLE

ANDREW J. RECK

R. M. MARTIN

PAUL WEISS

First Considerations

An Examination of **PHILOSOPHICAL EVIDENCE**

SOUTHERN ILLINOIS UNIVERSITY PRESS

Carbondale and Edwardsville

FEFFER & SIMONS, INC.

London and Amsterdam

Library of Congress Cataloging in Publication Data

Weiss, Paul, 1901-
  First considerations.

  Includes indexes.
  1. Philosophy. 2. Evidence. 3. Reality.
4. Methodology. I. Title.
B53.W387   100   77-23242
ISBN 0-8093-0797-9

158623

BOOKS *by Paul Weiss*

BEYOND ALL APPEARANCES *(1974)*
CINEMATICS *(1975)*
FIRST CONSIDERATIONS *(1977)*
THE GOD WE SEEK *(1964)*
HISTORY: WRITTEN AND LIVED *(1962)*
THE MAKING OF MEN *(1967)*
MAN'S FREEDOM *(1950)*
MODES OF BEING *(1958)*
NATURE AND MAN *(1947)*
NINE BASIC ARTS *(1961)*
OUR PUBLIC LIFE *(1959)*
PHILOSOPHY IN PROCESS, *Vol. 1: 1955–1960 (1966)*
PHILOSOPHY IN PROCESS, *Vol. 2: 1960–1964 (1966)*
PHILOSOPHY IN PROCESS, *Vol. 3: 1964 (1968)*
PHILOSOPHY IN PROCESS, *Vol. 4: 1964–1965 (1969)*
PHILOSOPHY IN PROCESS, *Vol. 5: 1965–1968 (1971)*
PHILOSOPHY IN PROCESS, *Vol. 6: 1968–1971 (1975)*
PHILOSOPHY IN PROCESS, *Vol. 7: 1975–1976 (forthcoming)*
REALITY *(1938)*
RELIGION AND ART *(1963)*
RIGHT AND WRONG: *A Philosophical Dialogue Between Father and Son,*
    with Jonathan Weiss (1967)
SPORT: *A Philosophic Inquiry (1969)*
YOU, I, AND THE OTHERS *(forthcoming)*
THE WORLD OF ART *(1961)*

PRINCIPAL CONTRIBUTIONS *by Paul Weiss*

AMERICAN PHILOSOPHERS AT WORK, *edited by Sidney Hook (1956)*
AMERICAN PHILOSOPHY TODAY AND TOMORROW, *edited by H. M. Kallen and*
    Sidney Hook (1935)
THE CONCEPT OF ORDER, *edited by Paul Kuntz (1968)*
CONTEMPORARY AMERICAN PHILOSOPHY, *edited by John E. Smith (1970)*
DESIGN AND AESTHETICS OF WOOD, *edited by Eric A. Anderson and George*
    F. Earl (1972)

Determinism and Freedom, *edited by Sidney Hook (1958)*

The Dimensions of Job, *edited by Nahum N. Glatzer (1969)*

Dimensions of Mind: A Symposium, *edited by Sidney Hook (1960)*

Evolution in Perspective, *edited by G. Schuster and G. Thorson (1971)*

The Future of Metaphysics, *edited by Robert Wood (1970)*

Human Values and Economic Policy: Proceedings, *edited by Sidney Hook (1967)*

Law and Philosophy, *edited by Sidney Hook (1964)*

Mid/Twentieth Century American Philosophy, *edited by Peter A. Bertocci (1974)*

Moments of Personal Discovery, *edited by R. M. MacIver (1952)*

Moral Principles in Action, *edited by R. Anshen (1952)*

Perspectives on Peirce, *edited by R. Bernstein (1965)*

Philosophical Essays for A. N. Whitehead, *edited by O. Lee (1936)*

Philosophical Interrogations, *edited by S. and B. Rome (1964)*

Philosophy and History, *edited by Sidney Hook (1963)*

The Relevance of Whitehead, *edited by I. Leclerc (1961)*

Science, Philosophy, and Religion: Proceedings *(1941–)*

Studies in the Philosophy of Charles Sanders Peirce, *edited by C. P. Wiener and F. H. Young (1952)*

EDITED WORKS *by Paul Weiss*

Collected Papers of Charles Sanders Peirce (six volumes), *editor, with Charles Hartshorne (1931–35)*

To My Critics

CONTENTS

PREFACE

FIRST PHILOSOPHY is primarily concerned with principles presupposed by what is known, and with the God it takes to be presupposed by whatever else there be. More often than not, it is pursued by men who are rationalistic in temper and theological in orientation. But a rationalism reflects only one of a number of legitimate, partial attitudes; a God may be but one of a number of finalities.

An adequate account encompasses what is usually divided among the separate enterprises of ontology, metaphysics, and cosmology, where the first is occupied with what is real, the second with what is beyond the reach of empirical agencies, and the third with the interplay of actualities under universal, objectively imposed conditions. The principles for such a study are the concern of this work.

Issues close to those here examined have been dealt with by me on a number of occasions, and the results reformulated many times. Almost every topic was restated and the results judged and sometimes rejected, after I had achieved both a psychological and a reflective distance from it—usually years later. The present study exhibits another fresh effort. This time, though, I have tried to be even more severely critical than I had previously been. As a result, this is perhaps my best and last attempt to understand what it is that we daily confront, the evidences this provides of final realities, and the process by which one can move from what everyone knows to what everyone should understand.

The musculature of a systematic account is here exposed. It lacks flesh and the attraction that flesh provides. In compensation, it enables one to discover lesions and weaknesses that otherwise might not be easily discerned. Its primary stress is on the transition from appearances and actualities to ultimate, persistent, conditioning realities—finalities. It can be said, therefore, to supplement *Beyond All Appearances,* which was primarily occupied with an account of appearances and the way these led to actualities. Though that work also concerned itself with the adventure of reaching the finalities, it did not do so at length or in detail. That defect is here remedied. An earlier work, *Modes of Being,* was devoted in good part to an examination of the finalities themselves and their bearing on one another. With obvious modifications, exposed in the reflections of later years, that work can be taken to supplement what is here presented.

An ideal summary of what I have thought over these years would require the use of the present book as a nucleus and a guide, helping to determine what was worth preserving in the others. Were this done, the result would perhaps approximate a single, satisfactory work in philosophy. But the present adventure is pursued in independence of my previous efforts; its outcome is to be judged without reference to what has already been attempted.

There is much in my other writings on appearances, actualities, and finalities that I here do not even touch upon and which, I think, can still withstand criticism. But where the discussions overlap, what is here said, I believe, is better stated and more adequately justified than I had been able to manage before. In any case, at each critical juncture I have tried to exhibit both the grounds and warrant for what is being claimed. To make it easier for others to join in the speculative struggle that characterizes the whole, I have introduced it by means of a quasi autobiography. This starts where all of us initially are, and progresses through a series of reflections dealing with more and more basic questions, to end finally where the work itself properly begins.

I have asked a number of philosophers, whom I did not expect would agree with me, to subject this work to careful scrutiny, and to give me the privilege of responding to their remorseless criticism. Some were not interested. Of those who wished to see the manuscript only a few seem to have read it, and fewer still have given me the benefit of their judgment. It is quite possible that the issues that have been raised by those who have answered are not too far from those which would have been dealt with by the others. Perhaps it does not matter. Schools come and go, and the more surely their members cut themselves off from problems that are at the root of theirs, the less significant is a consideration of what they have to urge. I am grateful to those who have given me an opportunity to clarify and expand on issues which apparently would otherwise have remained more obscure than they need be. Their observations and my replies are the substance of the second part of this work.

For the last half dozen years, I have had the privilege of discussing with my colleagues many philosophic issues, a good number of which are germane to the present work. I can not imagine how an inquiry could have had a more challenging and desirable accompaniment. I am most grateful to Jude Dougherty for having made this possible.

PAUL WEISS

Washington, D.C.

July 1976

1 / First Considerations

*

TENTATIVE PROBINGS

1 QUITE EARLY IN LIFE I learned the ways of many things. I mastered the use of spoon, fork, and knife, the intricacies of dressing, and the peculiarities of lock and key. Tentative, timid experiments, worked through by trial and error, pieced out with occasional reports, many admonitions, and half-heeded advice, soon taught me that stoves and stairs, dogs, streets, and cars were to be approached with caution. I also somehow learned to master common speech well enough to make it possible to communicate my most pressing needs, without undue difficulty. But even today, almost seventy years later, I am again and again taken by surprise. Too often I am baffled and confused. I am not always sure just what I should say or do to maximize my advantages, to minimize hurt to myself or others, or to live undisturbed. At almost every moment I encounter details and developments I had not expected. Some of the most familiar objects—my pen, my glasses, my telephone—at times set problems for me I can not readily solve. Still, for the most part, I have adjusted fairly well to the things I come across in daily life.

Rarely am I embarrassed or irritated by my lack of knowledge of what is to be publicly said or done. I am not usually in need of help, and what help I need I usually obtain. I seem to have most of the responses and habits that are needed to enable me to live unreflectingly and unselfconsciously, without undue discomfort or pain, and without much risk of being blocked or disdained.

2 I am not now and never have been as sure-footed in my dealings with people as I am in my dealings with familiar objects. I have always had some difficulty in avoiding struggles with my brothers, playmates, and schoolmates. Again and again my mother had to direct and redirect me. I was scolded, I was advised, I had to be reassured. Sometimes I was punished. Mother, father, teachers, brothers, friends, and, later, wife, children, and colleagues made evident to me that there were many things I should not have said or should not have done.

3 Today I am in possession of a rather large and useful set of rules, backed by warnings, modified by habits and beliefs. Some of those rules were passed on to me. Others I picked up in the course of observation and reading. Still others were distilled from what I

learned in daily living. This is one reason why I have managed to avoid having much difficulty or trouble with what I daily encounter.

4 Fairly well adjusted, there is still nothing on which I can completely count. Almost everyone expresses himself in ways I cannot always anticipate. Each seems to have some singular wants and values. I do not always know how others will speak or act.

5 One of the things I have also learned is that there is little in the story of my maturation which is not duplicated by others. Though I have known only a comparatively few men, and though my observations have been casual and often biased, I am confident that no one has fully mastered the ways of things, and none is perfectly adjusted to his fellowman.

6 Romantics, sceptics, and relativists, for different reasons, deny that I can warrantedly claim that everyone has experiences similar to mine. Let their contention—undemonstrated though it be—pass unchallenged for the moment. It still remains true that I believe that I, for one, have not fully grasped what else there is, what it does, and what it might do. Since I disagree with these other thinkers, they must allow that we both know that I am ignorant of some things.

7 I am confident that others, too, are ignorant of some things, for if they were not, they would have no future, or they would know it already. Also, there would be no past that had elapsed before they existed—or they would know the past without the help of an as yet unwritten, perfect history. In effect, they would be eternal and omniscient beings. But I was speaking of the kinds of men I have been able to encounter.

8 My adventures with things have led me to distance myself from them in thought and in fact, and yet to use them in some accord with what they promise and what I desire. I also maintain a distance from men as well. The distances I have from both are the outcome of an accumulation of many hardly noticed efforts to reach a position where losses in pleasure, power, status, or ease, for myself, and sometimes for them, are minimized and the gains maximized.

9 I do not attend to most things or to most men. Occasionally, some of them violently intrude into my life, challenging honor and strength, and perhaps survival. At times I am beset with a fear of what others think, or of what they might do. They make me aware that I am not always in full control of myself or of all the situations in which I find myself.

10 Among the men I daily encounter there are only a few in whom I am interested, or of whom I am forced to take account. But I do not find it easy to maintain a steady proper relation even to them. Sometimes I find that I am too remote, not sensitive enough to what they intend. Sometimes I find myself assuming an intimacy or familiarity far greater than that which they expect or will tolerate. Even my relations to those with whom I have built up strong bonds are not exactly what they should be if I, or they, or both of us are to prosper, or at least are never to get in one another's way.

11 I am aware of what is present, not as it in fact is, but as it appears to be, filtered through a multitude of hardly noticed suppositions. Only some of these suppositions are freshly forged by me. Created or acquired, the suppositions affect what I take to be the case. Both when I am distant and when I am close, I face other items, not as they are in fact but as they seem to be to me—this partly habituated, not too well-organized, somewhat conventionalized member of a half-deciphered world.

12 I do not want to give up the many habits and beliefs that have served me so well every day. Nor do I want to set aside the homely wisdom that I have so slowly learned. They enable me to remain more or less steadily in consonance with my fellowman, and to deal effectively with common things.

There will, I hope, be a time when I will be able to benefit from the systematic doubts of philosophers; if so, they will help me come to know what is certain and what is not. It may also be a time when I will be able to make use of the sweeping scepticism of the young; I will then be forced to be more alert to any unwarranted steps that I have taken and to question the unjustified conclusions to which I have come. But their doubts and questions have no role to play at present, for I am now seeking not some single truth on which I might pin a set of theses, nor something that cannot conceivably be denied, but a way of breaking through the particular barriers that now keep me in some accord, as well as in some disaccord with whatever things and men there be.

13 Doubts are reflective acts, but what I now want are practical guides for making theoretical discoveries. I would also like to free myself from the conventional and somewhat arbitrary limits within which I normally think and act. But, unlike the doubting philosophers and the impatient young, I want both to know and to pass through these limits, and not merely to set them aside.

14 When I gradually come out of a deep sleep, when I relax at the beach and let my eyes roam idly over the slowly breaking waves, or when light music sweeps over me, I come close to having a pure, aesthetic experience. For a while I lose myself in a variegated panorama, indefinite in magnitude. No particular objects are there distinguished, and I cease to be aware of myself standing in contrast with anything. The arbitrary limits with which I daily live are left behind. When I join in a joyful celebration or excitedly engage in team play, I sometimes experience a similar loss of self. Strong fear brings me to a nuanced but undivided immediacy by still another route. In these and others ways I esape from classifications and suppositions which I may have introduced, and which, in any case, may have no warrant in fact.

15 The more closely and persistently I approximate the state where I lose myself and all else within an undifferentiated experiencing, the more closely do I seem to move toward that unconceptualizable ultimate of which many Eastern and Western mystics speak. Or do I, instead, approximate the condition of a sensitive oyster when water of differing temperatures seeps in and out of its shell? I am not sure. But I do know that though I may move toward either state I cannot now attain it.

I have too many surfacing needs and vagrant thoughts to be able to lose myself in immediacy for long. I discriminate and set myself in contrast with other men and things. Thought and action conspire to keep me from sinking into a state of simple experiencing, without a sense of self or other. I can let myself live for only a short while with an unfocussed mass of qualities and movements, or with some singular unarticulated reality at the base of all that I know. Inevitably, I make distinctions. And it is wise that I do so. Otherwise nothing will be dwelt upon, remembered, expected, or understood.

16 I see that it is desirable to avoid making additions to the world on behalf of social stability and effective practice if they veil from me what is there in fact. I must try to attend to what is more than the product of habit and need. I also know that I should not rest content with the distinctions that daily force themselves on my attention if I am not sure just how basic they are, or even whether or not they are objective, expressing more than some interest of mine. But I don't want to abandon all I think I know as a price for getting to what may prove to be of little worth.

My hesitation would not surprise mystics and others who seek to become one with a One that is ultimately real. They say that I must give up this insistence on myself and my little store of minor truths, and submit to the teachings of those who have already reached what is ultimate and perfecting. The final goal, they insist, is not to be achieved unless I free myself from finite involvements. And this, they go on to say, requires more than a simple relaxing, feeling, or celebrating. A long and arduous but worthwhile self-disciplining lies before me if I am to reach what is unsullied by human and societal additions.

I am not confident that I can carry out such a program, nor am I sure where it will take me. I am willing to make a great effort, but I do not see how I could possibly get to what is real if that requires me to sacrifice self, knowledge, practice, society, and the pursuit of the arts, sciences, history, reason, and reasoning.

17 A program that requires me to annihilate my familiar self, the familiar world, and what has been learned over the course of civilization can at best lead me to only a part of what is real. I know that some of my thoughts and desires have led me into saying and doing foolish things, but that is not enough to make imperative the extinguishing of all my thinking and wanting. Rather than give up so much that seems worth retaining, I will first try to find other ways of getting to what is apart from me and society.

18 My thoughts introduce divisions and interpretations into what I face. They add personal notes, and tempt me to occupy myself with sterile abstractions. One way of avoiding these undesirable consequences is for me to withdraw within myself to the point where no concepts are entertained or used. Whatever I deal with from that position could well be what is objectively real, particularly if I then find myself living in considerable consonance with it.

By getting rid of all thinking, I get rid of the distortions that concepts involve—but at the same time I also lose what they enable me to know. I may then be able to live in harmony with what else there is, but unless I also think, I will not understand what it is with which I have made peace. Nor will I have anything I can use in inference, or as a base on which I can build with care. At best, I will merely allow one satisfying moment to give way to another.

19 I often live emotionally when I forego thought. But my emotions are not always in perfect consonance with what I confront. Sometimes they make me miscalculate, and leave me frustrated and bewildered.

Instead of giving up the use of all concepts for an unreflecting emotional life, it seems better to keep on thinking, but to make use only of highly general, steady ideas, referring to what is to be found everywhere and always. In that way I can avoid intruding personal and momentary elements into what I confront. Unfortunately, the range of applicability of an idea offers no guarantee that it is unbiased, unaffected by alien meanings and values. The greater its range, the more items it might misconstrue. Nothing is gained by my accepting more general ideas if they are not more trustworthy than the more limited ones I have already found wanting.

20 Detachment allows me to remain calm, to observe with care and at ease. If I can maintain myself at a distance from the world, perhaps I can keep the intrusions of self and society to a minimum. Perhaps if I do not care whether or not I am pleased or pained, satisfied or dissatisfied, I may be able to discern what is real.

Attending to what is before me in the most detached manner possible does not, unfortunately, enable me to know the difference between what holds only for that moment and what is true at other times as well. I will not yet know whether or not what I discern will remain, or remain unchanged the moment I no longer attend to it.

21 I know that sometimes I introduce considerations that are not in harmony with what is there in fact. I think there is no step before me and I stumble; I seem to hear a sound in the kitchen but my friends are talking in the living room; I think I have enough change but I have too little. These errors are expressed in the course of daily living. I correct them in passing, without abrogating the differences separating me from other things. But I do not yet have any assurance that I have not left untouched many similar errors which I have had no occasion to test or correct.

22 No empirical investigations or observations can help me learn if there is anything that holds everywhere and always. Empirical knowledge is particulate. If it covers wide territory, it is through the agency of extrapolations and generalizations. Are these more than hopeful guesses, or at best empirically encountered particulars shorn of their distinction from one another?

23 To know if there is anything that holds everywhere, and what its nature might be, I must refuse to immerse myself completely in what I confront, and yet refuse to withdraw wholly into myself; I must also refuse to attend solely to local and transient patterns or to take a stand with conventional truths. There is neither truth nor error if there is not something that is defiantly in accord with the one and in disaccord with the other.

24 When I err I am defied. Indeed, it is the defiance that makes me aware that I am in error.

An error is a claim defied. To know I am mistaken is to be aware that there is something that defies me. I correct my claim in the effort to be in better accord with what is there. I then credit what defied me with the power to accommodate the resultant claim to know it.

When I know I err, I know that there is more to what I confront than what I focus on, remark, or articulate. When I correct the error, though, I continue to be defied. My correction evidently does not destroy all defiance; instead, it respects and takes account of a nuclear defiance which persists whether I claim truly or falsely.

25 Let what I face be anything at all. It exhibits a defiance in opposition to me. It also seems to oppose others and, with them, to oppose a background.

Might not this triple fact express nothing more than my decision to face the world in a special but avoidable manner? After all, if I take up a position between the extreme of immersing myself in experience and retreating within myself, it is one that might well be marred by personal notes. Let it be so. No matter what I do and what I add, I always contrast with some items which contrast with others and with a larger undifferentiated background. The transient and even questionable distinctions I make specify more universal, stable ones distinguishing me, what I attend to, other objects, and a background.

26 These distinctions, fixed and universal though they may be, might they not conceivably be just boundary lines within which different kinds of roles—private awareness, the insistence of distinct objects, and the persistence of background—are carried out? Or might they not reflect controls which affect the operation of what takes place within their confines? Perhaps. But, for the moment, the matter is of little importance. It is enough for me now that the distinctions are not idle.

27 Fixed, universal distinctions could conceivably have been introduced by me in the act of attending. My understanding, even from a position which does not allow for the intrusion of particular concerns and interests, could itself be the cause of whatever distinctions are noted. I would then be constitutive of what was acknowledged. The fact that I accept only what is general and fixed does not suffice to show that I did not myself create these. If I did, though, it would be in the guise of 'anyone', as a knower who is like every other.

28 Were I 'anyone', the source of what is universal and fixed, what is said of objects in relation to a subject and of those objects in relation to a background will then have to do, not with realities as they exist by themselves, but with them as modified by a knower in general. What I individually know will be subject to conditions which all acts of attention and knowledge, my own or any other's, will illustrate.

29 I am a distinct particular reality. But as an 'anyone', indistinguishable from any other, I am at best a subject in general, who might not know anything in particular.

30 A particular subject, who knows particular things, is able to attend to them as present in a way they may not be present to others. If I alter what I confront, I may do so in a distinctive way, reflecting my peculiar bias and present position. At the very least, I see it from this position backed by an accumulation of experiences peculiar to me.

31 A particular subject is not made distinct from what it knows by the action of another subject. If it were, the latter would have to be distinguished by still another subject, and so on without end. Nor can the distinction between a particular subject and object be supposed to be the outcome of the act of that subject, without once again forcing one back over an infinite regress.

32 Were there no subjects, there would be no objects. Were there no objects, there would be no subjects. When one is present, so is the other, and then necessarily in opposition to one another. Their distinction is necessary and presupposes their presence. There could, though, be entities not faced by any subject.

33 It is conceivable that the distinction between subject and object might be the outcome of an act of self-differentiation. To begin with, of course, there would then be no subjects or objects. Instead, a primal reality would have to set a part of itself in opposition to itself and there produce a state where a particular subject and an object were set in opposition to one another. That outcome, though it yields a genuine oppositional subject and object, does not yield evidence of

9

the supposed prior self-differentiation of a primary reality into these two parts. The success of the operation precludes that presumed primal reality from being known. Since I have to begin and end with the fact of opposition, the supposition is only a fancy whose realization makes no difference to anything I in fact know.

34 There are objects in the foreground for me now. They stand away from all others. Might they not, apart from me, sink back into the background? If so, that background would still be something *for* me. It would so far not be constituted by me, but would maintain itself in opposition to me. And so it would remain, as long as I functioned as a subject.

35 If objects or background are only so far as they are correlative with me, with my vanishing they would also vanish. But objects or background might have different natures and functionings from what they had when they were there for me. That possibility is eliminated if I can know what holds even when I am no longer present.

36 When I attend to anything, I set it within a boundary. The boundary turns it into an object which is there for me, setting it apart from other objects and the background.

The boundaries that I introduce make that to which I attend be objects *for* me. The objects are not then controlled by the boundaries. They defy the boundaries, resisting and retreating before them, for those boundaries are only expressions of me.

What is within the boundaries that I introduce is a doubly oriented content. It is confined within the boundaries, turning it into an acknowledged object. At the same time, it is distinct and independent of those boundaries, defiant of them and me. Confined, it is an object of attention; independent, it is objective, something not yet understood or controlled.

That on which I focus is confined within the boundaries I introduce, thereby enabling me to have it as an object for me. But it also escapes conditioning by those boundaries, defying me, whether I know truly or falsely. I am aware of the fact that the boundaries I introduce, though not necessarily distortive, are not integral to it. Were it to escape completely all connection with the boundaries I impose, I would not be able to know it.

37 An object may have boundaries which I did not impose. Its boundaries and the ones I contribute, could coincide. When this occurs my knowledge is of an object as it is apart from me. I have such knowledge whenever I face a number of items that retreat from the boundaries I introduce while I maintain touch with them as they continue to be separate one from the other within the limits marked out by those boundaries.

38 No matter how precise and accurate the knowledge I obtain, no matter how confident I am of my claim that such and such are the limits within which this or that item exists apart from me, I never eliminate the possibility of having made an error. This or that item could in fact vanish, or be absorbed within the background as soon as I cease to attend to it. There is nothing of which I am sure that it will continue to be.

39 I know that what defies me so far maintains itself apart from me. It can not therefore be I who enables it to be a distinct item. And I know that just because I no longer attend to it, it does not necessarily cease to be or fail to stand away from the background.

40 It surely is conceivable that all separations are overcome on some deep level where even I become united with all else in a single undivided ultimate reality. I have now no way of knowing whether or not this is the case. What I do know is that there are distinctions not made by me, and which divide me from particular entities, and these from one another and what is beyond them all. If they and their background are creations by me or something else, I nevertheless cannot always avoid facing them as apart from one another and from myself.

41 I know that the objects to which I attend contrast with a background. This is an indefinitely large, diffuse panorama standing away from me and the objects to which I attend. The content of that background changes as I focus now on this and then on that object. What I would now like to know is whether or not there is more in the universe than myself, objects, and that background.

42 The objects I face are maintained apart from me, in independence of my boundaries and my judgments. They resist me, and pull away from the boundaries I impose; they change and function in ways which do not fully accord with what is controlled by the boundaries. Either they have a core which is independent of me, or they are the products of entities which are free of the limitations characteristic of objects.

43 So far as it is I who affect them, objects are subjectified appearances.

44 Left over when my contributions are abstracted from are objective appearances. What provides a locus and support for these are 'actualities'. What conditions all objective appearances, and all actualities as well, are 'finalities'.

45 An object exists only so far as it is in relation to a subject and a background. Apart from these, it is an objective appearance, the product of the interplay of actualities and finalities.

46 Objects and background, and any realities which are presupposed by the one and are within or behind the other, could all conceivably be expressions of some more fundamental reality. But I can not know if this is so unless I am able to extricate evidence of such a reality from appearances or from the actualities that remain after I set aside what has affected them.

47 It is not possible for me to escape from this task by taking refuge in my daily outlook. Since I can criticize my society, and since there are scientists, poets, and religious men and mystics who affirm what commonplace men do not, I can not confidently assert that my society and common sense provide that position from which all final questions can be raised or answered.

48 Mathematics, logic, and science have a greater range than my daily outlook. They seem to show what things are in fact and not what they have been made to be for a society of men. The existence of a plurality of geometries, alternative logics, and conflicting scientific interpretations of the same facts, however, closes out this possibility for me. And if it did not, there would still be the fact that there are realities known through other agencies—art and history, for example.

49 Mathematics, logic, science, art, and history are all specialized enterprises. Each makes assumptions the others do not. To know what is, I must engage in a more neutral and better based activity. This is systematic, philosophic inquiry, requiring metaphysical thinking.

50 When I realize that a background is for a foreground, and conversely, and that what is to the fore is a multiplicity of objects, constantly changing in membership, that some of its members are interlocked, that I can confront the selfsame entity from different positions, and that objects are relative to subjects, I become aware that the absence of subjects still leaves something defiant—either objective appearances constituted by realities, or the realities themselves.

Why am I so sure that even when it sinks into the background, something in it or pertinent to it continues to be distinct, and defiant of me and others? Is this not because I am also aware, dim though that awareness be, of an actuality inseparable from the object?

Why am I so sure that even while something is maintained apart from me and everything else that it is also related to me and everything else? Is this not because I am also aware, dim though that awareness be, of the effectiveness of final conditions governing everything?

If this is so, I now know that some widespread views about philosophy, and particularly about its pivotal enterprise, metaphysics, are not tenable.

51 Those who maintain that metaphysics is impossible because thoughts, knowledge, language, and inquiries are unavoidably oriented toward the empirical, transitory, and sensible, unduly limit thinking, knowledge, language, and inquiry. I can make sense of much more than these critics allow, for at the very least I am aware that appearances occur together, and thus are subject to conditions they themselves do not provide. I also know that if their actualities, while maintaining themselves, are interrelated, those realities must be conditioned together.

52 Those who maintain that metaphysics is impossible on the ground that its concern is with conditions but that those conditions are empty or idle, overlook the fact that the conditions convert independent entities into related ones, and that they do so no matter what the nature of those entities be. Conditions are not bare forms but, at the very least, governing, and empowered.

53 Metaphysics can not properly stop with a purported description of the pervasive features of experience or of language. It is not possible to know that there are such features without knowing that there is a power capable of making them present everywhere, and therefore able to make them not only be pervasive but also unavoidable—necessarily pervasive, always.

54 Whatever the ultimate realities be, they can not all be generalized or magnified forms of particulars, for some persist and insist on themselves in opposition to these.

55 What makes a difference to particulars—appearances or actualities—is not to be found by abstracting facets from those particulars. That could leave one with what is integral to the particulars, but made inert. One must instead distinguish what is not native to the particulars and trace this back to its source.

56 If I try to leap beyond what I confront, I leap I know not where. If I try to avoid all conceptualization so as to intuit what is confronted, I will perhaps feel it and share in it, but I will not know what it is. If, instead, I depend on revelation, or on the achievement of some special state of mind, I will not know whether or not I am being deceived. Nor will I know just what it is I then find.

57 I can not use the method of analogy, for this fails just where I am most in need of help—when I wish to move from particulars and their background to the source of their ultimate conditions, that is, to finalities. Analogy requires some likeness between a beginning and an ending; but particulars are conditioned and finite, finalities are governing and encompassing.

58 I can not make use of a Platonic or Hegelian dialectic to lead me inescapably from shadows or abstract factors to substantial, noble, unlimited realities (even if the shadows and factors are thin versions of the realities at which the dialectic is to arrive), for I must first locate those shadows and factors in realities other than themselves. Since the Platonists and the Hegelians reject actualities as unreal or as incapable of maintaining themselves in opposition to the final realities, they have nothing left but an all-powerful reality. Why did this allow anything else to be? Why does it take time to go from the beginning of the dialectic to the end?

59 My appreciations, acknowledgments, hypotheses, boundings, and evaluations might introduce irrelevant items, or might rearrange what is confronted. My judgments could be wrong. If I am to correct them I must attend to what is present. Though I am the author of the connections my judgments introduce, my corrections depend on the fact that I am not the creator of the items that are connected, or of all their connections.

60 But, surely, in groupings and classifications, use of language, practice, and evaluations, I impose controlling unities? Do I not then yield to what is nevertheless my own creation?

Sometimes items, as governed by my conditions, are also produced by me, for example, in poetry or in an act of self-expression. These are to be distinguished from what an indifferent nature produces, and from what is operative everywhere. In both cases, so far as items oppose the conditions I introduce, they stand away from them.

61 Just as the conditions I impose in limited situations are themselves, before they have been imposed, purer and have a greater range than they have as applied, so they in turn may be limited forms of much more basic, more extensively operative powers. Not only are the rules of my language special cases of the rules that govern all languages, but these in turn instance still more general and more widely applicable ways of ordering items. Were this not so, it would not be correct to say that there are many languages, and that these all illustrate a common character.

62 I know the contributions I make in limited situations when I know what there defies me. And I know what there defies me when my contributions, despite their limited range, match conditions which operate apart from me. That there are such objectively operating conditions I know when I encounter them not only here but also elsewhere.

63 With the students of analogy and dialectic, I see that it is wise to move slowly, cautiously, methodically. But first I must make sure of my beginning. This can not be with actualities, since I have to arrive at these by getting beyond the appearances which I face when I attend. Nor can the beginning be with what is entirely cut off from actualities, without making appearances be appearances of nothing, and therefore either illusions or irreducible realities. But illusions presuppose that I, at least, am real enough to be deceived, and therefore face what is real enough to present me with what I do not want, while irreducible realities directly confronted leave me knowing ultimates without error—in effect, actualities which never appear.

64 I think I can now see where a systematic investigation must begin, and can anticipate some of its main contentions. And I think I can also see the kind of defense that is to be made on behalf of its claims.

a) Subjectified appearances result from a change in perceptual conditions, from a blurring of distinctions, or from an intrusion of personal and social notes. When perception, awareness, personal and social notes are set aside, what is left over are still other appearances, objective appearances, the result of the interplay of exhibitions by distinct realities.

b) Individual men often make a difference to what they confront, intruding their interests, beliefs, purposes, and experiences. A number of them, particularly when sharing in the same tradition, using similar tools, and speaking the same language, often face appearances which differ from those faced by men in another group having a different tradition, practice, and language.

Personal and social conditions contribute to the constitution of confronted subjectified appearances. If these appearances were wholly constituted by individuals or by members of groups—or more generally, by knowers or consciousnesses of limited scope and with special biases—there would be nothing which all men could acknowledge, except by a happy coincidence.

If, instead, individuals and groups simply overlaid actualities with irrelevant additions, the result would be just hidden actualities. The addition could then imaginatively be undone to reveal what was there, unambiguously and without error. But we know that we can not do this.

c) Objective appearances are the products of counteracting realities, one of which is maximally effective and supportive, with the other less intensive but still contributive. Were there no appearances, there would at best be a single entity and nothing, therefore, which it could confront or which could confront it; a number of realities, each wholly by itself and therefore unreachable from the position of any others; something real which was merely altered by others; something completely passive able to be entirely assimilated by a reality, leaving nothing over; a product of realities which maintained itself, and did not belong to either; or realities which made equal contributions to the constitution of a product and thereby precluded the crediting of the product primarily to one of those realities. There are appearances because at least two realities, differing in effectiveness act on one another. Together they constitute a distinctive appearance of the dominant reality.

d) Since an Aristotelian form is imposed on passive matter, simply enhancing it, the form does not turn the matter into an appearance. Since a Kantian category gives a passive manifold a role and meaning, the manifold fills out the category, but does not produce an appearance of it, for it, or of the manifold itself. Interplaying realities produce appearances only when their product, while distinct, remains inseparable from and dependent on them.

1 5

e) Individuals and society change objective appearances into subjectified ones. By subtracting what perception and social outlooks contribute to what one confronts, one arrives not at an actuality but at its objective appearance.

f) Personal and social notes can be abstracted from, and sometimes what they overlay can be discerned. This which is left over might conceivably, at least in part, be constituted by something added by every consciousness or knower. If so, the result would vanish with a loss of consciousness. But, apart from all awareness by men or other living beings, actualities exhibit themselves in opposition to one another under common conditions. The objective appearances which result are preconditions for perception and other modes of experiential confrontation.

g) Some objective appearances form sets whose members come and go, while the object to which they are accredited remains self-same. In the absence of such an object a number of appearances—its shape and weight or color—would either be ultimates, or would belong to distinct objects. If ultimate, they would be realities, not appearances. If they belonged to different objects, at least one of the constituents of each appearance would have a unique source. There would be an 'apple-green' but nothing that was also apple-shaped or which could become red. Nothing would be able to change; nothing would act or be acted on.

h) A source of one of the constituents of an objective appearance may exhibit itself differently at different times, and therefore account for a difference amongst the appearances credited to it; or an exhibition may be countered by others originating at different places, and the differences amongst the appearances accounted for by the fact that an actuality is affected by other actualities in different ways; or a plurality of exhibitions, originating with different actualities, may be countered in a single common way to constitute a set of objective appearances, having at least the common trait of being together in the same domain.

i) Connected objective appearances can not be constituted solely by the interplay of exhibitions of different actualities. As merely interacting, the actualities would produce objective appearances, but those appearances would not necessarily have any relation to one another.

j) Both when they stand apart and when they interact, actualities produce exhibitions which are subject to common conditions. Those conditions are grounded in realities which contrast with any and all particulars. Because of those conditions, all objective appearances are able to be together.

k) Objective appearances can be known. Not only can one sometimes substract personal and social contributions and think of what remains over, but one can also note what both resists inclusion within our judgments and provides a test of the accuracy of those judgments.

l) Knowledge of objective appearances does not add another appearance to them. Instead of affecting the nature of objective appearances, knowledge enables them to be related to whatever else one acknowledges, entertains, believes, or knows. This gives the appearances new roles.

m) Personal and social notes are not present in objective appearances. Consequently, on being known, objective appearances could at most be affected by whatever constant conditions there be for knowing. Since appearances are inert, they would be altered by those conditions. But then we could never know what they were; what we said of them could never be known to be in error.

n) The presence and nature of the constituents of appearances—whether these appearances be subjectified or objective—are not discernible in them. Appearances are seamless, undivided, genuine products. One can not read off from the appearances the sources of their constituents.

o) We would be cut off from the sources of the constituents of appearances if those constituents did not continue to be connected with those sources. The exhibition of a reality is a continuum of intensities with a maximum at the reality, and with a stretch of ever weaker intensities, some of which function as constituents of an appearance.

p) An appearance has a depth to it. Between it and the reality to which it is to be credited is the exhibition in the role of a texture fringing the appearance. That texture, because continuous both with the constituent and the reality, enables one to know the nature of the constituent, and to pass beyond the appearance to the reality.

Though we can not read off the nature of an actuality by attending to its appearances, or find the constituents of an appearance by analysis, we can learn what an actuality is by moving continuously in depth, beginning at the texture.

To learn the nature of the other constituent in the appearance we must move in the opposite direction, through a condition, toward a finality, its source.

q) Objective appearances are subject to common conditions. The acknowledgment that an appearance is together with others is inseparable from the acknowledgment of those conditions. The conditions are continuous with less intensive interrelations of the appearances and with more intensive final realities.

r) It is possible to move experientially from a texture or condition toward an actuality or finality by a symbolizing act. One thereby participates in the actuality or finality.

Unlike conceptualization, symbolization is always involved with realities, since it begins with attenuations of them, and moves in depth. Unlike intuition, symbolization is precarious and needs guidance. Its success is tested by and, in turn, tests what is conceived when personal and social notes are subtracted.

s) By symbolization one penetrates into realities. Emotionally toned, symbolizing brings the initial content more and more under the control of the reality it enables one to move toward. There is no preassignable depth beyond which one then might not reach, though no one ever gets to a reality in its full concreteness, self-centered and apart from all else.

The proper, final terminus of symbolization is a constituent of an appearance, but denser, more unified, insistent, and independent of the confronted appearance with which the symbolization begins. What a reality is like can also be speculatively known by foregoing such a participation and reflecting on the difference between an objective appearance and what produces a constituent for it.

t) Each actuality stands apart from all others, and from all the finalities. It exhibits itself in a number of ways, each a continuum of lesser intensities.

Were there no actualities, there might be events. Events have no potentialities, no power, no ability to act or react. A world consisting of them is where nothing can be done, and therefore one in which there can be no work, no art, no politics, and no writing of books on process philosophy.

u) Each actuality is intruded on by finalities. They qualify it, thereby unifying it.

A qualification differs from an objective appearance in not being available for perception, or for the introduction of personal and social notes. It characterizes the entire actuality without annihilating the actuality as an independent, self-centered reality; the actuality in turn, specifies it and limits its range.

v) An actuality is given substantiality, being, intelligibility, extension, and value by the finalities. Since it is conceivable that it be one of these without also being the others, its different qualifications must evidence independently operative finalities.

w) By internalizing qualifications, actualities make themselves into epitomized instantiations of the finalities which are the sources of those qualifications. The actualities are then able to function independently of that which they instance.

x) Actualities are of different grades depending on what kinds of qualifications they internalize. All internalize the qualification produced by the finality, Substance. But only man is able to internalize the qualifications which originate with all the finalities. Consequently, he is at once one among the substances that there are, and is an actuality with a privacy that is richer than that of any other.

y) Each actuality is qualified by all the finalities. But it is not then necessarily related to the other actualities. Qualified actualities are not yet members of the same cosmos.

To be members of the same cosmos, the actualities, despite their independence of one another and of the finalities, must function in relation to one another. This is possible because the finalities not only qualify each, but govern them. Together the finalities form a single constant, defining the possible ways in which the actualities can be together as members of one cosmos.

z) Each finality is irreducible, self-centered, independent of the others. Each provides a controlling contextual constituent for all appearances. Each also controls the actualities, intruding on and qualifying each, and interrelating all of them.

Without finalities, there would be no objective appearances and, therefore, also no subjectified ones; nothing to interrelate objective appearances; nothing intruding on each actuality; nothing making them similarly qualified; and nothing making them into members of one cosmos.

65 The foregoing remarks are philosophical only in the way that a prospect or summary is like the work that is done to realize the one and to ground the other. It is therefore necessary to go beyond the point I now am—aware of some philosophic truths but without a systematic grasp of them. It seems wise, though, not to move on until I become a little clearer about the nature of philosophy, what it does, what it can do, and how it can proceed effectively and with surety.

*

THE TASK OF PHILOSOPHY

1 PHILOSOPHY IS NOT MATHEMATICS or science; it is more than logic or analysis. Whatever procedures are successful for these can not be confidently used to yield the results philosophy is to attain. Unfortunately, description, dissection, or the articulation of a private vision or insight are not viable alternatives, since they lead to the acceptance of what is doubtful. A worthy alternative to the procedures of mathematics, logic, and science is not provided by yielding to vagrant movements of the imagination, or by accepting the contingent presentations of experience. There is no alternative but to note the distinctions that are exhibited in the daily world, and to use them to begin a self-critical quest for what is real.

2 By foregoing criticism I allow myself to be easily betrayed into error and confusion. I leave too much to chance and conjecture, and, more likely than not, I will be led to overlook much that should have been considered. I will not know when an account is completed; not know what should be included; not learn whether or not questionable suppositions had been made; nor if and when prejudices had been introduced.

3 Were the outlook of ordinary men, the import of their daily discourse, or the evidence of experience entirely satisfactory, there would be no warrant for ignoring, denying, or changing them. Unfortunately, what is daily known is a partly inchoate, unsifted mixture of the sound and foolish, of the willful, arbitrary, and undeniable. We are all in danger of being betrayed by commonsense maxims and summaries, of being lulled by ordinary speech and established habits, and of being content with what has proven itself useful in practice.

4 Philosophers, like scientists and historians, must begin where all men initially are. And this is with the objective appearances. None can ever end with a warranted rejection of all that is found there, without thereby destroying the very ground which sustains their denials.

5 Commonsense views and practices could be set aside when they fail to cohere with what is maintained in some theoretical account. But the denial, with equal justification, could go in the opposite direction. In any case, no one has been so perpetually and thor-

oughly betrayed that he must set aside all that is daily known and claimed.

6 To justify a rejection of some commonsense acceptance on theoretical grounds alone, those grounds must be shown to illuminate and be satisfied by other portions of common sense. If they did not do this, what was not experienced or observable, or based on these, would arbitrarily replace what was in fact encountered and reliably used.

7 All studies begin with confronted, particular, commonplace items. But none deals with what is objectively so, unless it also puts aside the questionable overlays which carelessness, habit, prejudgment, practice, tradition, and belief add to it. To cut beneath these is not yet to lose oneself in a mere experiencing. One can still attend to objective appearances and to the conditions that govern all that is or appears.

8 By attending to universal governing conditions, one stands outside both the limitations characteristic of particular items and the accretions which practice, society, and self introduce. Those conditions are forceful, interplaying with what actualities present. To become aware of what governs everywhere is to achieve a knowledge of what is both universal and effective.

9 By withdrawing, one is able to face conditions before they interplay with what actualities exhibit; it is then possible to know what those conditions are. It will thereupon become apparent that though the conditions have little power of their own, they can qualify and interrelate the actualities, because they are attenuated portions of effective finalities.

10 Conditions govern actualities, and their exhibitions as well. The conditions are imposed on the exhibitions by the same powers which, in a more intensive form, intrude directly on actualities, severally and together, thereby enabling the actualities to be alike in many ways, and to be part of a single cosmos.

11 Each actuality maintains itself against all intruders. If it did not, it would not be imposed upon except by being annihilated, and so would not help constitute an objective appearance.

12 To get to the finalities one must refuse to become involved either with the actualities or their appearances. One must, instead, retreat just so far within oneself as to be able to note what is intruded or interlocked, that is, what qualifies actualities, or both constitutes and fringes objective appearances.

A satisfactory method for reaching what is universal, constant, and real attends to what intrudes on actualities or interlocks with their exhibitions. It then extricates the intruded or interlocked factor, moves to what this evidences, and ends with a claim that holds of the source of the intrusions.

13 The tracing of factors back to their sources is controlled and guided by those sources. One is thereby enabled to remain persistently directed toward what is sought. A basis for criticism is also provided; what is defective in one's procedure is exposed as resistant or distortive, thereby promoting its rectification.

Any activity which is being pursued is obviously not yet at its end. But it can come only to the end of itself. Its success demands its cessation. Its ending stands in the way of the activity achieving anything, unless what it ends with can be held apart from it. If the ending is to be more than a dead abstraction, it must also be more than a mere arrival point; it must be capable of being sustained by something beyond it.

14 Only by holding on to the end of an inquiry, while yielding to what sustains that end, can one come to know the object sought.

15 Since every man is unavoidably the product of his time, culture, and studies, since at his best he is confused, ignorant, biased, limited in vision and insight—in short, finite as mind and body—none can ever hope to achieve a perfect, all-encompassing, neutral, articulate account. No man, not even a multiplicity of them, could forge a full satisfactory systematic philosophy which was without serious flaw or omission. But the effort must be made. Not only is it desirable to try to push back the limits within which one had unreflectingly lived, to try to avoid arbitrarily assuming what should have been examined, and to try to reduce the number of unreliable, derivative, unexplained, and unexamined judgments that are made, but it is good to expose to the critical eye of others, and hopefully to one's own at some later time, the weaknesses as well as the promises of a philosophy, and thereby alert all to what next should arrest attention.

16 The most proper philosophic attitude seems at first to be the most pretentious, for it is nothing less than a determination to grasp those ultimate truths that only a divine mind could fully know. But it is, in fact, most modest, since it seeks to place every joint, warrant, and argument plainly in view, asking all to discover how inadequate it in fact is. Carried out with rigor, a philosophy is set in a system so as to force crucial issues to the fore, regardless of one's predilections. Difficulties, defects, omissions, and irrelevancies as well as unsuspected connections and explanations will then be made most evident.

17 An occupation with isolated problems allows one to neglect what does not happen to appeal. A system, instead, demands that certain questions be answered before one can move on. It weakens the temptation to leave unexplored what might make a great difference to what is being maintained.

18 The inadequacies of a systematic philosophy are not known to a serious author; otherwise he would change it. Nor will they be known by others, unless these attend to the philosophy in a highly critical spirit, sustained throughout by an effort to read carefully and to understand. Undoubtedly, the system will rest on inadequate evidence and will limp to questionable conclusions. But if it makes it possible for others to see this in an account which has overcome the kind of errors that haunt other views, it will, at the very least, make it possible for something better to follow.

19 Many of the errors made in a philosophy could be avoided if what is said and thought were limited in range and hedged in by disclaimers. But one will then be only a short step in advance of commonsense practice, with its fragmentary, unexamined, and often unsatisfactory claims.

20 No one is required to engage in philosophy. It is not an agency for discovering new matters of fact, or anything of practical value. Its outcomes are so readily a prey to doubts and so entangled with subtleties that it rarely yields what is exhilarating to contemplate.

21 One philosophizes because one is not content with accepting any authority, whether this be tradition, common sense, science, or other philosophies. What is accepted, nevertheless, must cohere with some of what these others affirm, for they too, have withstood considerable criticism and severe tests over time. Inevitably, of course, a new philosophic account will also go counter to some of their most central theses, as a consequence of its fresh, free examination of what they unquestionably assume.

22 No one can know in advance just what will withstand philosophic scrutiny, and what must give way. All that can be said with confidence is that there is no contention which a thoroughgoing study may not show to be unwarranted, or to require modification. It is also true that no one can say in advance that this or that conclusion can not forever stand.

23 From the first and throughout, a philosophy should offer itself as more than a set of fictions, unwarranted suppositions, or imaginary states of affairs. It should always be more than a coherent, arresting, or original view, for it claims to speak of what is, and not merely of what might have been or could possibly be.

24 A philosophy starts with and never completely rejects all the claims of common sense, all common uses of terms, or the lessons of experience. If it did, it would, more likely than not, be unintelligible, and where intelligible would fail to provide a purchase on what else there might be. But it can not remain there. Like science and history, or any other discipline, philosophy demands an objective examination of what is initially encountered, and uses the result as the beginning of a controlled course of inquiry which knows where it is to go and why.

25 Each philosophy stands in the precarious position of refusing to abandon everything maintained apart from it, all the while that it knows that there is nothing which may not have to give way. But if it dismisses what it can not accommodate, or belittles this as the product of a confusion in thought or language, it supports dogmatism with arrogance.

26 A philosophy inevitably challenges the established judgments, not only of common sense, but of science and theology, in part because, though it speaks with them of what is encountered, of nature, and of what is forever, it proceeds independently toward a goal which is not entirely identifiable with theirs. In part, too, it is in disaccord with these others, because it looks at its own presuppositions, seeks warrants for whatever it claims, and analyzes, classifies, and organizes what the others stop with.

27 Philosophy's main concern is not with what the others maintain, and not even with what they presuppose. Its object is with what is irreducibly real.

28 Philosophies die, not under the sharp knife of criticism, but from neglect. And they are deservedly neglected when they are unable to allow room for any of the central facts that everyone knows—birth and death, love and hate, growth, change, and decay, motion, action, and rest, thought and fact, present, past, and future, truth and error, man and nature, social and personal experiences, what these entail and what these depend on.

29 A philosopher always travels alone, suspicious of all road signs, even when his pace is similar to others, and even though he may arrive where many have been for a long time.

30 To philosophize is to set off on a road where much that is familiar and reliable proves to be as untrustworthy as what is new or unsatisfactory. A philosopher, to be sure, has old friends and allies; he never allows time to set him apart from great thinkers in the past. But if he is to exhibit something of their spirit, he never simply borrows from them. Whatever he accepts is freshly examined—and may be modified. While refusing to deny or minimize claims widely held, he looks at them sharply, aware that some of them may have been misconstrued or misstated, perhaps by a multitude, and for a long time. Some views may withstand his most severe scrutiny; his modifications of others may keep him fairly close to established doctrines or to the ordinary man's unreflecting understanding of the value and import of what is encountered. If they do not, he will slowly, reluctantly, but confidently modify or abandon them on behalf of a more coherent and adequate understanding of what there is and can be known.

31 In this post-Hegelian age, it would be foolish not to take advantage of some basic truths which Hegel so brilliantly used and sometimes abused: what is real is already discernible; what is real is already involved in what is encountered; what is real is knowable; universal conditions are ontologically based; universal conditions make a difference to the particulars they govern; there is no stopping at any point without a premonitional advance beyond it. These truths are not necessarily tangled in a quasi-historical dialectic; they are more than resting places on the way to an absolute; they do not require a slighting of particulars. But they do keep one from going back to periods before Hegel for philosophy's beginning or method. They do not, though, require one to be an Hegelian. In a post-Hegelian period one needs another philosophic outlook than those which either he or his predecessors provided.

Hegel held both that we already are in possession of absolute knowledge and that we do not yet have it. He was surely right on both counts. But he failed to give sufficient value to the distinction, because he did not allow genuine independent reality to actualities, oppositional to and sustaining what a finality provides; nor did he consider whether or not there was more than one finality.

32 From the very first, one is in contact with the finalities; all the while there is a distinction between where one now is and the finalities themselves. From the first, and throughout, one remains in a world of particulars; from the first, and throughout, one is involved with what is independent of these.

Hegel insisted that there is always more meant than said. In a progressive, one-directional system, such a view leads to an endless, incompleteable progress toward an absolute (Peirce's view); to a confession that there is something meant which can not be said (Wittgenstein's conclusion); or (Hegel's position) to the attempt to show that one can eventually say all that was meant. But though there is nothing meant that can not be said, there is always something meant that is not said. A correct speaking of the finalities leaves over something meant about actualities. If what was meant about those actualities is then said, there will be something further that is meant but not said about the finalities. The saying of what had been meant about those finalities will be richer than what had been said before, resonating with what had already been learned. But then there will be something meant but not yet said about the actualities, and so on without end.

33 A carefree journey is often a pleasant one. But it leaves too much room for carelessness. Because philosophy is a discipline, it must have a structure that can be independently tested for possible weaknesses, and which will allow one to see clearly what the affirmation and rejections imply. An unstructured philosophy is at best a set of detached observations. Lacking interconnection, these do not sustain one another. Separated, they might be alive, but not together.

A philosophy is a creative work. It must be quickened by insight; it must adventure, dare, be imaginative and free. If it is to contribute to thought it must both break new ground and by its very presence raise questions about itself and other accounts.

34 In a systematic philosophy each part supports the others; each carries out the intent of the whole. Though it begins at a definite point and ends at another, its beginning is not left behind, but accumulated and embodied throughout. Ideally, each step is demanded by its predecessor, and prefigures its successor. It attains its proper end when it reaches what begins a justification for its having begun where it did.

35 Errors in philosophy are unavoidable. In its attempt to encompass all that is, a philosophy is defeated by man's limited vision and grasp. The history of the subject is a history of errors committed in the attempt to allow nothing to escape scrutiny and explanation. Each error, however, is as much an achievement as its truths. No one can master the one or the other unless he works through the philosophic work in which they occur, for it is then only that he is forced to go beyond them.

To learn the errors that indelibly mar the Hegelian account one must allow it to force one forward to a position from which those errors are seen to be intrinsic to that view. The defects in the succeeding philosophy will themselves have to be discovered in a similar way. If the account is right in the main, those errors will have to do with the manner in which one rests with or passes from actualities to finalities to actualities, directly and indirectly.

36 From a beginning with intruded and therefore alien content, a move is made to what is evidenced. Finally, a claim is forged about a reality. What is then learned illuminates the initial beginning. If one returns to that beginning, it is found to be even more arresting than it had been before. The circle from beginning to end to beginning is to be traversed again and again. The outcome is greater clarity and coherence. Sooner or later, there comes a time when the gains diminish appreciably. That is when what has been thought and what has been seen are to be offered to the sympathetic and critical examination of others who are also interested in discovering what always is, and can be known.

37 Inevitably every philosophy fails to satisfy what is demanded of an account which is to be all-comprehensive, vigorous, rational, and true. Every one is defective, making conspicuous the fact that the enterprise has a future as well as a past. All that any one thinker can do is to make the present be the future for that past, and be the past that can be used to realize a still wanted future. Still, there are undeniable truths. Here is one: It is not possible to deny that one is attending or knowing, without at the same time reinstating what the rejection tries to take away. To deny that one attends or thinks is to deny the denial.

No one can reject such a self-certifying observation. But it has no reach and no richness. It takes one nowhere. To move from it, use must be made of principles outside its scope. It does, though, prompt a question: May there not, in addition to statements, be realities which never can be set aside? I think there are. They have already been remarked upon. I call them 'finalities'.

38 Philosophical truths have an ontological base. These can be known if the conditions of speculative knowledge are identical with those constant conditions which govern men and other actualities. Did men not have within them, though in as yet an unsatisfactory form, the very answers that they sought, they would have to grope without guidance. Nor would they ever know that what they said was true.

The claim that men are entirely cut off from what they seek to know, presupposes a knowledge of what it is they presumably can not reach. One must be content either with saying that one never knows whether or not one is right, or must affirm that man already has within himself a way of determining whether or not something is finally so. The affirmation follows from the fact that whatever there be is qualified by and, in the case of man, internalizes what is forever.

39 A finality is a necessary reality. Otherwise it would not always be present, everywhere, and also be apart from all actualities. There is no moment or place where it is not, at the same time that it is outside all moments and all places. Otherwise something would escape its control, or it would not provide an unavoidable condition. A finality maintains itself apart from the conditions it imposes and that which is thereby conditioned.

40 An understanding of finalities is the outcome of an adventure. At its best, nothing is affirmed that is not necessary for explanation. Excessive foliage disfigures the tree of knowledge. But nothing must be avoided which must be acknowledged in order to know that the finalities are, to understand their natures, how they function, and the effects they have.

41 Philosophical knowledge is subject to the same controls that operate on what is experienced, and on what lies beyond this. It starts from experience. That experience, though, is one which the finalities help constitute, and where they always leave evidences of themselves.

*

EXPERIENCES, APPEARANCES, AND KNOWLEDGE

1 Eₓₚₑᵣᵢₑₙ𝒸ₑ' is an ambiguous term. Used with the greatest possible latitude, it refers to a conscious involvement with any content. The content need not be exhausted in the experiencing. The fact permits one to say that thinking is one kind of experience and appreciation another. Also, expecting, perceiving, recollecting, hoping, feeling, dreaming, believing, walking, talking, and eating would all be allowed to be experiences.

2 The termini of different kinds of experience differ in objectivity. Some, like imagining, terminate in what is constituted in or by the experiencing. Others, like observation—even of one's feelings—end with what resists the experiencer. And some, like self-consciousness, terminate in the man who has the experience. Objectivity, evidently, is not identical with externality.

3 Different kinds of experience make use of different agencies. Perceptual experience needs the help of the senses. Appreciation requires sensitivity. The experience of a proof in mathematics must be mediated by technical knowledge. Religious experience presupposes faith.

4 "Mere experience" is an abstraction from specific mediated ways of terminating in confronted content. Were there such an experience, it would not make use of any channels, and therefore could not be learned, improved, or guided. Specific experiences might fill it out, but they would not be able to complement or support it. It would end with what was neither seen, heard, felt, tasted, appreciated, demonstrated, or reverenced. We approximate that state when we neglect everything in a relaxed, somnolent, unfocussed frame of mind, but even then interests and bodily dispositions occasionally force some items to the fore.

5 All the kinds of experience merge in a single experience of what is common to, but also beyond their diverse termini. That single experience presupposes a start with some particular mode of experience, and never gets entirely free from this. A single experience of what is common to all kinds of experience is still not free from more limited encounterings.

6 Some kinds of experience lead to still further experiences. We learn from experience not only what is present but sometimes how

this connects with what is still to be directly confronted. Inquiry and inference not only terminate in both the proximate and remote, but involve an effort to make the remote proximate. An experience is not necessarily punctuate or episodic.

7 The termini of different instances of the same kind of experience may differ in location. Instances of denotation, observation, and searching terminate at different places. Instances of inquiry and inference terminate at different times. Some instances have termini nearby, others terminate in what is at a distance. There are also nonlocated termini—the finalities, the objects of pure mathematics, ideals.

8 Were there something with which no one was consciously involved in any way at all—emotionally, linguistically, conceptually, practically, inferentially, or imaginatively—no one could know that it was there or what it was like. Yet, though what can not be confronted in any sense can not be known, there could be realities which are not experienced or even experienceable. In any case, knowledge is not restricted to *sensible* experience.

9 When 'experience' is restricted to sensible encounters it is usually also given an honorific import, as at once primary and normative, the standard in terms of which all other uses are to be measured. Though lived through, dreaming and imagination are then taken to be experiences, either derived from the sensible or constructed on its base.

10 Experiencing does not stop at the limit of an experience, but entrenches on a limit *for* experience. That limit sustains and thereby makes it possible for there to be a limit *of* the experience.

11 What limits an experience is independent of that experience. The limit therefore faces two ways—toward the experience and away from it. As turned away it is encompassed in an experiencing.

12 There is content beyond the limit of an experience, and of the experiencing which continues further. Made the limit of another experience, the content will have a side which is beyond that limit.

Beyond the experienced limit there is further content into which an experiencing passes imperceptibly. For that content to be made into a limit of an experience, still another experience is required, beyond which is another experiencing of content, and so on without end.

An experiencing continues indefinitely into content. Any distinguished proximate portion of this is connected with one that is still more remote, into which the experiencing passes without ever reaching a terminus of its own.

13 Experiencing and content are continuous with one another. Though it can not be maintained that there is nothing in the latter beyond the reach of the former, it is always true that there never is a moment when the former encompasses all of the latter. Experiencing always passes into what is beyond the point where the experiencing might become only an experience of a terminus.

14 We are able to know that there is something independent of an experience because the experience occurs within the compass of an experiencing; and this is not separable from the content which provides the experience with a limit at which it terminates.

15 Because experiencing continues past an experienced terminus into a retreating content, one is always experiencing more than is experienced, and is always opposed by what is more than the experiencing. Something is always there for us to experience.

Experience is stopped by what is beyond that experience. When the stop is made at the terminus of an experience, the act of stopping is still left over. There can be an experiencing of the stopping, but this will still leave the act of stopping as not yet being experienced, and so on without end.

16 Knowledge and reality are not necessarily coextensive. Neither are ignorance and unreality. They could not be, unless knowledge produced its own objects, or reality necessitated that there be a conscious involvement with it. But if knowledge produced its own objects there would be no errors, and therefore no knowledge. And if reality necessitated that someone be consciously involved with it, the world could not exist before there were conscious beings, and there then would be no place where these could come to be.

17 What is real can not be entirely caught up in experience. Experience and experiencing presuppose something to experience. Nor is anything precluded from being the terminus of an experience, or set beyond the reach of all experiencing. But every experience and experiencing has something beyond it which sustains the terminus of, and provides a limit for the one, while slowing the progress of the other.

18 Experience needs something beyond it to enable it to be an experience *of;* experiencing needs something beyond it to enable it to be an experiencing *with.* Denied a limit, an experience turns into an experiencing; separated from what is stopping it, an experiencing turns into a private feeling.

19 Different kinds of experience often supplement one another. Sense experience may be backed by a conceptual experience. We see a green and a blue and know that they are two.

20 The demands of practice and the effect of habit tempt one not to observe with care. As a consequence, the effect of the emotions on observation and perception is usually ignored. Emotional experiences fasten on the remote, but pass through and qualify other experiences which are occupied with what is near. The emotional experiences are not more basic or genuine or reliable than the others, but are just more involved with what is not to the fore.

Emotional experiences color and may distort the experiences

through which they pass on the way to their termini. Maximal qualifications are produced by elicited emotions. If fear, terror, hope, ecstasy, anger, love, or hate is elicited, one tends to ignore the qualifications to which those emotions subject other experiences through which they are expressed. Though what is observed may then be seriously misconstrued, one is usually unaware of the fact or of the degree.

21 One can live through emotions as directly, unreflectively, and confidently, as one lives through other experiences. The emotions, too, may at times terminate in what is independent of them, and they usually take one past any discernible experienced terminus.

22 An outburst of emotion, not articulated by what is confronted, overflows it. It is raw emotion, not given satisfaction by a particular. In the ordinary course of life we learn to express ourselves with considerable appropriateness in connection with the items we encounter. If a raw emotion is then also evoked, it remains not fully engaged by those items.

23 A primary experience terminates in a particular which is defiant of it. The experience thrusts toward this in an effort to make it focal. Other kinds of experience—emotional, religious, speculative—also do this. To take one of these to be more genuine, reliable, simpler, or accurate than the others, would be arbitrary, unless one appeals to something other than their natures or claims.

A rational experience with what was clear and distinct satisfied Descartes; it is not intrinsically superior or inferior to a Humean experience of what is encountered through the agency of the senses. From the standpoint of the first, the second is unreliable, streaked with contingency, and open to error; from the standpoint of the second, the first is derivative, a pale copy of a rich original. For both, emotional experiences are neither primary nor reliable.

If mathematical exactitude is preferred, the Cartesian choice should be made; if it is decreed, instead, that the senses must be used, the Humean. But if it is joint use of mind and body that is wanted, recourse must be had to emotional experience and experiencing in terms of which the worth and accuracy of the others can be measured.

Whatever type of experience or experiencing is chosen as a standard, it will require that the others be taken to be minor, derivative, or to make claims which are unwarranted. But the kind of warrant that the rejected is unable to yield is simply the kind that the chosen alone can provide, or which it provides to a greater degree.

24 Unengaged emotions are provoked in an experience with art. Their objects are remote from what is perceived and observed, not in space or in time, but in depth and in availability. That is why the arts can teach one about the course of the world, and help one to check the deliverances of speculation.

25 What is ultimate is emotionally felt and can be speculatively known. The emotionally reacted content tells us that what we daily accept may not offer reliable reports of what is objective; speculation clarifies and makes evident the power of art to take one to what is permanent and basic. Both offer tests of perception's more superficial acceptances.

26 A *confronted appearance* is affected by an experience of it. Relative to and partly constituted by the experiencer, it is subjectified. An *objective appearance* is more than what is sensibly or perceptually confronted.

Both kinds of appearance are derivative and inert, and therefore differ from what is real. This can be reached in sympathy, be known speculatively, or terminate the emotions. The acknowledgment of what is reached, known, or terminated in justifies an unwillingness to stop with a knowledge even of objective appearances.

27 Perception confronts an appearance, at the same time that it continues, as an experiencing, into and beyond this into an objective appearance. A confronted appearance, though, may elicit so sharp a response that it obscures the fact that the appearance is unaffected by that response. The confronted appearence may even be so obtrusive that the presence of an objective appearance may be neglected and even denied.

28 Many men, despite their idiosyncracies or distinctive traditions, can experience the same things. All can attend to common content, only partly hidden by their additions. No man, consequently, need be wholly cut off from what other men confront.

29 Objective appearances are the outcome of the interplay of two factors originating with different types of reality. The factors constituting objective appearances do not have equal weight; one dominates over and limits the other. The result is to be credited to the source of the dominant factor. A shape is attributed to a particular object rather than to space, because the shape, due to the object, dominates over the extension present there. In contrast, a body localizes a larger extension. The localized extension, as within the larger, dominates over the distinctive insistence of the body. A shape is an objective appearance of an actuality; a localized extension is an objective appearance of a finality.

30 Each factor in an objective appearance is insisted on against the other. Each, therefore, both qualifies the other and resists an assimilation by it. Were a factor devoid of all insistence, there would be no appearances, but just independent fulgurations on the part of distinct kinds of reality.

31 Part of the insistence of a factor is due to it; part is due to a power transmitted through it. Each factor, therefore, at once insists on itself and is forced on the other factor. Were only the self-insistence to occur, a factor would be able to act apart from its source, and in effect be a reality itself; were only the intrusion to occur, one factor would not of itself make a difference to the other. A common extension and the shape of an actuality do not exist by themselves; yet they limit one another to constitute a distinct world of appearances (attributable to actualities), and the appearance of an extension (attributable to a finality).

32 Factors can be held apart from one another in thought, but only partially and precariously. Each can also be distinguished in an abstractive act. There it is less than it was in the appearance, when it was supplemented while being limited by the other factor.

33 Factors stretch from constituting realities to appearances, preventing the appearances from being products which were irreducibly real, cut off from their sources.

34 Could the factors exist in the absence of their sources they would yield appearances of what never appeared. If a reality did not make an appearance, we would not be able to begin to move systematically to the reality.

35 An appearance is continuous with a reality, via a factor which the reality provides. The factor helps constitute the appearance and textures it.

36 Appearances without textures would not allow one to know what appears. Realities are reached by starting with textured appearances; were they cut off from the textured appearances, they could conceivably be reached only by leaps—but no one would know where to leap or how.

37 We cannot know what is real by examining appearances. Appearances do not mirror realities. They are, though, continuous with realities; the factors which constitute appearances continue beyond them, into the more and more intensive, denser, unified realities.

38 A reality is a singular source of factors, each exhibiting it in an attenuated form. The further back one is traced into its source, the less distinguishable it becomes, and the less, too, is it constitutive of an appearance.

39 Each source is a reality in its own right, and can be reached only by getting rid of what is alien to it, due to another. The further we move into a source, the more is a factor freed from the limitations introduced by another reality.

40 The closer we come to its source the less is a factor effectively countered by another. The dominated factor may be so feeble that it is not able to interact with the dominant to constitute an appearance. At that point, the dominated factor is just an attenuated continuation of its reality. We are, consequently, never entirely cut off from realities, though we are never at their centers.

41 We can progress toward realities as they are unaffected by anything else, and that beyond any preassignable point. Sooner or later, we find that we can go no further. The reality is then faced as brute, impervious. We can start there and get beyond the point where we had been stopped, but we then find ourselves faced with what defeats that attempt, and so on without end.

42 We cannot produce the world by taking thought; nor can we turn it into nothing but a thought. It is there for us to think about; and it continues to be, no matter what we think. But we can also come to know what it must be like in order for it to be more than a thought. One way of discovering this is by noting that knowledge necessarily bounds what is there to be known, that those boundaries are effectively defied, and that the defiance is known when we attend to what we are bounding.

43 Attention to one or a number of appearances depends on the imposition of a boundary separating what is focussed on from what is neglected. If what is focussed on was initially separate from other items, attention will duplicate a boundary already there. Whether it did this or not, however, what we knew would still be bounded by us.

44 An objective appearance is not conditioned or controlled by the boundaries which we impose in attending to it. Its career in the world is determined not by those boundaries, but apart from them, by the way its factors function together.

45 Were appearances wholly confined within our boundaries, they would be objects of attention but not objects *to* which we attend. Attended to, the appearances contrast with themselves as belonging to and continuing into actualities. As the one, the appearances are constrained by the boundaries we introduce; as the other they are indifferent to them.

46 Objective appearances are appearances to be credited either to actualities or to finalities. We can arrive at the one by efforts of our own; but the other must guide and lure us. Both hold objective appearances apart from the boundaries we introduce when we attend, and from the additions we add as individuals and conventionalized beings.

47 A bounded appearance can be distinguished from itself as unbounded, and then brought to bear on this. The bounded appearance thereby achieves a status relative to itself as unbounded. It is then enabled to function as though those boundaries were not there. It is *objectified*.

48 In becoming objectified an appearance is divided into facets—a designation, a meaning, and an adumbration. The adumration relates the designation and meaning to their common base in an objective appearance. The objectified appearance is thereby able to provide an articulation of the objective appearance.

49 The various facets distinguishable in an objectified appearance are isolated and combined in judgments and claims. They also are dealt with separately or together in language, concepts, memory, inference, and expectation. They can be abstracted from.

50 In a judgment the unity of an objectified appearance is restored, but on the side of man. The result is a judged, known, objectified appearance. If adumbration is given prominence there, one moves toward the objective appearance. If that appearance is given prominence, one is then involved with what tests the judgment.

51 In knowing, a claim is made by means of an *assertum*, something judged of something else. The assertum is warranted if inferences drawn from it keep in accord with the consequences which follow in fact. But we do not always remain with what we know; sometimes we leave what we know behind to involve ourselves with what is confronting us, and which tests and corrects our claims to know.

52 Perceiving thrusts beyond the appearances to which we attend. Related observations are pertinent to actions, exhibitions, and insistencies—indeed to all arrivals at any position. There is no stopping at any point except so far as one also at the same time goes beyond it. Otherwise we would never have it as a terminus, but would merely end at it, not be able to face it, not have it stop us, not have it function as a limit.

53 Knowledge of an objective appearance involves an experience of an absenting of the appearance from the act of knowing it. The absenting is more certain and complete, the more the factor which was dominant in the appearance achieves independence from the other factor. Since actualities control what they contribute to objective appearances, to get to an actuality one goes back over the route of that control toward the actuality.

54 Factors are exhibitions of actualities having the role of constituents of appearances; facets are distinguished aspects of objectified appearances. An adumbrative—ideally expressed by the copula in the guise of an orienting agent—roots the facets in an appearance, and roots the factors, which constitute the appearance, in the actuality which possesses that appearance.

55 Adumbration is the converse of the act of contributing a factor to an appearance. Because it is possessed by, it can lead one into the actuality. At the same time, it has the role of a facet in an articulated claim. It there orients the other facets in an objective appearance and, through this, in the actuality. That is why we not only know the known but know something beyond the known.

56 A facet is oriented in an objective appearance at the same time that a factor in that appearance is oriented in an actuality. The adumbrative's epistemic role merges into an ontologic as one moves from a concern with appearances to a concern with their actualities.

57 Though we are active when judging and claiming, at the end we are receptive, awaiting support and perhaps correction by objective appearances and actualities. There would be no reason to await anything were it not that we already have some grasp of what is needed to make our judgments and claims right or wrong.

58 'This is a dog' separates distinguishable facets in a confronted appearance attended to, and then unites them in a judged claim which awaits sustaining by the objective appearance. Nothing is here said about the objective appearance; it is merely adumbratively reached as a base. Nothing is here said about the factors in the appearance or as continuing beyond it; a different kind of judgment deals with them. And nothing is here said about the actuality beyond the appearance, though the adumbrative continues into that actuality.

59 Knowledge of an appearance is inseparable from an *attitude* which ignores but does not remove the boundaries that attention introduces. That is why one can be ready to deal with other bounded appearances.

Knowledge of what is here and now is a base from which an attitude of expectation takes its start to mark out an area where one is ready for what is relevant to what is already known.

60 A satisfactory knowledge of the known and expected together is assured, if they are preestablished to be in consonance, if an attitude dictates their relationship, or if the relationship governs the attitude. But a preestablished harmony requires the action of a harmonizer who could have refused to allow the items to be independent in the first place. Since an attitude can not prescribe the relations that hold among objective appearances—for those relations are there before they are attended to—the reverse must be the case, and the expected therefore must be capable of being satisfactorily united with the known. Because this is so, we can be intelligently receptive of appearances that had originally been set aside, and of appearances yet to come.

61 Dominated factors in the appearances of actualities also have a dominant role in the form of *contexts*. As subjugating the factors contributed by actualities, the contexts themselves have the status of appearances, attributable to final realities.

62 Because they are under the dominance of a counter insistent context, the factors produced by all actualities together help constitute a variegated, punctuated, single appearance of a final source of that context.

63 Knowledge can terminate in objective appearances; in what is actual; in what determines the way in which appearances are together; in a complex, single contextualizing appearance; in what produces a context; in what qualifies and controls actualities in their severalty; and in what determines the way in which actualities are together.

64 Knowledge is a contingent product; it need not occur and may be blocked by errors. If one proceeds persistently and properly, one eventually moves toward what is either necessary in itself— finalities— or with what is necessarily presupposed—actualities.

65 The more surely an appearance of an actuality has a status of its own, the more surely is it continuous with various unities—an intensive unity characteristic of the actuality to which the appearance belongs, and others which interplay with this.

Were there no such unities, there would be just present surfaces, each separate from all else. But whatever one confronts is penetrated to some degree; one inevitably reaches into the intensive actual unity to which different appearances belong or into the final sources of contexts in which those appearances are together with all others.

66 The imposition of an idea of a contextualizing unity on an appearance yields an interpretation of it. If the interpretation is sound, it brings a conceived unity to bear on what a real unity helped constitute.

67 To interpret a societal or personal form of an appearance, one must make a unity relevant by specifying it, and then approach the appearance in terms of that specification. A perception presupposes a specification of a region of indifferent space; the specified region demarcates the area in which something appears.

68 The unities which interconnect appearances are usually attributed to a knowing self. This will not do. It overlooks contexts and their bearing on confronted appearances. A knowing self, of course, may add to the unities that in fact interconnect the appearances of actualities. A recognition of its contributions can not, though, require a cancellation of the unity that the items have as already together; otherwise they would not be available for the contributions that the knowing self provides.

69 Ontologically effective unities are not sensed or perceived, though what is sensed and perceived continues into them. Nor are they the objects of a detached mind, though one can come to know them. They terminate emotions in which bodily and mental efforts are intertwined. Initially they are not clearly distinguished one from the other.

70 When one penetrates into actualities, there is a beginning with appearances and a passage to what is more intensive but beyond the reach of bodily agencies. When one moves to finalities, there is a passage to what is more and more comprehensive but never fully conceptualized. Reflection distinguishes and draws the entailed consequences from both of them as able to be reached emotionally.

71 An infant initially neither penetrates nor withdraws from what it confronts. Instead, it faces all the unifying contexts vaguely together. Metaphysics recovers what the child initially grasped, but without losing the fact that the appearances of actualities are known, and have objectivity and contexts apart from knowledge. It distinguishes what the child blurred together, and at the same time attends to the fact that all appearances are interrelated in and by a single, complex, unifying *Context*.

72 A metaphysical endeavor would be stopped at the very start could one show that neither appearances nor actualities were related; that there are no actualities; or that all unifications could be accounted for solely by attending to actualities or their appearances.

73 Were either appearances or actualities not interrelated, neither would be together with others. One of them could not be larger or smaller than another, more or less similar to it, near to or far from it.

74 Since some appearances are exhibited independently of others, and since actualities sometimes act independently of one another, for all the appearances to be together and for all the actualities to be together there must be powers able to transform them from independent into interconnected items. And since actualities, despite a multiplicity of parts or roles, function as singulars, each of them, too, must have been subjected to a unifying controlling power. To account for the different unifications one must look beyond actualities and appearances to what prescribes to, is imposed on, transforms, and governs them all.

75 If one takes a stand inside some language—that of ordinary men, logic, mathematics, or science—what is said in another language can be dismissed as nonsense or confusion. Nothing, though, is gained by such tactics, except the pleasure of remaining consistently within arbitrary limits.

Each language has a distinctive role; none covers everything; nor is any so pure that elements of other types are never present, offering helpful guides to other languages and what they enable one to state about reality and what can be known of it. Each, too, presupposes men, a society, learning, history, the difference between truth and falsehood, and the difference between correct and incorrect usage. None could condition and encompass all that is, including its users, and whatever occurs when and where men are not. None can therefore constitute all that is or can be known.

76 The acknowledgment of intruded unities is one with the acknowledgment of evidences in a world of interrelated appearances, in a cosmos of interrelated actualities, and in individual actualities. Those evidences can not have their source in a mind unless this has a cosmic range, encompassing all the appearances and all the actualities. Such a cosmic mind would be hard to distinguish from the finality, Possibility, when this is arbitrarily credited with a consciousness.

77 Possibility is one of five finalities, all ultimate, all reachable, all sources of intrusive, omnipresent governing evidences. A set of such evidences is provided by the Context within which all the appearances of actualities are confined.

*

CONTEXTS

1 Wᴇʀᴇ ᴀɴ ᴀᴘᴘᴇᴀʀᴀɴᴄᴇ simply by itself, it would not be 'an' appearance. It is an appearance because it is one of a number. This requires it to be together with others. But it can be together with them only if all are subject to one or more conditions interrelating them.

2 In the absence of all common controlling conditions each appearance would be solely by itself. To know a number of appearances a man would then have to break himself into fragments, each occupied with a distinct item. Or he would somehow have to be able to stretch over them all, and thereby condition them together. Objective appearances would all be radically separate, not able to be members of a single many. Subjectified appearances alone would be together.

3 Were the insistencies of separate actualities to mesh in harmony, they would help constitute conjoint appearances. But actualities sometimes oppose one another at the same time that their appearances continue to be together. And sometimes actualities operate conjointly at the same time that they continue to maintain distinctive holds on their appearances. Appearances, evidently, depend for their conjoint existence on more than actualities.

4 Conjoint appearances are all in a single domain because the exhibitions of different actualities are countered by common controlling conditions. As a result of the union of the exhibitions of all the actualities with a single countering condition, the former are turned into appearances together in context.

5 Objective appearances are constituted by diverse factors, each expressing a reality. Because the appearances are credited to the source of the dominant factor, once can speak of the factors as though they themselves were appearances. Consequently, one can refer to what is within a context as appearances of actualities, just as well as one can speak of them as exhibitions of actualities dominated by a context.

Since a context contributes to the constitution of a world of appearances, when the context is dominant over the contributions of actualities one can speak of it, too, as an appearance. And since such a context will be an appearance in which what is real, apart from all actualities, has a dominant role, it is to be credited not to any or all actualities, but to a finality.

6 Various appearances have *affinities* with one another in different degrees and ways. Canary yellow is gay, brown is flat, a square has solidity, a triangle is hard. Red, says the blind man, is like the sound of a trumpet. There are sounds, colors, shapes, tastes that readily harmonize; others clash; still others have little affect on one another. The appearances may belong to the same actualities or to different ones, to actualities close by or to actualities far away, all without apparent effect on the nature or force of their affinities.

7 The affinities of appearances compel the knower. They can not therefore be produced by him unless he somehow can turn around on himself and make himself submit to what he has himself produced. If he could do this, he should be able to undo what he has done, unless he is himself in the grip of forces over which he has no control. But then it becomes a mystery why the forces should make him act on himself in just these ways and not others, and why it is that at various times he is able to misconstrue or ignore what presumably so overwhelms him.

8 A number of men, not necessarily acquainted or in the same culture or time, acknowledge the same affinities. If one could compel himself to relate appearances, he still would not compel all the rest of men to do so. It is also true that not all acknowledge the same affinities. White is the color of mourning for the Chinese.

9 Affinities are compelling but not irresistible. They can be misconstrued, distorted, and modified, and sometimes ignored, defied, and even cancelled. They do not have control over our judgments or tastes. But were they not objective, there would be no discords in fact and no laws of harmony; nothing would be mistaken; there would be no aesthetic better or worse. It is because they dictate to but do not wholly determine what will be approved or rejected that there can be poor aesthetic judgments, misjudgments, and bad taste.

10 The affinities of appearances can not be due to actualities in their severalty, for they solely concern the ways in which appearances are interrelated. Actualities might mesh with and oppose one another. That fact, though, relates not to the appearances themselves, but to the contingent and alterable ways in which the actualities were being made present together.

11 Congruous appearances sometimes belong to radically opposed actualities. The same kind of ferocious look, bristling of the hair, and coloration characterize fighting bucks; males and females sometimes dislike one another despite aesthetically compatible guises. The affinities of appearances are not necessarily due to the actualities working together.

12 The affinities of appearances are a consequence of their subjugation to a common insistence, which is transmitted through a context that helps make those appearances be affiliated in various ways and degrees.

13 Each appearance is not only affiliated with others, in various ways and degrees, but has the role of a term in an internal relation of equality to them.

14 One appearance is not more an appearance than another. There are bright blues and faded blues; there is pink and red; high notes and low, shrill notes and bland; the sweet, bittersweet, sour, and bitter. One of these is not more of an appearance or less of an appearance than the appearance of a dog, a child, or a king.

15 One might not want all appearances to be equal. Yet, each is present with the others in a single domain of appearances. Nor is their equal status, enjoyed no matter what their modality or symbolic role, due to the action of a number of men. If it were, the men themselves would have to work in harmony to make possible common ways of getting the appearances to be together. This they do not always do. A number sometimes acknowledge the same set of appearances, but one of them may note what others do not. Some see but do not hear, or hear but do not see what others hear and see. And what they all see or hear may have a different tonality, specifications, or import for each.

16 The equal status of appearances can not result from the activity of independent, unrelated actualities. Such actualities would be isolated universes, little absolutes whose expressions would fail to make contact with any other.

17 There is a dominant context which keeps all the exhibitions of actualities on a footing, no matter what they are like or where. The result is a single set of equalized appearances.

18 Appearances are also rationally related to one another. The contextual connections amongst them are intelligible. There are laws dictating how one can rationally pass from an actual circle to an ellipse, from one end of the spectrum to another, from C to A on a violin.

19 The intelligible connection of the appearances of actualities is not due to individual men. It is this they try to know. They may not like what they encounter; they may misconstrue it; and they may try to defy it. Unless a man submits to the structure which contextualizes all the appearances together, he will have to live through impressions having no intelligible connection with one another.

20 Men in a society share common ideologies, and look out at the world in terms of common ideas, prejudices, expectations, and fears. But some appearances are intelligibly together for more than the members of a single society; and some are intelligibly together sometimes for only a few men in any one society. It can not, therefore, be because men think in similar ways that appearances have intelligible relations which men know; rather, because there are such intelligible relations, a number of men can both know them and make predictions about appearances not now present. Humeans deny this; but they forget that if their impressions are radically independent, the impression that next is met may be non-Humean, and may then, on their own view, be rationally connected with all the impressions that follow and all that preceded.

21 We learn from experience that appearances are related to others in various ways. To account for the fact that the patterns are fixed, widespread, persistent, understandable, and usable in predictions, reference must be made to what enables an intelligible structure to have appearances as its terms. Apart from their use of appearances as terms, laws are interconnections of variables, structures to be filled out. When an appearance instances one of those variables, there are demands imposed on other appearances, present or still to come. The demands issue not from the initial appearance—since this is being made to function as a term in a relation—but from what enables the structure to encompass this and the other terms.

22 Intelligible relations interlock with factors issuing from actualities. So far as the intelligible relations are in ascendancy, the two constitute a variegated intelligible context. When there is an opposite stress, the two yield rationally contextualizable appearances of actualities.

23 By working together, actualities could conceivably connect their different appearances, but the actualities could not produce intelligible relations which act in opposition to and govern what all the actualities contribute. Such relations depend for their presence and nature on what is other than the actualities.

24 The intelligible relations connecting the exhibitions of actualities are insistent, maintaining themselves in opposition to opposing individual insistencies. They also transmit an insistence which enables them to dominate over those exhibitions. As a consequence, they provide a context in which all the appearances are intelligibly together. A search for the source of the dominant insistencies leads away from the intelligible relations to what is able to impose these on the contributions of all the actualities.

25 The appearances of actualities are also extensionally together, and this in three ways.

a) They are contemporaries, no matter where in space they are, what their causes, how known. They can be at the same next moment, no matter how sluggish or quick their actualities are, for they are all subject to a time which has them under its single control.

b) The appearances of actualities are spatially related; they are in contact, or they are at a distance in a geometrized whole where they remain for indefinite temporal stretches, playing various roles in relation to one another. They are located units within a single geometricized space.

c) Appearances have differing careers. Some come to be, and pass away before an event is over; others last as long as it does; still others outlast it. They all, despite these differences, have places within one dynamic whole.

The temporal, spatial, and dynamic relations of appearances, though independent of one another, are operative at the same time, to make the appearances extensionally related in a threefold way. As so related, the extensions of those appearances become just limited regions of larger extensions. Apart from the relations, each appearance might have an extension of its own, but this would not be extensionally related to the extensions of other appearances.

26 The various appearances are forced to function as extended terms, related to one another by extensions continuous with those terms. The power to convert the appearances into extended terms extensionally related is obviously no creature of those appearances. If the conversion be credited to a mind, that mind would also be the source of an insistent space, time, and dynamics large enough to encompass all appearances.

27 Individual knowers can not produce the extensional connections of the appearances. It is because men confront the same extended world that they can severally acknowledge it. Those who do not acknowledge the same extended world can not calibrate their watches in terms of the same observable occurrences, cannot acknowledge a common geography, and can not identify the same casual processes. They would be able to act with others only by accident.

28 Though men live and act together, this does not enable them to produce the extensional connections which keep appearances together. Even when the men work in harmony and share the same traditions and preconceptions, they sometimes find themselves compelled to acknowledge extensional connections which they dislike. Some rebel, some acquiesce, some introduce modifications, but all, to be in consonance with what is there, have to take account of the temporal, spatial, and dynamic relations that in fact connect the appearances.

29 The extensional connections amongst appearances can not be the work of individual actualities. Those actualities yield what is being extensionally connected; they cannot produce what both limits their contributions and dominates over them. Though a number of actualities functioning in harmony could produce common connections amongst the factors that those actualities individually exhibit, those actualities could not produce extensions which encompass and govern all those appearances.

30 The exhibitions of actualities together are subject to a temporality, spatiality, and dynamism that neither the exhibitions nor their actualities control. There is an insistence characteristic of those extensions that the actualities cannot annihilate; in addition, there is an insistence which those extensions transmit. Together these insistencies enable the extensions to dominate over the contributions of actualities, and thereby turn these into nuances inside a single extended context.

31 All appearances also merge imperceptibly into one another. There is an evaluational hierarchy to their world despite their differences. Each is more or less distant from the highest point of the hierarchy. The nearer, the higher its value.

32 No individual knower is the source of the valuational totality of all the appearances. Each man must try to know it if he is to free himself from his individual overpersonalizations. He will then be able to face appearances, not as they are oriented in their different actualities, but as subordinate to a final value.

33 No multiplicity of knowers can be the source of the totality in which distinct exhibitions of actualities are valuationally together. Since all men may fail to observe it, the existence of that totality can not be due to them. If their failure to observe made it vanish, there would be no world of evaluated appearances that they could come to know or possibly misconstrue.

34 To share in a common value, each appearance must be converted from an isolated item (rooted in an actuality) into a unit term. That conversion requires the exercise of a power able to produce related values. Apart from control by that power, the appearances would still be affiliated, equalized, law-abiding, and extensionally connected, but they would not be terms which are comparable in terms to a single value. Nothing less than a primary value is needed if there is to be a value for each relative to the others.

35 Five dominating, omnipresent powers connect the appearances of actualities. The powers conjointly but independently express themselves to constitute a single fivefold Context for all appearances. Because of those powers, the Context connects the appearances by affinity, coordination, rationality, extensionality, and by value. These connections provide evidence of the Context and, through this, of the finalities beyond it.

36 Instead of attending to the Context in which all appearances are embedded, one can attend to the exhibitions of different actualities. When those exhibitions are traced back along the lines of their insistencies, one penetrates further and further into the actualities. But no matter how far one goes one always finds something escaping his grasp.

37 Everyone penetrates into actualities to some degree in sympathy and love; the acknowledgment of men's rights, the appreciation of their distinctiveness, communication, and the use of proper names and terms of address are inseparable from a passage below the surface of encountered men. All seem to know this, though it is not often remarked by philosophers.

38 The reality of actualities has already been acknowledged. They are the sources for the fillings of the Context; they enable the Context to stand away from its sources; and, apart from the Context and what they contribute to this, they themselves sustain a number of different types of evidence of the finalities.

.

*

1 N O MATTER HOW FAR exhibitions of an actuality are traced back, one fails to reach an actuality as it is centered in itself. There is no preestablished limit to the process. At whatever point one stops, one is not only in the actuality, but is involved in it beyond the point where one had stopped.

2 An actuality always escapes one's grasp. But it can be partly experienced and known in new acts, once again leaving over something with which one is involved and which is to be known by engaging in still other acts. What is beyond all penetration can be understood by reflecting on what it is to be an actuality able to be penetrated while still able to maintain itself beyond the reach of any penetration.

3 As perceived, an actuality is attended to within the boundaries which attention imposes, and thereby is made into an item in knowledge, able to be related to what else is perceived, believed, expected, and remembered.

4 A perceived actuality is within boundaries which enable it to be an item in knowledge, but it is not controlled by them.

5 As existing apart from all perceiving, each actuality has a limited range and power, leaving room for others. Each comes to be and passes away. Its duration is finite, with a magnitude undeterminable in advance. Did it not have this status, an actuality would be only while and as perceived, within boundaries of our making, and would not resist us or be able to act apart from us.

6 Conceivably, actualities might be understood in one of four inadquate ways.

a) They could be taken to be irreducible complete units. But such units could be forever; there is no reason why they should come to be and pass away.

b) Actualities could be the outcome of the interaction of irreducible units. That would leave over the question as to how and why the interaction should ever have begun or why it should ever end, and therefore, why the resultant actualities should not exist forever.

c) Actualities could be the contingent products of the interplay of factors belonging to other irreducible realities. The actualities would then be indistinguishable from the appearances of those realities. They would lack power of their own; they would not act; they would not be by themselves; nor would they together interplay with common cosmic conditions.

d) Actualities could be identified with events which begin with parts interconnected in one way, and end with them as united in another. If they were, we would be faced with a number of unanswerable questions: Why should there be such a beginning? Why does not the ending remain forever? How distinguish the supposed actualities from appearances, since they then are inert, having their whole existence exhausted in their becoming? No answer is ever final which raises unanswerable questions.

7 When an appearance is abstracted from an actuality what is left is the *actuality in itself*. This ranges in density from a minimum—the terminus of the exhibition of the actuality—to a maximum, which is the actuality at its center. The Kantian manifold is a thing in itself, blurred and cosmologized.

8 Were there no actuality in itself, there would be nothing which was open for determination; there would be nothing particular to be acted on; nothing which could interplay with an intrusive power; nothing which would help constitute an appearance.

In itself, an actuality is irreducible, incomparable, self-maintaining. It can be approximated to any degree by freeing the actuality imaginatively or in fact from externally imposed determinations. One then arrives at the same content that is left when one abstracts an appearance, but in a denser form, closer to the center of the actuality.

An actuality in itself holds itself away from all others; it is single, undivided, solidified. No actuality, though, ever succeeds in being just in itself. It is always subject to intrusions and is always multiply expressive. As just itself it is neither real nor unreal, independent nor dependent, present nor absent, neither this nor not this, not unique, not duplicable, for these are all determinations due to insistent intruding powers.

9 An *actuality itself* is the actuality in itself so far as this has been affected by an intrusive determining insistency. As itself, the actuality is inseparable from the actuality in itself, precluding this from ever being fully indeterminate.

10 An *actuality by itself* is the actuality itself united with what intrudes. It is complex, always more or less joined with an intruder without ever becoming completely so.

11 Each complex actuality is conditioned. The conditions are partly expressed in the form of a power which provides the determinations of the actuality itself.

12 Starting with an actuality in itself, an actuality by itself is the outcome of the interplay of the actuality in itself with an alien, insistent power. Starting, instead, with an actuality by itself, an

actuality itself is a constituent which matches determining insistencies with counterthrusts.

13 What passes away are complexities. With their passing, what they are in themselves also passes away, not because they are extinguished, but because the actualities no longer mesh with what is intruding on them. Conversely, actualities by themselves come to be because there has been a meshing of the actualities in themselves with what is other than them, insistently intrusive.

14 An actuality in itself is present in every determinate actuality itself as its limit and, therefore, as the actuality itself at its most indeterminate.

15 Within an actuality by itself, there are two opposing insistencies. One of them is provided by the actuality in itself, the other by an intrusive power. The one gives the intrusive power a degree of specificity, the other gives determinations to the actuality itself.

16 An alien power reaches to actualities in themselves at the same time that it functions in the actualities at points in between, stopping at these in its passage beyond them. The selfsame power that operates on an actuality itself passes beyond to the actuality in itself.

17 An insistency operative on an actuality, but as not yet met by a counterinsistency from it, is part of a *transcendent* condition.

18 A transcendent condition is an ontological, omnipresent, controlling universal. It makes each actuality so far like every other.

19 Each actuality provides evidence, in the guise of a transcendent, of what insistently imposes itself on that actuality.

20 The insistence of a transcendent is countered by an insistence originating with the actuality in itself.

21 An actuality itself is *unique* to the extent that it has been made determinate by an alien insistent power. Its uniqueness has degrees, ranging from a minimal characteristic of the actuality in itself which is part of it, to a maximum above which the actuality itself is an integrated part of an actuality by itself.

22 An actuality by itself has one of an endless number of possible degrees of *density*, ranging from one limit where its constituents are maximally joined, to another limit where they are minimally joined together. As comprising the actuality itself and the insistent power which provides this with determinations, an actuality by itself is an individual, at once complex, determinate, and dense.

23 The individuality of an actuality provides evidence that there is something operative on the actuality by itself, which is not due to the actuality in itself.

24 When an actuality in itself exerts more thrust than an intrusive power does, the result is an objective appearance of the actuality.

25 An actuality itself has degrees of *reality*, ranging from a minimal where it is relatively indeterminate, to the maximum where it is fully subject to an alien insistence. Depending on the extent to which it is interlocked with the source of determinations it has a degree of *facticity*.

26 An actuality is real only as interplaying with an alien insistence and therefore as made determinate by this.

Were an actuality real apart from the determinations provided by an alien insistence, it would be able to act and react, insist and resist, and yet not be given the opportunity to do anything. It would be an indeterminate with a status of its own, standing in opposition to all other actualities in themselves, though there was no way in which they could be distinct and together.

27 An actuality by itself has *being*. Were it to have that being in itself it would be irreducible and coordinate with other beings, and there would be no reason why it should not be forever.

28 Because an actuality itself has reality it provides evidence of a counterinsistency which operates on the actuality in itself. Because an actuality by itself has being, it provides evidence of a power which is expressed as a transcendent, characterizing that and every other actuality.

29 Taken as including its constituents, an actuality by itself has being precariously, since its being depends on the way in which it is joined with an alien insistence. But whatever the degree of its being it is also a determinate complex, with facticity.

30 An actuality itself is *intelligible*. This has degrees. At one limit it is almost formless; at the other it is articulated but undivided.

31 Because an actuality itself is intelligible only so far as it interplays with an alien insistence, its intelligibility is evidence of a counterthrust. Were it to be intelligible without the aid of this, it would be intelligible even when at the limit of indeterminateness, and there would be no reason why its intelligibility should vary in degree. It would be a sheer form which was present, and that was all.

32 An actuality by itself has a *nature* which provides evidence of a power expressed as a transcendent, characterizing it and all other actualities by themselves.

33 The nature of an actuality can not be accounted for by referring to the actuality in itself, for this is too indeterminate to have a nature or to produce anything that is determinate. It cannot be accounted for by referring to the actuality itself, for this is too self-contained to have anything distinguishable within it. It can not be accounted for by the actuality by itself, for it is this which it helps constitute. To account for it we must look beyond it.

34 An actuality by itself has degrees of *organization*. At one limit the counterinsistencies are perfectly meshed; at the other, they interplay only minimally. At one limit the organization is complete; at the other it is hard to distinguish from an aggregation of the elements. An actuality by itself, consequently, is at once complex, determinate, organized, and possessed of a nature.

35 An actuality itself is spread out. It is *self-distended.* Not divisible into parts, it does not have any distinct regions.

36 A distended actuality occupies no space or time or causal process, because it is not yet in a space, time, or causal process. It neither moves nor rests. Yet it could be said to be spatial in itself, because all its distinguishable points are symmetrically related; temporal, because it issues from a past and terminates in a future; and in a causal process, because it interplays with a counterinsistence. But it is these in isolation, and not within environing regions.

37 A distended actuality has degrees running from a self-centered simplicity to a radical expansiveness. Depending on the extent to which its constituents mesh, an actuality by itself has degrees of *effective expansiveness.*

38 An actuality by itself has an *extension* with a distinctive structure, not accountable by the parts within it, since that structure is maintained apart from these. The fact that an actuality has an extension evidences a larger extension of which the actuality's is a subdivision; the actuality is an occupant of an extension spreading beyond the borders of the actuality.

39 At one and the same time an actuality by itself is complex, determinate, expansive, and extended.

40 Finally, an actuality itself is a *unity,* modulated, diversified, but not divisible. In itself, though not a plurality or a manifold, it is still not yet a *unit*.

41 Were an actuality a unit in itself, there would be no accounting for its coming to be and passing away. To account for these, reference must be made to that with which the actuality meshes more or less.

42 A complex actuality has a degree of *singularity,* expressive of the extent to which its constituents interlock. But no matter what the degree, the actuality remains a unit. Because it is a unit it provides evidence of a counterinsistency which operates on the actuality in itself. By itself, it is a complex unit, determinate, and singular.

43 An actuality is at once a unique individual, a real being, an intelligible nature, a distended existent, and a unified unit. It is all of these at the same time, for though the various powers intrude on it independently, they do so together.

44 An actuality by itself has a degree of density, facticity, organization, effective expansiveness, and singularity, reflecting the degree to which what it is is interlocked with intruding determinants.

45 Individuality, being, nature, extension, and unity are transcendents. Each is a constituent in a complex determinate actuality, enabling this to govern the interplaying insistencies within it.

46 The presence and power exerted by transcendents, as well as the characterization which they bestow on an actuality, are to be accounted for by turning away from the actuality to what is able to intrude on it.

47 A transcendent controls the counterthrusts of actualities in all their degrees, at the same time that it is distinct from those actualities and their counterefforts. It affects each actuality; it also controls all of them, making them members of the same cosmos.

48 *Compounds* have parts which are also actualities, each in itself, itself, and by itself. Those parts are sources of the dominant factors of their own objective appearances.

1 IN A *compound actuality* a number of complex actualities, its parts, function together.

2 The *cosmos* embraces both ultimate particles, each of which is a complex but not a compound actuality, and compounds of these. The particles are the concern of a theoretical physics; the compounds are the concern of chemistry, biology, sociology, politics, and any other enterprises concerned with observable actualities.

3 Actualities by themselves within a compound are together in a number of independent ways. As a consequence, actualities can not only be multiply united in a single compound, but may remain united in one way while they cease to be united in others.

4 One way in which actualities may be together is as distinct parts, all located within the same compound actuality. As parts, they are actualities by themselves, only some of which may be compound.

5 A relation of the parts in an actuality, though it does not exist apart from what it relates, contrasts with them. As distinct from the relation, the parts are still together. That fact requires one to refer to a power which operates on all of them, to make them be together.

6 The parts of a compound may be allied or disjoined. So far as they are allied, they *cluster*. Without losing their independence as distinct parts, they are there interconnected without regard for the distances between them. A part here may be allied with one there while being indifferent to or while repelling another close by.

7 A compound does not have the power to ally or disjoin its parts, though it is able to have consequences and relations of its own. Its parts can not cluster of themselves; of itself a part is able only to *interplay* with others. When it does more than merely interplay, it has been empowered to do so.

8 That parts are clustered in various ways and degrees within a compound is an additional fact about them. That fact evidences the presence of a power transmitted through the compound, making the parts function together within that compound.

9 Distinct parts may either be merely with one another or more intimately connected, reflecting the way they are turned toward one

another through the agency of the particular compound in which they are. As the former, they constitute a *set,* as the latter, a *whole.*

10 In a whole, parts are turned toward one another in one of an endless number of degrees. At a maximum, the relation of the parts reflects the nature of the compound; at the minimum, the nature of the compound plays no role, leaving the parts to be just members of a set.

11 Whatever the degree of intimacy, the parts are independent of one another. Their actions are not controlled by the compound in which they are. All bodies fall at the same rate under ideal conditions, because their parts are not under the governance of the compound. Organic bodies, of course, do control their parts, as their locomotion shows. But not always, as is evident from the fact that their rate of fall is no faster or slower than that of any other compound.

12 A compound may have linked parts having various roles in relation to one another. Some of the parts may be pivotal, others subordinate, still others mediative in role. They can be in an hierarchy, a chain, a circle, be mutually supportive, or sustain multiple relations to some or all of the others in an *arrangement* or an *order.*

13 An arrangement is a product. An order is imposed by a compound which, without affecting the independence of the parts and therefore the kinds of relations they might have on their own, governs those parts.

14 A compound transmits an insistency. This compels its parts to be positioned with reference to one another. The positioning varies in intensity in accord with the variations in the amount of force that the compound transmits. But whatever the degree, its members have prescribed places and roles. Together they change their places and roles in accord with changes in the kind and amount of force that the compound transmits.

15 The various parts of a machine are arranged, usually with some of them in distinctive pivotal roles. Through the action of its maker, the parts also have designated positions and roles, making them parts of an engine or a mill or an incinerator, or some other special kind of machine. Energy is fed into the machine in consonance with the nature of the compound, and the parts are then set in action in a distinctive way and with distinctive tasks.

Were a machine to have its parts positioned through the imposition of a power expressed through a compound, the machine would not have to depend on the infusion of energy within it before its parts could have distinctive roles in relation to one another in a definite order.

16 Within the limits of a compound the parts may be compelled to make a difference to one another in various ways. They may affect one another mutually, they may inherit from one another, they may condition one another. When the parts function independently of one another, they constitute a *bundle*. This changes in nature and career as they change in their relations to one another within the compound's limits.

17 The parts within a bundle have relations to what is outside it. Those relations may be exactly like those that other realities have to one another, but those others will not make a bundle, because they are not parts of one compound. Yet a compound has no power to control the coming and going, the acting and reacting of its parts.

18 In a *colony*, parts are subject to a new condition; those within the confines of the compound act on one another in ways they do not act on what is outside those confines, even when they are related to what is outside in the same way they are related to those inside the confines of the compound. Their roles inside the compound, in contradistinction from those that they can have with respect to what is outside, betray the presence of a power transmitted through the compound.

19 In daily life a distinction is normally made among things, living beings, and men. All of them are compounds of complexities. Within the confines of any one of these there may be no interplay, set, arrangement, or bundle of parts, and therefore no evidence that there are powers which enabled them also to be members of clusters, wholes, orders, or colonies. Or there may be some parts which are just arranged and others which are just bundled, and so on. Nevertheless, all compounds are subject to the same imperious powers.

20 There are latent powers. The fact becomes prominent in the more elementary lower organisms. Their parts lack arrangements and order for a while, only to achieve them at some subsequent date. The latent power awaits for its operation on an appropriate arrangement before it can give them an order. Were there are no arranged parts—to take this as an example—within a compound, those parts could not be ordered, for the power to order them is unable to operate until the parts are arranged. The power is then latent in the compound, coming to expression only when the parts are in the suitable condition. This might be achieved in the ordinary course of change or growth, or even through the play of chance.

21 Living beings are *organic*. The parts within them are not simply confined by the compound through which a power is transmitted. The compound itself effectively governs what is within it.

22 In abstraction from effective control by a compound, parts *coalesce*. Though they then belong together, they may interact with what is outside that coalescence with as much effect as they have on one another.

23 A compound adds to a coalescence the condition that the parts belong to the compound. It controls its parts, at least in part, through a power received, and which it loses when its parts are removed. When the parts are no longer available, a compound ceases to be, but the power which it transmits continues to operate on what is left.

24 Organic beings come to be and pass away; they grow and they decay. Each dictates to its parts, not only where these will be in the course of an organic movement, but how some of them will function on behalf of the organism.

25 In the case of men and other highly compound and complicated organisms, reproduction introduces a new problem. The sperm and cell are themselves organic beings with compound natures embracing at least an actuality in itself and a determining counterinsistence. There are compounds and complexities in each as well, all subject to a power transmitted by, and also under the control of, the distinct compound natures of sperm and egg.

When sperm and egg are joined, their compound natures give way to a single compound in which sperm and egg are transformed into termini in a new relationship. Had the sperm and egg remained, there would be no new organic compound with its own distinctive contained compounds and complexities; instead, there would be something like a whole, cluster, an order, or colony of sperm and egg. But their union results in a compound that is as fully organic as they were, operating in new ways on the actualities that were within both sperm and egg.

26 The objects known in daily life are compounds of compounds of compounds. . . . Those compounds seem to be so clearly connected in an hierarchy that it is tempting to suppose that the lower temporally preceded the higher in an emergent evolutionary process that produces ever higher level realities in the course of time. But a compound that embraces other kinds of compounds need not come to be after those others; a particular compound which embraces other compounds may come to be and pass away at the same time that its included compounds do.

27 A compound does not stand above whatever compounds it may embrace. Instead, it is integral to them, giving them the status of terms. Together it and they make a single *complex compound.*

28 In a complex compound, complexities are governed by a transmitted power, transforming the ways they were together on their own. The transmitted power may be different from that which had been transmitted through the compounds that are now terminal.

29 A complex compound does not allow complete independence to its complexities; it requires some transformation of them and the way they are together.

30 A highly complex compound, such as man, has complexities under the goverance of a relation connecting what are relations of relations . . . , until one comes to terminal compounds which embrace complexities of determinate actualities, and countering and controlling powers.

31 The power transmitted through a compound might be quite distinct from that which its parts originally suffered when they functioned outside that compound. But whether or not the power be the same, it owes its presence to what is outside the compound.

32 All compounds, complex or not, are subject to the same finalites. Actualities differ in grade in accord with their ability to internalize them all.

*

INTERNALIZATIONS

1 ACTUALITIES ARE SUBJECT to alien powers. These enable the actualities to be conditioned together and, so far, to function as terms in relations. They also enable compound actualities to govern their parts.

2 Were there no powers subjecting the actualities in these ways, each actuality would stand apart from the others, or would be diffusely together with them, and only by accident would all exercise the same type of governance over their parts. Actualities are in the same cosmos together, and are there subject to firm, persistent cosmic controls. Each also is made determinate by the selfsame conditions and is therefore *an* actuality. Each, too, governs in common ways the particular parts that are within its confines, and can therefore be *a* compound actuality.

3 Nominalists are concerned with actualities in their full concreteness. They give full value to the irreducible status of individuals in themselves. Realists remark on what is common to all actualities. They rightly insist on the fact that actualities must be enabled to be together by something other than themselves, and that they all mediate common conditions and are therefore understandable in common ways. The two views are compatible. But they should be supplemented by an account of the sources of the conditions. Otherwise, we will lack an explanation of the insistent presence of governing conditions.

4 An actuality in itself counters alien insistencies with insistencies of its own. So far as the alien dominates, the actuality is characterizable as other actualities are, as an individual, with a being, nature, extension, and value.

5 The power of an alien insistence can not be absolute, without the actuality being controlled by what is forever, and thereby ceasing to be that which has its own boundaries, status, structure, actions, and demands.

6 A *transcendent* partly transmits a power; it also partly embodies it, and thereby controls a determinate actuality. That part of the power of an alien insistence which is not spent in making an actuality in itself be determinate, is spent in controlling the result.

7 The power that a transcendent possesses enables it to function as a *qualifier*.

8 A qualifier characterizes an entire actuality at the same time that it keeps the actuality connected to the power expressed in and through that transcendent.

9 The very same power that makes compounds possible, enables all actualities to be members of the same cosmos. When the power takes either form, it is limited by the actualities in which and on which it operates. As a consequence, the actualities are then and there qualified; made to be substantial individuals and not merely unique; to have beings and not merely to be real; to have natures and not merely to be intelligible; to be extended and not merely distended; and to be unit values and not merely demanding particulars.

10 An actuality tries to internalize its qualifiers. The effort at internalization may not be successful. Whether or not it is, it prompts the actuality to thrust itself out against the power, so as to constitute, through its aid, an objective appearance of the actuality.

11 An actuality has status of its own, and that is never swallowed up by any other reality. Otherwise there would be nothing on which the transcendent could operate. Yet, from the position of a qualifier, there is nothing more than a center for it, a mere point at its limits.

12 A qualifier encompasses the entire actuality from a position outside the actuality. From that position there is no aspect of the actuality that could then be said to be untouched by the transcendent.

13 An actuality is completely qualified, making the actuality adjectival to a reality over which it has no control.

14 A qualification does not prevent an actuality from continuing to be independent of and indeed opposed to what is qualifying it. The presence of a qualification is inseparable from a reply by the actuality.

15 There always are appearances because actualities are always qualified, and are thereby prompted to exhibit themselves in opposition to the reality that is qualifying them. Were they indifferent to their qualifications, they would either be without insides, or these would be discrepant with what the actualities were made to be on the outside. What they were made to be together, also, would be without bearing on what they were by themselves.

The acknowledgment of different kinds of insides makes possible a grading of actualities; the acknowledgment of a discrepancy between inside and outside makes possible an account of the need for the kinds of exhibitions the actualities provide; the acknowledgment of the bearing of them as together with others on what they are by themselves makes possible an understanding of the way the actualities can function independently and yet be in a world with others.

16 Actualities differ in their ability to internalize what qualifies them. Those of the lowest grade internalize only the qualifications produced by one finality; those of the highest grade internalize the qualifications of all. The one is a thing, the other a man. Other grades of actuality lie in between. The actualities in these between grades are able to internalize the qualifications of more than one finality, but cannot internalize all. The exhibitions of each kind of actuality reflect the kinds of qualifications it has internalized.

17 As an exhibition of an actuality comes into the open it is modified along the way by the transient responses of other actualities. These responses tinge the actuality's persistent reply to what persistently qualifies it. As a consequence, all the appearances of actualities are not only inside a Context where they share constancies, but reflect the particular adventures of the actualities with one another.

18 As merely qualified, an actuality is not yet a substance, but just substantialized. Only when it internalizes the qualification is it able to be a substance. It then takes that qualification into itself, and from within becomes the substance that it has been qualified to be.

19 A substance makes whatever it touches into a dependent possession. Denied this ability, an actuality would not be able to so reply to an intruding insistence that it contributes to the production of its own appearance.

20 Were an actuality just qualified, it would not help constitute an appearance. If the actuality did not internalize the qualification, but was provoked to help constitute an appearance, the actuality would make an appearance possible but would not itself appear.

21 A *factor* is an exhibition of a reality interlocked with the opposing attenuation of another reality. So is a transcendent. But while a factor ranges from a dominant to a recessive position, a transcendent always remains dominant. A factor issuing from a finality has a cosmic range; a transcendent, in addition, governs and controls particular actualities.

22 A physical object, or *thing*, is a substance, able to be, act, react, change, and move. What a thing can do, all other grades of actuality can also do. That is why physics and chemistry can have an application to them as well. Their theories, though, fall short of what actualities are, not only as qualified in other ways, but as having internalized those qualifications. They know nothing of what things are from within. But that is where things possess what they exhibit, and the appearances that thereby result.

23 Ignoring the fact that all actualities are qualified, and that all internalize some qualifications, does not make the fact vanish. No account can be satisfactory which allows only things to be real yet takes them to be not substantial and unable to move or act.

24 Different grades of actuality are functions of different abilities to internalize the qualifications to which all are subject. The grades may or may not come to clear and observable expressions. Grading does not preclude the acknowledgment of an evolutionary passage from one grade to another, since that passage depends on new opportunities for some actualities to internalize what they could not before.

25 There is no clear observable line marking off things from the lowest grade of living beings, and no clear observable line marking off these from higher grades of living beings.

26 Different types of qualification are imposed on all actualities at the same time. An actuality is thereby provoked to internalize and express itself in a number of distinct ways. Since a thing can internalize and express no more than one type of qualification, that stemming from Substance, the other types of qualification imply nothing more than that it is subject to other finalities.

27 The lowest grade of living being, like a thing, internalizes a qualifying substantiality, and is thereupon able to have appearances which are affiliated and disaffiliated with the appearances of other actualities. The living being, in addition, pulls into itself an extension that had qualified it and thereby made it extended. Its appearances, consequently, have a position in an environment where it has a special pertinence to a few others.

The appearance of an oak is positioned in relation to the appearances of soil, water, other oaks, and other trees. The space, in which all these appearances are, is distinct from the space of a cosmos where their actualities interact under the aegis of cosmic laws. The one is a context filled out, the other is a condition setting the limits within which the actualities function.

28 A living being that is a grade above the lowest living being is, like it, positioned in an environment at the same time that it is affiliated or disaffiliated with others. It also internalizes the unity that qualifies it. As a consequence, the living being is able to be a member of, and help constitute an appearance in, a group.

29 On higher level still, are those living beings that incorporate within themselves the intelligible possibility which qualifies them. They reply to the presence of the qualifier by contributing to the constitution of appearances in a structured world of appearances.

30 Appearances are intelligible so far as they are united by a common structure. The intelligible relations they then have to one another is independent of the rationale of the actualities to which they belong. The one is constituted by a single intrusive power, the other by internalizations of limited expressions of that power.

31 A man stands above all other actualities. He can not be entirely understood in the terms they provide; we can, consequently, no more understand him from the vantage point of the primates than we can understand a mammal from the standpoint of a reptile. To understand a man it is necessary to escape the frame within which other living beings are completely confined, and see him as one who alone has internalized a qualification due to Being.

32 It is not possible to mark man off clearly from all other types merely by referring to his making or using tools, or to his having or using a language or a mind. These are not altogether absent from lower levels. One could, though, refer to his science, art, religion, history, philosophy, laws, traditions, myths, and conventions, and then to his making or using tools, language, or mind for the sake of or because of these. But, detached from man as expressing himself as a being, these are only patterns of public activity. Other actualities, or combinations of them in the form of a machine, can duplicate such patterns. What they can not do is to produce the science, art, and so forth, in which the patterns are created or creatively used.

33 A man is to be accounted for in ways which require no break in continuity from those that are relevant to an understanding of lower grades of actuality. He goes beyond the point they can, but only because he alone succeeds in internalizing all the qualifications to which every actuality is subject. Since he alone internalizes a qualifier produced by Being, he alone functions as one who not only is given but encompasses a being.

1 EVIDENCES ARE EFFECTS present in something alien, and affecting this. If metaphysical, they are also produced by, are informative of, and enable one to begin a movement to their sources. Unless there be atomic units lacking all determination, there is nothing which can not yield metaphysical evidence.

2 A number of different evidences can be in the same place. This is true even when the evidences are not metaphysical. The quality of a piece of paper provides evidence of the way it was made and of the pulp from which it was made; the writing on it evidences the date of composition and, therefore, possibly the perpetration of a hoax or a fraud.

3 The evidences of different finalities are copresent, the result of the independent functioning of distinct powers. Five different types are to be distinguished.

a) *Context.* This persistently dominates over the exhibitions of all actualities, making it possible for those exhibitions to stand apart from the actualities, as factors helping constitute a world of appearances.

b) *Alien insistencies.* These give determinations to the actualities themselves. The determinateness provides evidence of intrusions, and these in turn provide evidence of what intrudes.

c) *Transcendents.* These govern actualities in their entirety at the same time that they are interlocked with what the actualities insist upon. Transcendents hold on to what they help make possible.

d) *Qualifiers.* These affect actualities in their entirety but, unlike transcendents, are not constrained by or interlocked with anything in the actualities.

e) *The cosmic pattern.* Actualities are together in a cosmos. The manner of their togetherness evidences distinctive powers able to keep them together, despite their independence as self-centered realities acting on their own.

4 Context, insistencies, transcendents, qualifiers, and the cosmic pattern interconnect actualities in distinctive ways. The Context interlocks with factors contributed by actualities; insistencies interact with the actualities in themselves; the transcendents are inter-

nally differentiated by what they condition and control; a qualifier subjects each actuality to a single governance; and the cosmic pattern makes the actualities function in relation to one another.

5 Though some parts of exhibitions and of actualities are recessive and others to the fore, some pivotal and others peripheral in place or role, all are made to be together. The Context is germane to all exhibitions of actualities, giving them an equal status, no matter what the dignity of their sources. An alien insistence operates on all actualities in themselves in the same way, no matter how different they are. A transcendent is effectively involved with each actuality, in all its variety. A qualifier characterizes all actualities, no matter what the grade. And a cosmic pattern connects all actualities, no matter what their magnitude, value, or function.

6 Categories are classifying meanings of such scope and ultimacy that every character necessarily falls within their confines. Evidences categorize what they are involved with.

7 In the Context, what was dominant in the appearances of actualities is recessive. The result is a single categoreal domain for those appearances. Insistencies give things in themselves the categoreal status of determinate entities. Transcendents give actualities by themselves the categoreal status of controlled pluralities. Qualifiers give complex actualities the categoreal status of dependents on the finalities. And the cosmic pattern gives actualities the categoreal status of cosmic entities. In each case categorizing evidence provides a new import for that on which it operates.

8 Without an evidencing category there could be determinates, conditioned and controlled pluralities, and cosmic entities, but no one of them could be understood to be so. Each would function in an unduplicable way, exhausting its meaning in the exercise of its role. Categories allow us to stand apart from actualities so as to be able to understand what actualities can do and be.

9 Evidences encompass the items on which they have been intruded. The encompassment makes that on which the evidences operate be bounded as separate, and yet be part of one world as together. This is obviously true of the Context and the cosmic pattern, for these are areas within which a number of distinguishable items are together. But though insistencies, transcendents, and qualifiers operate only on distinct actualities, each intrudes, interlocks with, or affects every actuality in the same way.

10 Evidences control that on which they operate. The Context dominates over the contributions of actualities; insistencies keep actualities in themselves dependent on them for determinations; a transcendent turns an actuality into content for it; a qualifier has room for every feature of the actuality; and the cosmic pattern makes all actualities belong to one cosmos. Without such controls, actualities, their parts, and their exhibitions would be just places at which

these evidences were; instead those evidences also have a new import and role there.

11 Evidence is located as well as controlling. This is obviously true of what is distinguishable in a Context and a cosmic pattern. It is also true of insistencies, transcendents, and qualifiers; operating on distinct actualities, they operate on all, positioning them in relation to one another.

12 Actualities, as well as contextualized appearances, are units on the same level as, and continuous with, their interconnections. Their interconnections are relations internal to them, allowing them no independence. Actualities and appearances are, of course, also more than related terms; each is distinct from the others, with a density and depth peculiar to it.

13 Whether or not appearances and actualities have values of their own, they have values because of the roles they have in relation to the evidences that they carry. Appearances in the Context are involved with one another in various ways and degrees to yield a single aesthetic value. The attainment of determinations due to the operation of an intrusive insistence enables an actuality to have the value of a distinct entity by itself, contrasting with all others. A transcendent enables an actuality to share in the status of that which is everywhere and forever. A qualifier, instead, enables an actuality to belong to what is final. And the cosmic pattern enables all actualities not only to belong together but to make a difference to one another's functioning.

14 There are no evidences except so far as there are carriers of them. Otherwise the evidences would never get to the stage of being present. Instead, they would be expressions of powers which never were impressed anywhere.

Were anything without a carrier, as classical theology takes the entire spatiotemporal-dynamic world to be, it could not provide evidence of a creator, precisely because it would not stand apart from him. Only so far as it adhered to something other than itself could it evidence the God who supposedly made it be. A supposed created actuality must have an existence distinct from the essence it carries. Taken apart from the existence, the essence would be just a possibility not yet realized.

15 A carrier of evidence and the evidence are not opposed to one another, as two independent realities might be; instead, the evidence, in making its carrier be for it, thereby gives the carrier an oppositional role for it. Apart from that role, the carrier has an integrity of its own, and as such, opposes all else, including the source of the evidence.

16 To characterize actualities in terms of the evidences they carry is to emphasize what is common and persistent in them. This overrides their idiosyncracies and contingent adventures; it, therefore, enables one to refer to the actualities in stable ways.

17 Evidence is part of a setting where it is connected with what it evidences. The setting for the evidence and evidenced may be a convention about causes, motives, or actions, or the product of a belief or memory. But if the evidence is metaphysical—the kind with which we are here concerned—it is always more. Metaphysical evidence is affected by its source, and is related by this to the evidenced. It is a term in a setting where what it evidences has the guise of another term. In the rules governing formal proofs of finalities, this feature of the evidence assumes prominence.

18 Evidence is always two-faced and doubly toned. Imposed by and never free from its source, it is sustained by and limited to its carrier. To attend to it as the one, it is necessary to neglect what it owes to the other.

19 The Context and the cosmic pattern are evidential of their sources, along a route of an intensification. Intruded insistencies depend for their power on their sources; they evidence what transmits a power through them. A transcendent refers to a power outside it, which both empowers and acts through it. Qualifiers are loci of forces but not transmitters of them, and are inseparable from what empowers them.

20 Insistencies, transcendents, and qualifiers are located singulars. The Context and the cosmic pattern, in contrast, are diversified by what they embrace.

21 A source in the very act of providing evidence also provides a correlative term for that evidence. The source of the evidence thereby points the evidence, not to the source, but to an evidenced version of the source, relative to the evidence.

22 Evidence, via the evidenced, symbolizes its source. In using it, one goes through a process in which the source is more and more penetrated, and enriches what has already been attained. If a symbolized version of the source be kept apart from the source, the symbol is made to function as a mere sign.

23 Context and the cosmic pattern, no less than insistencies, transcendents, and qualifiers, evidence finalities. All are enabled to be symbols by the evidenced; this, in turn, symbolizes what produced both it and the evidence.

24 Evidence is here and now; the evidenced is only possible, yet to be attained. Evidence is specific; the evidenced is relatively general. Evidence acts on actualities; the evidenced acts only on the evidence. Where the one is pluralized and offers a beginning, the other is single and terminal.

25 Evidence has a persistent, insistent source; it is consequently always being made present in something other than itself. Though in many places, it is a constant. Everywhere there is the same contextual determination, the same cosmic relationships, the same insistencies, transcendents, and qualifiers. But as involved with distinct entities, evidence has a specificity and career partly dependent on the way these function.

26 Since evidence is involved with particulars, that is, appearances and actualities alien to it, it can never be more than a specified, failed universal, connected with an evidenced universal which is indifferent to whatever particulars there be. All the while, actualities provide occasions for the evidence to remain outside the evidenced.

27 Evidence needs to be freed from whatever prevents it from functioning as a true universal, which is what it is regardless of what actualities are or what they do. It should be united with the evidenced in consonance with the way the source of both unites them.

28 Evidence exhibits a lack which the evidenced makes good. The making good, though, awaits the actual passage to and arrival at, and, therefore, the realization of what is now only a possible terminus for the evidence.

29 Evidence never becomes that which it evidences. If it did, it would vanish without a trace. Its success would be its destruction. The freeing of evidence from actualities and their contributions leads to a pairing of it with what it evidences.

30 The passage to the evidenced is a perfecting of the evidence. It does not annihilate the evidence; indeed, this continues to be carried by alien particulars.

31 There is an attachment of the evidence to the evidenced. As a consequence, the evidenced gives the evidence a direction, pointing it to the evidenced. The evidence is then related to the evidenced as a usable fragment is to the whole; there it no longer has limits imposed on it by alien realities. One gets from evidence to the evidenced by yielding the one to the other more and more, until the two form a single unit.

32 A distinguishing of evidence is to be followed by a directed pointing of the evidence to the evidenced, by a correlating of evidence and evidenced, by the evidenced's directing of the evidence toward the evidenced, and, finally, by a solidification of the evidence and evidenced. The distinguishing makes it possible to have evidence; the directed pointing is the evidence ready to be used; the correlating makes it possible for the evidence to be evidential; the use of the evidence by the evidenced makes the evidence part of the act of evidencing; the solidification yields the outcome of the evidencing.

33 Evidence is like a question open to its answer. Peirce translated questions into forms where there were empty spaces; these, when filled out, turned the questions into answers. Such forms do not show that the empty spaces are to be filled out, or by what, for they are not connected with anything that can fill them out. Metaphysical evidence offers a question connected with what will fill it out. What is metaphysically evidenced contains whatever is missing in the evidence.

34 The evidenced (or answer), though it contains what the evidence (or question) lacks, is itself incomplete. Though it can complete what asks for it, it itself needs completion, since it is itself a question directed at the source of it. But it also needs the evidence to point to it and fill it out, before it can properly symbolize its source.

35 The source of evidence is independent of it. It both provides the evidence and enables it to function as evidence. No one could return to that source unless aided by the source itself. But it is only through the agency of the evidenced that the evidence takes one to the source of both.

36 Evidence and evidenced satisfy one another when they are intimately united. What is missing from both of them together is provided by the source, and what is missing from that source—a relevance to actualities—is provided by the evidence.

*

NAMES

1 Evidence can be used so privately that others do not know that it is being used at all. Even when the use is accompanied by public acts, gestures, and words, the private use and the public accompaniments could be quite different in nature and career, or could be together adventitiously and irregularly.

2 Though public accompaniments may affect the way evidence is privately viewed, they do not enable another to know that evidence is being used, unless they are made part of the evidence.

3 If one is to know that another is using evidence, or if he is to know where another is acknowledging evidence, what that evidence is like, where it can take one, and where one arrives by using it, the other's private activities must be made known. The most readily producible, shareable, and variegated way of doing this is through language, when this is kept in accord with the main stages of the process of evidencing.

A linguistic expression can be made part of a qualified actuality; it can be held apart from the actuality to become a linguistic specification of the qualification itself; it can be connected with other expressions at the same time that their relation is made part of the relation between evidence and the evidenced; it can be taken to require the production of other expressions by being made ingredient in the process of evidencing; and it can be solidified with other expressions and thereby enabled to specify the way in which the evidence and the evidenced are united. Linguistic expressions then will have roles similar to those involved in the use of evidence. The understanding of the linguistic expressions, as a consequence, will be inseparable from an understanding of the evidential steps.

4 Were language to constitute a self-enclosed world, it would not only fail to provide a means of communication and cease to be a vital factor in the making of a community, but there would be no way to provide publicly usable indications that evidence was being privately used. The language used in discourse specifies objective states of affairs at the same time that it makes public that some one is involved with those states of affairs.

5 A language is analyzable in many ways. The previous discussions make desirable a division of it into five elements. Any particu-

lar natural language may lack some of these; a truly basic, good artificial language allows for all the distinctions that the use of evidences requires—the basic language settling for the broadest possible expressions, the other restricting these for special purposes.

6 Some linguistic expressions have a primary, while others have an auxiliary role. An expression in a primary role concerns evidence of high generality—an insistence, a transcendent, a qualifier, a context, or a cosmic pattern, functioning as something sustained, by itself, related, used, or completed. Expressions having an auxiliary role are at the service of these.

7 Since the evidence to which we initially attend is sustained by actualities, it is proper to begin a linguistic account with a consideration of the kind of words—proper names—that are involved with those actualities. Since evidence, to be used, has to be held apart from what sustains it, related to what it evidences, directed toward what it needs (and which needs it), and united with whatever makes possible the move from the evidence to the evidenced, use must also be made of auxiliaries as well—except where there are specific terms singularly appropriate to each of these states.

8 There are four distinct kinds of proper names: *adherent* and *exalted*; *honorific* and *arresting*. The first two are primary, pertinent to actualities and finalities, respectively; the second two are derivative, transposed versions of these.

9 Adherent names are united with individual actualities through an act of acknowledgement. 'Tom Jones', 'my partner', are examples. Such names are used when one attends to an actuality with sympathy or repugnance, or some shade in between.

10 Exalted names are the proper names of finalities. They are inseparable from deep emotions, such as awe, reverence, terror, by means of which one penetrates into the finalities.

11 An honorific name is obtained by using an exalted proper name for an actuality. We then say that the actuality is a substance, with a being, nature, extension, or unity. 'Saint' and 'genius' are honorific if they retain at least a trace of an initial involvement with a finality. An honorific 'king', 'lord', perhaps even 'father', is accompanied by an implicit promise that one will continue to have a subordinate role if a certain response to the name is forthcoming.

A *quasi-honorific* name is addressed to an expression of a finality when this is directed toward particulars which are controlled by it. 'The law-abiding physical universe' is a quasi-honorific name.

12 An arresting name uses the adherent name of an actuality—Buddha, Isaiah, or even the *ens realissimus* or the 'unsurpassable' to refer to a finality. Such a name, since it is derived from the world of actualities, is merely set in a deep emotion, and lacks its support. It does not involve acceptance, rejection, submission, avoidance, or penetration of the finality.

An arresting name remains on the surface of a finality. It contrasts with the exalted name, which is caught up in a penetrative act.

A *quasi-arresting* name is addressed to evidence which has been freed from its involvement with particulars and been brought under the aegis of a finality. Used in the course of a penetration into the finality, that name becomes merged with the evidence, and then functions as an exalted name of the finality itself.

13 All words—proper names and denotatives, no less than common names and predicates—are universals in discourse. They can be applied to many different entities. Only by being matched by an empty entity do they enable a man to say what he means and mean what he says—a universal.

14 Proper names and denotatives—'Robert' and 'this'—can be used to accompany a gesture, serving to mark off some encountered item. They can be used in a novel, and they can be misapplied. But their primary and proper use is to take one into actualities. This requires that they be used adherently as part of the very realities they name. Instead of having an empty entity matching a universal in language, one then reaches toward a dense, intensive center possessing all that it exhibits.

15 An ordinary proper name, 'Tom Jones', is adherent. Equally, it is a specification of a qualification of an actuality. The first formulation stresses the actuality, the second the qualification. The first is used when there is an inclination toward the actuality in itself; the second, when there is an inclination toward the imposed qualification. When speaking *to* Tom Jones we favor the first; when speaking *about* him we favor the second.

16 Could one know just what had been added to an actuality from outside it, a subtraction would leave one with the actuality. Conversely, a subtraction of the actuality would leave one with evidence of something else. But we can not know what has been added to an actuality until we are able to distinguish it from the evidence it sustains. When an adherent proper name is used, the distinction is not made. 'Tom Jones' is a qualified actuality in a specialized, intensified, linguistic guise.

17 To create an adherent proper name, one begins with some other proper name, or something less than this, and moves on from there to the position where the name is produced. To name the baby, the parents think of the proper name of some relative, saint, prophet, or patron, and in a process, like that of making use of evidence, move on until they have produced a proper name which is to be used adherently. They could have started with a common name of a flower or a type of belief, and ended with a 'Rose' or a 'Faith'. The possibility of starting with something other than a proper name shows that one is not driven back over an endless regress in the attempt to account for a particular proper name.

18 A man rightly resents being called 'that-man' because his depth is then ignored. He is rightly annoyed when his name is misdirected. He is doubly insulted when his name is given to a dog or a shoe, for these not only are distinct from him but do not deserve to be addressed by means of penetrative proper names.

19 When 'Tom Jones' deals with a man in depth, it is identical with a transcendent unity that has been made integral to him. To use the name is to make that unity present in a linguistically-tinged form, and is thus to offer evidence both of an individual and of a transcendent.

20 Since an adherent proper name adds a humanly produced public specification to a unified actuality, others are provided with the opportunity to be in a position where they, too, can specify the actuality by using the name adherently.

21 A listener exhibits an understanding of a proper name when he functions in accord with the actuality to which the name adheres. He might then also make an acknowledgment similar to that which the speaker made, and follow the acknowledgment with other expressions which are based on and are appropriate to what follows on the speaker's acknowledgment.

22 A child is taught proper names as well as the behavior that is appropriate to the actuality to which the name is to adhere. Initially the two are distinct. The child's maturation in part consists in its achieving the ability to have its behavior nor merely accompany, but to be more and more relevant to the actuality. Over the course of time, it refines the way it uses some such proper name, as (my) 'mamma', and thereby comes to acknowledge her as more than a source of satisfactions and commands.

23 A child, when affectionately speaking to its dog or horse or doll, does not make use of proper names. It externalizes its feelings when it speaks to them, but without then moving into that which is in or by itself. The names it assigns to these, consequently, are not adherent, but referential, marking out areas within which proper names can be used.

24 The names of famous men are given to streets, cities, epochs, and animals. The names are then no longer used adherently; they have been translated into other kinds of names. When 'Washington' names a city or a state, it is not used as a term of address, for it does not then serve as an agency for penetrating into them. A poetic 'O Washington' is a salutation, not a proper name.

25 In a savage's prayer before an idol arresting names are directed not at the idol but at a divinity supposedly mediated by this. His prayer, so far, differs from the prayers of civilized men, not in his use of different kinds of names, but in his use of certain names not acknowledged by the others.

26 When a proper name is used, there normally is at least an implicit use made of auxiliaries, spelling out details about what had been named. 'The brave man, Tom Jones', 'my husband, Tom Jones', make use of explicit auxiliaries.

27 'This-substance', 'this-being', 'this-nature', 'this-existent', and 'this-unity' are *honorific categoreal* names. They fall short of individual actualities for, despite their intended singular reference, they have a part which is appropriate to any actuality. That makes them all the more suitable to express a concern with metaphysical evidences. 'This-substance' refers to a qualification, publicly available.

28 By means of a proper name, an actuality is re-presented in a publicly available form. The respondent knows what is being said just so far as he grasps the name as adherent. Although what is done is no secret, what is done is more than speaking or writing, for the name is ingredient in what is being dealt with privately. Men reveal who they privately are and what they are privately doing by using proper names adherent to the actualities that are being privately acknowledged.

29 Most actualities are not given singular proper names, but are referred to by means of such compound expressions as 'that-man', 'this-book', 'there is the tree'. These, like the honorific categoreals, have a general component. Unlike the categoreals, the effect of the generality is overcome through pointings, gestures, and acts. They are proper names in function, not linguistically.

30 'Tom Jones', in primary use, specifies the evaluational unity which qualifies an individual man. To provide an opportunity for others to participate in the acknowledgment of the man as qualified in other ways as well, recourse must be had to such expressions as 'the sensitive Tom Jones', 'the real Tom Jones', 'the man, Tom Jones', 'the existent Tom Jones'. The different qualifications which these expressions take into account are on a footing with the evaluational unity expressed by 'Tom Jones'.

31 Anthropologists, sociologists, and psychologists do not usually attend to the ways in which linguistic and associated expressions are used by different men in the course of their private acknowledgment and use of evidence. Instead, they occupy themselves with associated expressions, functioning as a common ground between speaker and listener. Language is thereby taken to be an intermediary between the two, enabling the men to be members of a communicating community.

32 Where the listener is the individual addressed, a distinction is to be made between him as spoken to and as attending to the manner in which he is spoken to. In the second guise he functions toward what is said in somewhat the way a third person might attend to it.

33 A position of neutrality has to be assumed in order to explicate how public linguistic evidence can have private roles for speakers as

well as listeners. The linguistic expressions can then be examined in their own right, with the speakers and listeners dealt with as having the contributory functions of users and interpreters.

34 A man in himself has internalized qualifications originating with the different finalities. Account of that fact allows one to acknowledge him to have an individuality, rights, intelligence, identity, and value in himself. To know that he is being dealt with in one of these guises, attention must be paid both to the accompaniments of the names that are addressed to him, for these reflect the degree to which his independence and determinateness are being acknowledged, and to others which show that he is being treated as the locus of these dignities. Terms of respect—'sir', 'Mr.', 'Ms.', 'brother', 'comrade' have the latter function.

35 'You', and its cognates, are adherent when accompanied by expectations of a response toward oneself in the role of a you.

36 A proper name has not been used properly until the required reality has been reached. Confirmation that a proper name has been properly used is obtained when accompanying expectations are fulfilled.

37 One may not know a foreign language, but expressions of admiration, contempt, and the like toward oneself are sometimes readily recognized despite this. One then knows that a name or personal pronoun is being so used that it bears on one's dignity.

38 When an adherent term is applied to an animal, the expression should be accompanied by an indication of the fact that the animal is taken to be an independent actuality with some determinateness.

39 One must look to the behavior of a speaker to determine whether or not an animal is being accredited with the same dignities that men have. Whatever the decision, it does not affect the fact that an animal allows for the acknowledgment of evidence intruded on it, and that the use of that evidence can be linguistically known by means of names supported by behavior which makes clear to others what the accredited dignity is.

40 Normally, a thing is not spoken to or addressed. But it, too, provides evidence of alien intruding powers.

41 The import of exalted philosophic terms is grasped by taking them to follow on a discussion in which their import is distinguished from the somewhat similar terms used to refer to transcendents or qualifiers, to the actualities as affected by these, or to the two of them together. A philosophic discourse, consequently, can be thoroughly understood only by one who treats its various expressions as parts of a technical language. The discussion which precedes their use has a role similar to that provided by the habitual practices of a society in which one learns the established ways for using proper names.

42 'Tom Jones' may have been mistakenly used of a mirror image, a dummy, or someone who had been wrongly supposed to be Tom

Jones. 'Du', the intimate 'you' in German, is used when speaking to God, servants, dogs, and children, as well as to close friends. One precariously relies here on a difference in gesture, tone, and other noticeable accompaniments to differentiate the uses. A foreigner sometimes, and a native occasionally, might therefore speak as though he were using a penetrative humanly applicable name when he in fact is not.

43 A successful venture in communication ends with a private recognition of what another acknowledged and which he publicly expressed. The listener's private acknowledgment, just like a speaker's, can be known by the way in which his subsequent expressions accord, in consonance with the grammar and syntax of the language, with what had been noted, done, or said.

44 The exhibitions of actualities are subject to an all-embracing Context with which they constitute a single set of appearances. It is possible for others to know that one is attending to a particular dimension of that Context by saying 'this *goes* (does not go) *with that*', 'this *and* (not) that', '*if* this, *then* (not) that', '*here* this, *there* (not) that', 'the *unification* of this and (not) that'. 'This' and 'that' here refer to different exhibitions of different actualities, and implicitly refer to something visual, oral, and so forth. 'Goes with', 'and', 'if then', 'here, there', and 'unification' are *operatives,* keeping one linguistically in accord with the ways in which the exhibitions of actualities are associated, coordinated, intelligibly related, located, or unified.

45 A poet will incline toward associating words so intimately that they melt into a metaphor; a sensitive observer will tend to stress the association of the words within a limited frame. Normally, one stands somewhere in between, associating the words while attending to the associations that occur in fact. Sometimes more emphasis will be put on the one and sometimes on the other, but this emphasis rarely equals a poet's or a sensitive observer's. Ideally, words and the items associated with them are associated to the same extent and with the same consistency as the items to which the speaker applies them.

46 The primary terms used in a scientific cosmology are *operative proper names of operators.* Each names the manner in which actualities are objectively connected, at the same time that it interconnects the names of those actualities, hopefully in a concurrent way. A philosophical cosmology, in contrast, names the distinctive ways in which actualities are cosmically governed by affiliation, coordination, law-abidingness, extension, and evaluation. It does not speak of the particular ways in which specific actualities are in fact related.

47 Despite the fact that there are different ways in which actualities and their exhibitions are affected by alien realities, they all yield the same usable evidences. 'Substantializer', 'coordinator', 'structuralizer', 'existentializer', and 'unifier' name these. The listener shows that he has understood them by setting what is named in opposition to himself, and using it as evidence.

48 The transition from an acknowledgment of evidences as involved with alien realities to the evidences as held apart from these, is conveyed by replacing sentences, where names for the evidences function as predicates, by the names of those evidences. Both 'Tom Jones is a substance' and 'this is a substance' are to be replaced by 'substantializer'. This names evidence of Substance, detached from the actuality.

49 When used in a sentence and assigned a predicate, a proper name has the role of a common name. By retaining the proper name within a sentence, it is possible to maintain a hold on the fact that it has to do with an insistence, transcendent, qualifier, context, or cosmic pattern.

50 In 'Tom Jones is a substance', 'Tom Jones is a being', and even 'this substance is a substance', 'this being is a being', the grammatical subject has the role of a common name with a generality that allows it to escape the confines of an actuality.

51 A name in a sentence does not have full generality; this it can have only when it is in no way limited. It can then be the name of evidence detached from the world of actualities and their appearances.

52 Detached evidences do not allow for the distinguishing of their different roles in particular actualities. They allow for distinguishable references to Substance, Being, Possibility, Existence, or Unity, and that is all.

53 Sentences governed by established custom can belong to the world of writing. In the absence of that governance, the sentences are no longer in that world; instead, they are in some other, where they have different natures subject to a different governance.

54 A written sentence (in English) ends with a period. The period prescribes that the beginning of the sentence come to an end with the last word. That period becomes just a dot, that is, a mark having no function in a sentence, when one moves away from the world of writing.

55 Unintended, set down by accident, a set of words may be followed by a dot. The words and dot become part of a sentence with its period when the words are subjected to grammatical rules, one of which is that a period end a sentence.

56 A domain of entities is identified by means of an arresting name. This functions either to *mark off* the domain from others where the entities are governed in different ways—a dot is related to other marks; or it *establishes* a domain in which the entities are transformed and then subjected to distinctive conditions—a dot is made into a period for a sentence; or it *fixates* a domain in contrast with others merely possible—a dot and other marks, as they occur in fact, are contrasted with what they might have been, had they, let us say, been set down at random.

57 The domain of writing has room for sentences and periods, but not for just words and dots. To name it 'a domain of writing' is to mark it off, establish it, or fixate it. In it sentences with their periods are enabled to be unities having nuances, but they have no parts distinct from and independent of one another.

58 Each sentence is bounded off from others which, together with it, are under a common governance. The totality of sentences is in the domain of writing; selections from that totality—those in a book or a paragraph—are in specialized delimited portions of that domain.

59 A precise language would refer to each distinguished type of domain by a different name. It makes for clarity to write the name as 'a domain of writing', 'a domain of art', 'a domain of men' in each of which there are bounded entities together with others, from which they can not be taken without being transformed. But for most purposes, the same name can be used if given different roles.

60 Dots produced without intent exist in a domain distinct from that occupied by periods. The domain of dots is named and has a determinate status because it has been set in contradistinction from others. When subjected to the customary rules of language, the dot (or, more precisely, the mark we use for a dot) achieves the additional status of a period in a domain where it is not separable from a sentence.

61 A monkey can set down dots; periods are not in its world. The paper on which the monkey writes must be taken away from it; it does not know when it has come to the end of a sentence. Its dots become periods when brought into another domain and there subjected to the rules of language. A writer, instead, begins by intending a period, the mark for which has the status of a dot in another domain.

62 It takes a man to refer to the domain where dots occur.

63 A sentence not known to have been man-made has for us the same status as a man-made work which is not being attended to. This status is also achieved by products of a machine or an animal when those products are subjected to the customary rules of language.

64 What is true of dots is true of words as mere sounds. The sounds are occurrences in a unitary domain where all are subject to the same governance. That domain is there only for one who has marked it off, established, or fixated it. He identifies it by using a quasi-honorific name having one of these roles. If it is a domain where sounds are temporally related, it is marked off in contrast with one where the sounds are related by assonance and dissonance; established in contrast with one where men speak and thereby keep the sounds under the governance of the rules of language; or fixated in contrast with one where sounds might be related by laws that do not now prevail.

65 One can mark off, establish, or fixate a domain without naming it, through attention and the adoption of a consistent attitude and way of acting. By using a name for the domain, though, one is able keep it in focus as that which has been set in contradistinction with other domains.

66 A written sentence—"this is a leaf"—can easily mislead one to suppose that it is made up of distinct words alongside one another, or that 'leaf', or the idea of it, might be predicated of the 'this' or the referent of it. 'This is a leaf' is an undivided unity in which the words are interlocked. It would be more correct, therefore, to write it as "This-is-a-leaf." Used in perception that unity is made to provide a limited domain to which a plurality of items is to be referred—the items themselves also being unified in realities beyond them and the perception.

67 Judgments can not subsume one item under another unless the latter is a governing unity. There is, therefore, no matching of the constituents of ideas, concepts, categories, theories, hypotheses, or rules by distinct particulars, but only an acceptance of those particulars as belonging within the limits of those unities. If a judgment is correct, certain particulars are governed by a unity beyond them in a way counterpoised to that in which they are governed by the unity of the concept, idea, or similar domain.

68 In 'I know that this is a leaf', 'I suppose this is a leaf', 'it is possible that this is a leaf', the unity, 'this-is-a-leaf' is accompanied by an indication of the kind of unity it is—known, thought about, a possibility. It is intensional, not in the sense that it had to be intended, but in the sense that it is a unity, not to be treated as though it were made up of distinct parts to be added together.

69 A similar observation is to be made about 'This is a leaf', though it, unlike the other expressions, refers to an object permitting generalizations and the substitution of equivalent terms—'the lateral outgrowth of a stem of a plant' in place of 'leaf', for example. The object, a 'leafed this', makes the expression true. That object, in turn, is sustained by what is there in fact—a leaf possessing a localized extension.

70 What is generalized and allows for substitution is not the unitary expression 'This is a leaf', nor the entity by itself, the leaf located, but the 'leafed this', standing in between the other two.

71 'This is a leaf' is a unity directed at a delimited portion of the world where it will have or is expected to have an object which makes it be true. 'It is true that this is a leaf' says that the unity is being responsibly offered, as that which in fact has an object. The expression is no less intensional than 'it happens to be the case that this is a leaf', and is no more intensional than 'this is a leaf'.

72 'For every x, x is ϕ', and 'for every x, if x is ϕ then x is ψ', seem to be made up of distinct parts, and the 'for every x' seems to allow us to put any constant in place of the x's that follow. But 'x is φ' and 'if x is φ then x is ψ, are undivided unities. 'Every x', in the one case, tells us that it applies to everything; in the other, that if anything is identified with one of the constituents it is to be identified throughout. The 'for every x' in these cases is both intensional and extensional—the one because it relates to the unity, telling us where the unity is to be referred, and the other because it refers to distinct items to be subjected to the unity. It tells us that we are using a quasi-honorific name, and also where we are to use it.

73 One difference between intensional and extensional logics is that the intensional attends to what the extensional assumes and uses. Extensional work occurs under the aegis of the intensional, whose presence it ignores.

74 A precise logical notation will distinguish $φ$-a, which is an intensional expression, brooking no divisions and no generalizations, from $φa$ (i.e., a is $φ$'d) to which it refers and which allows for generalization and substitutions, and from ($φa$), the unitary entity that allows us to confront an object, $φa$.

'All', 'and', 'implies', 'not', and 'or' are intensive counterparts of the finalities, Substance, Being, Possibility, Existence, and Unity. Like these, they are prescriptive, and have universal application.

75 Intensions are replaceable by quasi-honorific names. A unit object is named by '$φ$-a'. $φ$-a is a bounded portion of an indefinitely large domain of truths or knowledge, and of special limited cases of these—what is knowable to an indefinite, persistent community of inquirers; what is knowable in some discipline such as science or history; what is knowable by me. It can not be set within some other domain, such as 'what I have been told', without being altered, since it then is no longer bounded off simply as a truth, but has the status of something learned.

76 The bounding off of anything within a domain leaves over a stretch through which one must move in order to get to something else in that domain. In activities which require material to be worked over, the bounding requires one to act on what is not in the domain. The move from $φa$ to $φb$ in a domain embracing both, takes time and energy because it involves the exclusion of $φc$.

In thought, boundaries are imaginatively produced. In judgments of fact, one acknowledges something external which justifies the remaining within the confines of a boundary made within a domain. If the acknowledgment is verbal, one uses the bounded portion of a domain as a quasi-honorific name. Such a name presupposes and delimits the range of the encompassing domain, just as 'Tom Jones' presupposes and delimits the range of the name, 'man', where the latter refers not to a character or essence 'human', but to the human beings with whom the user allies himself.

77 We can encounter, understand and name evidence, and use it to get us to a finality. We can also understand and name the way in which what we isolate is transformed and adopted by a finality. The two accounts are distinct, each starting with a different irreducible reality.

Each reality incorporates, without preassignable limit, something of the other, but still has the other forever beyond it. The two realities meet in nameable evidence. As suffered by one reality, that evidence is distinct from itself as possessed by the other.

78 When evidence is freed from an involvement with one type of reality, it is already involved with another. To express the fact that the evidence is taken away from its lodgment in an actuality and therefore brought under the control of a finality, the quasi-honorific name of the evidence should be replaced by a quasi-arresting name of the finality. Instead of speaking of a substantialized actuality one then speaks of an affiliating or grounding Substance. Used in the course of a penetration into the Substance, the quasi-arresting name functions as an exalted name of the Substance. Similar observations are pertinent to the names of the evidences of the other finalities.

EVIDENCE AND EVIDENCED

1 INITIALLY, all of us are caught up in practical activity. If we restrain a practical act, even if only preliminary to another, we have already begun to distinguish an actuality or its appearance from what is alien to it. We have, therefore, already begun to make evidence available.

2 The beginning of metaphysics is where practice has not completely taken over. Its first task is to understand the nature of alien items when these are freed from that on which they intrude.

3 That something is a hammer is practical knowledge, directed at an undivided object. When the object, as it serves practice, is given a cognitive role, boundaries are imposed on it by the knower. The knowledge is quite different from an intent to use the hammer, since one then faces it mainly as related to its incipient future.

4 Well before there is any question of having a concern with what is not related to practice, living beings are faced with the problem of getting to the point where a complete immersion in practice is preceded by preparation to act. This is an evolutionary result; the further down the scale, the less room is available for a preparation to act.

5 A preparation to act requires the isolation of an aspect of an object as the base in terms of which one is to act toward that object or toward something else.

6 At the lowest level, living beings live through rhythms, passing from one beat to another after an interval. In order to maximize the use of available energy, a stop is made in that interval by higher beings as a preliminary to a better use of the stage that follows. The stop can occur without consciousness or intention, for it requires nothing more than a habit of awaiting a subsequent satisfaction.

7 Whatever is involved with a being's attempt to increase satisfaction through delay helps constitute the nature of the interval. Such efforts have survival value. A living being improves its chances of continuance by excluding practical matters for a while, preliminary to a plunge into practice. Use of evidence carries on that effort on a new level.

8 The isolation of evidence is a complicated process, though taking place very quickly. Evidence is oriented toward actualities and appearances and is affected by these. Its stress must be considerably altered before it can be at once relevant to and related to the evidenced so as to function as the beginning of a process of getting the evidenced.

9 When a controlling factor is acknowledged, contact is also made with what is being controlled. As a consequence, the factor is acknowledged both as helping constitute what is being faced and as passing beyond this to help constitute what lies beyond.

10 For a controlling factor to function as evidence, it must be extricated from the object it helps constitute.

11 Evidence is first faced as involved with what is alien to it. No leap is necessary to get to it, except for one who is so mired in practice that he can not even prepare to act.

12 Evidence becomes available when control and controlled are distinguished. To be used, evidence must be held away from what it is controlling.

13 A controlling factor is alien to what it controls. By attending to the factor one is able to avoid penetrating into an actuality, and can, instead, make use of it as evidence in an act of evidencing.

14 Dislocated evidence needs support. It is not seen to need it until it is seen to be in disequilibrium, tensed mainly toward actualities or appearances, or toward a finality.

15 Though we normally attend primarily to appearances and not to actualities, it is also true that we rarely stop with the appearances. Instead we penetrate beyond them to the actualities that make them possible. This is done both when we speak of those actualities and when we act.

16 One way to know that another has a mind and what that mind is like, is by withdrawing sufficiently far to make possible an advance into a world from where one can match the expressions of that other with one's own.

17 A student of animal behavior withdraws much further than an animal did, for he is not trying to do what the animal did or even to understand what it understood, but rather to understand how the animal's mind functioned. The animal's behavior is taken by him to provide evidence of the kind of mind the animal has.

18 We perceive, not by attending to sensations, experienced items, and similar supposedly unintelligible data, and not by adding them up within ourselves, but by subjecting a confronted plurality of items to unities within our control. Concepts, categories, rules are brought to bear on what is confronted, and are there faced with a multiplicity which they are to accommodate.

19 A judgment subjects a multiplicity to a unity at the same time that the multiplicity is held away from it by an objective unity which, it is hoped, matches that which the perceiver provides.

20 Distinguished aspects are united in an actuality or an appearance, and are available for unification in a judgment because the actuality expresses itself in diverse ways. The aspects are united in a true judgment at the same time that they are united in the actuality or appearance.

21 Were there no judging, what were distinguished items would be just fulgurations of the actuality; were there no actuality, they would be units arbitrarily united; apart from both judgment and actuality, they would vanish. By expressing itself, an actuality provides judgment with elements to unite.

Neither the subjective nor the objective unifications annihilate the multiplicity; it is available for each, but only so far as each is also subject to the other.

Dealing with an actuality from the position of a unity which he provides, a man reaches no further than to the actuality fragmented into aspects. He connects the judged unity with the unity of the actuality by means of the 'is'. This relates the aspects at the same time that it connects the unity he provides with the unity of the actuality.

22 Perceptions impinge on what is external to the unities one brings to bear. The bringing to bear, though, is privately undergone. Men are involved in a public world from private sides.

23 It is possible to know that another has privately known something if he makes words and acts publicly available. One understands what he is saying if one listens to him, and does not simply hear him. That we have been listening we show by the consonance of our expressions with his. That we are listening, he and others can know only so far as our listening is publicly expressed.

24 What intrudes on an actuality or its exhibitions is not separated from that which is enabling it to intrude. To be able to use the intruder as evidence one can not therefore simply shift emphasis from the side where it is intruding to the other side where it is being sustained. That would leave one with no knowledge of what it is as a single, doubly tensed item. As a consequence, one would be a user of evidence who did not know what he was using.

25 To make proper use of evidence it is necessary to know it. Instead of allowing oneself to be carried by it toward and into what is being controlled by it, one then makes it into a limited universal specifying a more comprehensive one, the evidenced.

26 Evidence is specified by that which it controls. There is an emphasis on the direction where it is specified so far as one is acquainted with what specifies it, while lacking knowledge of what it is specifying. But that it is specifying something, we already sense when we become aware that it does not have the full range of a universal, applicable everywhere, and instead is tied down to something alien to it.

27 Since evidence points toward what specifies it as well as toward what it specifies, to use the evidence to lead one to finalities is to be forced to ignore a side of it.

28 An acceptance of evidence still leaves a distinction between what it in fact is and the power which it transmits.

29 Used evidence is held away from what it controls. To free it from all impurity, it must be brought into relation to the evidenced.

30 Supposed evidence, which had no connection with something for which it was the evidence, could not provide evidence for it, and therefore could not be evidence. To the degree that one succeeds in having it as evidence, to that degree one faces it as turned toward that for which it is evidence.

31 Both speaker and listener presuppose that the evidence they use is objectively related to the evidenced, through the agency of a governing condition. Were evidence and evidenced not so objectively governed, they would not be effective correlatives; there would then be neither evidence nor evidenced.

32 A withdrawal beyond the position necessary to detach evidence is needed if one is to have it subjectively correlative with what is evidenced. One is not yet, though, at a position where it is possible to go most effectively through the process of evidencing and arrive at the evidenced; evidence and evidenced must first be related as relevant to one another.

33 The subjectively produced relation which connects evidence and evidenced may not be used. Nothing then would be used as evidence. But there could still be something which was involved in alien content, was detached from this, was objectively related to a correlative, and was directed toward this.

34 Known or not, evidence is always related to the evidenced with a status and role which does not depend on its acknowledgment or deliberate use.

35 To use evidence properly it is necessary not only to detach it and subjectively relate it; one must pass to what it evidences.

36 A knowledge of what makes evidence available, objectively and relevantly related, and contributive to a final outcome, can be achieved if one is able to occupy a position apart from it.

37 Evidence is involved with actualities and their expressions; it is also objectively held away from these by its source. That is why there is evidence, and that is why evidence is available, and why its use by us can be assessed as adequate or not.

38 To understand what objectively, apart from any user, makes evidence be involved with actualities, detaches it, relates it to the evidenced, and passes from it to the evidenced, one must assume a position from which one can express himself in consonance with the way an impersonal, more persistent source does.

39 If a start is made from what is heard, use can be made of what already has the status of evidence only if one has matched the position of the speaker.

40 There is a difference between the deliberate effort to reach what objectively produces and controls evidence, and the effort to reach a position from which one can use evidence. The first can be known only by one who has successfully engaged in the second. The second, though, may be carried out without deliberation or reflection, and may come to an end with what is itself not known, though lived with and expressed; it depends for its success on the ability to end with what can allow one to be in accord with objectively determined evidence.

41 Animals use evidence in the form of spoors, smells, sights, and signals. Through their agency the animals move to what is evidenced, without self-consciousness. They do not know what they do. Yet they, too, approach commonly available evidence from within themselves and make use of it.

42 Unlike animals, men can attend to the evidences that are derivable from the actualities they name, and use these to reach toward the powers that govern all actualities and their appearances. Because men alone can withdraw far enough within themselves to be able to attend to evidence in the guise which enables them to reach what is final, only they can have metaphysical concerns.

43 A minimal withdrawal suffices to enable one to confront a complex in which evidence is a dominant factor. One can then use a proper name. Less than this would leave one merely experiencing, or so intimately interlocked with an object that there was no position from which it could be named, and so pulled by the confronted object as to make the detachment and use of evidence imagined rather than actual occurrences.

44 By being confronted from a greater distance than before, a complex is more emphatically remarked. The greater the withdrawal, the more deeply can one subsequently penetrate into what is confronted.

45 The arrival at a position which permits of a clear detaching of evidence, enables one to acknowledge a depth to an actuality that was not possible before. But one could be so involved in the task of keeping the evidence detached from the confronted, after he had attended to it from that distance, that he would not be able to do more than imagine it being turned toward the evidenced, and would not have it turned by him in fact.

46 Evidence and evidences are objectively relevant to and correlative with one another. As relevant they are turned toward one another; as correlatives they are inseparable from one another. As the one they have been made to be for one another; as the second they have been made to be for the relation between them. As the one they are distinct, subject to a power beyond them both; as the other they are termini within a single relational whole, which is maintained by the very power that enables them to be mutually relevant. Were they not relevant, there would be no evidence for the evidenced and nothing evidenced for the evidence. Were they not correlatives, they would not be together.

47 Evidence and evidenced are correlatives when and as they are mutually relevant. They are made mutually relevant by a power beyond them, and are made into correlatives by an expression of that power in the form of a relation which is continuous with them. Detached from the power they are just items alongside one another.

48 Evidence and evidenced are objectively turned toward one another apart from any use. That which imposed the evidence also holds the evidence apart, makes it relevant to the evidenced, and correlates them. There is no sequence here. Evidence and evidenced are embodied, held apart, turned toward one another, correlated, and subject to their source all at the same time. But the use of evidences by men requires that there first be an acknowledgment, followed by a detaching, a correlating of them, a turning of them toward one another, and a submission of them to their source. Men attempt to reproduce sequentially a single ontological state of affairs.

49 To make proper use of evidence, it is necessary to withdraw to a position from which the evidence and the evidenced can be paired—that is, made relevant to and correlative with one another. That epistemic pairing itself presupposes an ontologic pairing. Were there an epistemic but no prior ontologic pairing, the pairing of evidence and evidenced would be constituted by the user, and so far there would be no possible errors and nothing to learn.

50 How there can be an ontologic pairing can not be known until, through the use of evidence, one has come to know what can pair evidence and evidenced independently of and before anyone's use of evidence. Though an ontologic pairing precedes the epistemic, an epistemic pairing precedes a knowledge of the ontologic.

51 The epistemic pairing of evidence should accord with the ontologic. If it does not, one would have the evidence and evidenced connected solely on one's own terms. The two might then be connected in ways which would not permit the move from the one to the other; the evidence might be paired with what had nothing to do with it, or the evidenced might not be pertinent to its source.

52 A user of evidence, without knowing what made evidence and evidenced objectively relevant and correlated, could be sure to pair them in accord with the way they were paired apart from him, so far as the power he used in his pairing reproduced the action of a power constituting an ontologic state of affairs. He could know that the reproduction occurred if he could know that his activity conforms to what in fact operates on both the evidence and evidenced.

53 The use of evidence requires the exercise of mind. This pairs evidence and evidenced, hopefully so as to be in accord with what is ontologically the case.

54 Empirically, one pairs items that may be erroneously taken to be relevant and correlative. But a pure speculative mind, concerned with evidence that has been imposed on actualities and their exhibitions, is necessarily in consonance with the power that objectively pairs evidence and evidenced.

55 It is possible to err when speculating because one has not been able to free oneself from the persuasions of his empirical mind. Wholly freed from the empirical, though, the speculative mind is attuned to the power which ontologically pairs the evidence and evidenced; it, therefore, necessarily reproduces what had ontologically occurred.

56 A speculative mind differs from a finality. It is not an ultimate reality. It does not engage in the act of evidencing, but dissects and understands this. It takes account of actualities as independent of the finalities. It attends to the fact that the actualities and finalities are involved with one another in a number of evidential ways. It attends, too, to all the finalities in their severalty and as affecting one another. It is systematic and, therefore, when it comes to where actualities are joined with finalities, makes evident that they still maintain themselves in independence of one another.

57 To the degree that he frees himself from an empirical involvement, a man enables an intrusive power to be expressed as a speculative mind. The fact can be understood to be a consequence of the intrusion of an ultimate power into a man at a point from which he can exercise a speculative mind, or to be a consequence of his withdrawal within himself to the point where he can tap the power that so far had operated apart from him. The first approach is justified because a man, like every other actuality, is subject to intrusions that are universal and persistent. The second is justified because he slowly learns to free himself from empirical involvements. Both approaches have to be taken if one is to explain how a man can use evidence that had originally been produced independently of him.

58 A relation between evidence and evidenced is produced by a power operating apart from any mind. That relation is a structure terminating in correlatives. As sustained by and therefore as inseparable from the power which made evidence and evidenced relative to one another, the relation constitutes a *setting*. There always is an ontologic, and there sometimes is an epistemic setting for both evidence and evidenced.

59 A *prescription* is a setting viewed from the perspective of the power that produces it. A *rule* is a prescription produced by a man. A *principle* is a rule used by a speculative mind.

60 The power which is imposed on evidence and evidenced, through the agency of a principle, thrusts toward the evidenced to make the evidenced that which both is to be reached from and controls the evidence.

61 The same power which produces the evidence and evidenced puts the evidence at the service of the evidenced. As the one they are symmetrically, as the other they are asymmetrically connected.

62 When evidence and evidenced are correctly paired by men they are governed by principles; a justified passage from evidence to evidenced will keep within the confines of a principle.

63 All the finalities contribute factors controlling appearances and actualities. The factors need a grounding, mediation, clarification, quantification, or value, which they can get only from the finalities, and then only if mediated by the evidenced.

64 An emphasis on qualifiers enables one to start with what is comparatively pure, but qualifiers do not themselves so obviously need a ground as other evidences do. An insistence is most like a ground, but it is also comparatively difficult to free it from that with which it is involved. A transcendent provides a ground for that which it governs, but does not itself readily show the kind of ground which it itself needs. A cosmic pattern is closer to an ultimate ground than the others are, but it itself must be arrived at, since it is not something with which one can take a start in experience.

65 Evidence for a grounding finality can be obtained in these several ways. But because of their different limitations it is desirable to help each out by the others.

66 Despite evidence's independent objective locus, its distinctiveness when detached, and its symmetrical connection with the evidenced, it is related to the evidenced as that which completes it. Via a grounding evidenced, the evidence is related to the source as a dependent to ground.

67 A source enables itself to be evidenced by giving the evidenced the status of a ground for the evidence. As long as that ground remains distant from that which depends on it, it is only a possible ground. Not until the evidence is in fact grounded by it will the evidenced be an actual ground. That can not occur until it is itself grounded by the source of both.

68 Each item of evidence has its own integrity. But each also, from the standpoint of the evidenced, is evidence in the same sense that every other is. The evidenced faces all of them as so many special cases of itself. By itself, though, the evidenced has no power to do this. It can make the evidence instance it only so far as it mediates a power for which the evidence is also an instance.

69 Because philosophers with mathematical gifts or interests have dominated Western thought, it has mainly been connections of a formal nature that have been considered with care. Men want proofs which can be expressed in the ways mathematicians and logicians approve, and suspect any other way of going from evidence to evidenced, from the world of actualities to what lies outside these. But when evidence and evidenced are just formally related, the relation falls short of the fact that the evidence is completed by the evidenced.

70 Evidence formally implies the evidenced. 'The evidence implies that so and so is the case' is understood by those who can use both the sentence and the name in a similar way and produce sentences and names that are implied by these.

71 He who understands 'implies that' names what the speaker does; he who understands 'if . . . then' accepts a unity similar to that which the speaker did.

72 'The evidence implies that so and so is the case', is a single expression which can be used as a name. The hypothetical 'if this is evidence then so and so is the case' is also single, but it requires that one hesitate before the 'then' so as to mark off distinct items.

73 To name a situation in which evidence is dependent on, is for, or implies the evidenced is to leave them as they were, but within the situation. There the evidence and evidenced are also extensionally separated.

74 'Dependent on', 'for', 'implies', and 'separated' refer to intensifications added to a paired evidence and evidenced. 'Enhances' adds another, expressing the fact that the evidenced increases the value of the evidence.

75 A withdrawal adequate to the task of having evidence and evidenced turned toward one another does not take one deep enough within oneself to make possible an engagement in an act of evidencing. The move from evidence to evidenced requires one to express himself to a degree he had not before. He must not only attend but use, not only acknowledge the evidenced, but progress toward it.

76 A respondent may not withdraw exactly as far as one whom he is trying to understand. He may not go as far, or he may go further than the other. The child does not withdraw as far as its parent does; the parent withdraws further than the child does. Consequently, the child does not get the full import of what the parent is saying; the parent reads into what the child says more than the child intends. Sometimes, of course, the situation is reversed, but normally the child understands less than the parent does, and says less than the parent understands it to say.

77 Withdrawal may be only minimal; it may be maximal; it may be anywhere in between. The distance determines if and how well one can reach the evidenced. Success here is independent of a success in communication.

78 Withdrawal is not only essential to the use of evidence, but is also required in order to pass from an involvement with data to knowledge, from the words of a sentence to its meaning, from what another is like bodily to what he is doing, and from what another expresses to what he intends. In all these cases, it is necessary to retreat to that position from which one is able not only to recognize abstractable content in what is confronted, but to utilize this in order to arrive at other content which is itself to be embodied in what will enable that content, too, to be confronted.

79 The evidenced arrived at is filled out by the evidence. It is to be used in a claim directed at the source of both.

80 To isolate evidence is to depart from the world of actualities or appearances. To use that evidence as part of a claim is already to have enabled the evidence, more or less transformed, to become part of the source.

81 A finality, in accepting a claim, allows the evidence to be more intimately connected with the finality than that evidence had been when it was involved with actualities or their exhibitions.

82 A source corrects any errors that might have been made in one's claims. Its relation to a claim made about it, therefore, is different from that which actualities and their appearances have to what is claimed of them, for these do not make what is not altogether true be converted into what is entirely true of them.

83 Though a source corrects the claims one makes of it, thereby truing them, it is nevertheless desirable to try to rectify the unsatisfactory claims we make. An altering by a source still leaves what we are claiming not altogether true of it.

84 Since to be in possession of an unsatisfactory claim which the source corrects is not yet to have avoided making an unsatisfactory claim, it is desirable again and again to repeat the process of forging a claim, until we get one needing little or no correction by the source.

1 AN ACKNOWLDGEMENT of evidence is possible because the user of the evidence advances on it from a position which is outside the realm where the evidence is confronted.

Even the most extreme empiricist advances on his data from a nonempirical position. When he seeks to substitute a brain for the mind, behavior for thought, and words for meanings, in the effort to remain with the hard and palpable, he continues to assume a position from which he can use the evidence for the brain and its functioning. That evidence, to be sure, is not evidence of a finality, but that does not preclude the need to deal with it from a position outside the domain where the evidence is found.

2 Both the evidence that is to take one to the evidenced in the empirical world and the evidence that is to take one to what is evidenced of finalities presuppose the use of a mind which approaches and uses the evidence from a transcendent position. When it is occupied with empirical matters, that mind keeps its activities confined within the limits of empirical situations, but only after it has moved there from a position outside them.

3 The evidenced remains only a possible object of confrontation until one arrives at it.

4 The passage to the evidenced goes through a number of stages. Only at the last stage is it possible to have the evidenced fit for use.

5 Each of the stages in the progress to the evidenced has two sides. It is being attained, and it has been attained. As the one it is a prospect related to what precedes it; as the other it encompasses its predecessor.

6 Evidence is used in order to enable one to arrive at the point where the evidenced is faced apart from the process by which it was reached. The evidenced is then no longer a possible but an actual terminus, no longer that which is being reached but that which has been reached.

7 Used evidence and evidenced are distinct, with distinct loci. Their union is beyond the capacity of either. They are united in the course of the act of evidencing.

8 The use of evidence involves the user more and more in what is being evidenced. This is another reason why the arrived-at evi-

denced differs from the evidenced as it exists apart from the use of evidence to reach it.

9 Both the evidenced and the source are outside anything empirically confronted. The one is a prospect conditioning the evidence extricated from the confronted; the other is a power governing both the way in which the evidence and evidenced are paired, and the progress that is made from the one to the other.

10 The focusing on evidence, even while still involved with actualities and their exhibitions, is already an involvement with what is final.

11 There is at least an implicit acknowledgment of a finality when one identifies something as having been intruded on actualities or their exhibitions. The intruder possesses, coordinates, orders, locates, or assesses these. It is evidence of a finality and, therefore, belongs to it.

12 Evidence is involved with actualities and appearances. For their source to possess the evidence fully, it must go through a process of recovering it via the evidenced.

13 A user of evidence must pass from the evidence to the evidenced in accord with the structure which relates them. His movement requires effort, and should match the objective movement by which the source passes from evidence to evidenced.

14 Were there no objective movement to the evidenced, the source of the evidence and evidenced would be sundered from them both, and they would be forever estranged. Or it would already have attained the needed outcome, with the consequence that the detachment of evidence and the relating of evidence and evidenced would be only analytic phases in an unchanging absolute. Since that absolute would internally mark out evidence and evidenced, and relate them at the very same time that it had them indissolubly together, a man in using evidence could do no more than temporally illustrate in a limited way—and therefore inevitably distort—what was already fixed and eternal.

15 Unlike a man, a source is not finite. Why has it not yet been able to free evidence and evidenced, and thereby be able to complete the task of reaching the evidenced, which it sustains, from the position of the evidence which it had produced? Or if it has not yet had time enough to do this, why may not this effort be concluded at some particular moment in the future, so that thereafter there would be just a frozen absolute in which there was no longer a separation of evidence from evidenced?

16 One solution: The attainment of an outcome over time brings about a state where the entire activity of intruding the evidence, detaching it, relating it to the evidenced, and progressing to the evidenced must be begun again and again. As Indian thinkers have long maintained, a final reality temporally re-expresses itself without end. Why, though, if it succeeds in achieving its goal, should it begin the unnecessary activity all over again? Their answer is that the Gods are at play. But this answer merely throws the issue back a step, where further questions can not be answered—Why do they play? For how long? How do we know they play?

17 A second solution builds on the first. The evidenced reached is never entirely satisfactory. Each effort is an adventure that never fully succeeds, forcing still another attempt. If so, a man would have no sure guidance for his use of evidence, and there would be no period where a solution is achieved in fact.

18 A third solution builds on the second. By itself a source can not arrive at the evidenced from the position of the evidence which it had introduced into the domain of actualities and their exhibitions. But success is possible through the help of man. Men can arrive at the evidenced through thought and action; their success will enable the source to move beyond the point which it was able to reach by itself.

A view something like this is held by some religious men who think that their God attains his objective only if men, by their good deeds, make provision for his successful operation. Men supposedly guide the source. Somehow they dictate to it, even though they are finite, fallible, and comparatively powerless. In their absence, one then holds, an all-powerful source is forever faced with evidence and evidenced which it can not bring together.

19 A fourth solution builds on the third. The fundamental fact is the transition from evidence to evidenced. At every moment the desired end is successfully reached, only to be followed at once by a dissolution of it into evidence, evidenced, and source. Success yields a need to begin all over again. But then there would not only be an endless repetition of the same, but at each moment a perfected universe will come to be, only to give way to the production of another, no better or worse, and so on forever. Why should a perfect outcome be but the prelude to a need to start all over again? What guarantee is there that there will be an opportunity or occasion to do this?

20 A fifth solution builds on the fourth. Success at one moment is inherited by the next. What is achieved gives way to a situation where another attempt must be made, the new attempt utilizing what had been achieved before. As a consequence, the same task does not have to be monotonously repeated without end. There is no guarantee, though, that there will be a next moment following on a present achievement. Nor is provision yet made for the fact that over the course of time something is lost as well as preserved. And there still remains the difficulty that, at the end of a moment, what had been achieved has to give way to another attempt which has to go just as far as the previous one had gone.

21 A sixth solution builds on the fifth. A number of efforts must be made to reach distinct kinds of evidenced prospects from the base of distinct kinds of evidence. When an effort comes to a close, it has accumulated something from past achievements and lost something, too, to make its next attempt not altogether determinable in advance. But now there is no assurance that the successive efforts will be coherent. And no matter how long the process, the desired end will not be attained.

22 A seventh solution builds on the sixth. Different sources of evidence are involved with one another. Their different momentary successes are all framed inside a single longer stretch of undetermined length where they try to free themselves from one another. They are in a perpetual pulsational tension, never entirely involved and never entirely independent of one another, but passing from extreme to extreme for periods of no predetermined length. Since a source, together with its evidence and evidenced, is a self-contained totality, why should its entire activity not be over in an instant? Why must its success be momentary only?

23 A final, satisfactory answer builds on the seventh. Evidences are involved in actualities and their exhibitions. The use of the evidence is resisted by them. The source of the evidence is forced to struggle against that resistance at every moment. At every moment, too, it partially succeeds, only to have its expressions involved once again with actualities and their exhibitions, requiring it once again to struggle against the resistance these put in the way of its having the evidence (and therefore, also the correlative evidenced) in an independent form. At every moment there is some success and a need to try again, the one because evidence has been freed, and the other because the expressions of the source are inevitably involved with what is alien to them.

In addition, no source ever succeeds in holding its evidence and evidenced entirely free of an involvement with the evidence and evidenced that the other sources provide. Their independent efforts to get free of one another are matched by their efforts to impose themselves on one another, with the consequence that they are tensionally interlocked forever.

Since all sources independently but conjointly determine the kind of insistence, control, qualification, context, and cosmic pattern that will be imposed on actualities or their exhibitions, each has to struggle to free its own use of its contribution from those which the others make of theirs. This effort to be free from the others is distinct from and takes longer than any of its efforts to solidify its own evidence and evidenced. But in this, too, it never entirely succeeds.

24 Knowledge of the different finalities requires a taking account of the distinctive evidence which each finality introduced, and an understanding of how this is to be used so as to reach what is evidenced.

25 An objective dialectic would result if finalities dominated over one another in sequence. But there is no surety that such a sequence ever occurs. Nor is there any reason to hold that an objective movement from evidence to evidenced goes through a set series of stages, that it determines the course of history, or that it forever gets better and better results.

26 A partial union of evidence and evidenced by a finality is achieved in a single moment. That moment begins with the three of them distinct from one another, and ends with them almost solidified. The achievement is followed by the finality making evidence of itself present in and for all actualities. Each moment starts at a different place from its predecessor, since it follows not the free expression of the selfsame finality, but on its solidification of evidence and evidenced.

27 A solidification of evidence and evidenced is by and with their source. Since this is not separated from the partial solidifications of other evidence and evidenced by and with other sources, the various solidifications form a single block occupying an indefinite stretch of time. That stretch is punctuated by the moments in which the different sources bring distinctive, partially successful efforts at solidification to an end.

28 Evidence is objectively conditioned by the evidenced, and is under the control of their common source. When men engage in a process of reaching the evidenced they must try to reproduce that conditioning and control, the one by completing the evidence, the other by keeping within the compass of a principle.

29 A man deals with evidence properly when his use is in consonance with that to which its source subjects it. But, though it takes him time to arrive at the state where he can do this, he does not, like a source, have to struggle to hold the evidence apart from the distinct contributions of other sources. Consequently, the time he takes to use the evidence differs from the time its source does.

30 To know that a man is engaged in a process of evidencing, it is necessary to attend to what he says. He best states what he is doing by using such expressions as 'I am grounding this (evidence)'; 'I am showing that this is what I have evidence for'; 'I am inferring from this evidence that . . .'; 'I am encompassing this evidence in that evidenced whole'; 'I am yielding this evidence to that which it evidences'. The understanding of these expressions requires the listener to attain a position where he, too, can use expressions that reflect the use of the available evidence to reach what this evidences.

31 Evidence, when just paired with the evidenced, is like a runner at a starting line. That runner is not yet one about to begin. A starter is simply one who is where he should be if he is to be in the race; when he is about to begin he is tensed and awaits the gun. An effort must be made to change him from a starter who might run a race to one who is about to begin and is therefore prepared to run the race—and that change takes time.

32 A user of evidence starts a process of evidencing by accepting evidence. It is with this that the evidencing is to begin. If there is to be an actual evidencing, the evidence must be made into that with which one begins.

33 A user of evidence does not tamper with the relation that the evidence has to the evidenced; their relationship provides the limits within which he operates. When he detaches evidence from its involvement with actualities and their appearances, he both pairs it with the evidenced and faces it as that with which he will work. It is as if a runner were acknowledged to be at the starting line and about to begin, both at the same time. But while a runner assumes these roles in sequence, evidence can, in fact, have both roles at the same time. That the two roles are nevertheless distinct becomes obvious when the start gives way to a beginning while the relation of evidence to evidenced remains unaltered.

34 The beginning of a race comes after a runner is ready to begin. He awaits the gun. The gun goes off and he begins to run. Were he racing for a hundred yards, the way he sets off will be at least as important as the way he continues on his way.

35 At the same time that it is paired with the evidenced, evidence provides a beginning for a process taking one to the evidenced. But only after one has accepted evidence as that which will be used is there a beginning of a use of it in fact. Not only does it take time to get to this stage, but it requires the conversion of a controlled disequilibrium where one begins, into a beginning of an actual movement. This stage is properly acknowledged with some such remark as 'This is the evidence I am using.'

36 At the beginning, the evidence is in focus; there is then little discerned of the ending. Toward the end of the act of evidencing the situation is reversed; the evidence (as pertinent to an actuality or appearances) has faded, and the evidenced is to the fore.

37 At the beginning, at the ending, and throughout, there is always evidence, evidenced, and evidencing. At each stage of the progress, they differ in dominance and therefore in their relative importance.

38 The user of evidence tries to make it more and more integral to the evidenced; this requires him to identify himself more and more as their mediator. Since he is a mediator between what he himself makes possible—the evidence with which his act of evidencing is begun and the evidenced with which it ends—what he does will mirror what the source does if he keeps within the limits of a principle.

39 At the beginning of a process of evidencing a user accepts the evidence, and entertains the prospect of the evidenced. He comes to the end of the process of evidencing when he has completed the evidence by the evidenced. To be sure that he produces what properly expresses the source, he must guide his production of the evidenced, with which he is ending, by the evidenced that he initially entertained and had paired with the evidence.

40 A user of evidence tries to reach the evidenced as no longer paired with the evidence. Such a freeing depends for its success on an adoption of the evidenced by the source. For that to occur the evidenced must be made appropriate to the source—if not by the user, then by the source.

41 What is metaphysically evidenced is used in a claim made about a finality. Beginning with the evidence a user of that evidence passes to what is evidenced. This in turn is referred to finality. It is then distinct from itself as paired with the evidence or as arrived at from the evidence. The evidenced includes the evidence, enriching it and itself.

42 Because in using the evidence, a user makes himself integral to a temporal stretch in which the evidence helps constitute what will be claimed of a finality, his mediation between evidence and evidenced inevitably is also a participation in them.

43 Evidencing is an emotionally-toned act whose nature can be re-presented in rational terms.

44 Cosmological arguments, which take one from finite situations in this world to finalities, formalize actual, emotional, symbolizing, teleological movements from intruded expressions to the sources of these.

45 An argument is an inference which conforms to an implication. The inference is a process, the implication a static formality. Both are distinct from a conditional, 'if . . . then' which refers to the terminal points of a mediation, and from a concluding 'therefore'.

'I am inferring' names the process of inference through which I am in fact going—a passage that takes time and requires effort. 'Therefore' instead, rehearses what is accomplished in the inferring. It keeps the separation characteristic of the conditional 'if . . . then' and allows for the passage characteristic of 'I am inferring'. But since the 'therefore' simply abandons one extreme for the other, it makes no provision for the time required to pass from the one to the other, and can not, consequently, be equated with an inferring.

46 A passage from premiss to conclusion is from a dependent to what is not yet free enough from the user or the evidence to belong to what is outside it.

47 Evidence always has a limited magnitude, for the being, unity, and so forth, intruded on actualities or their exhibitions, are specified by these.

48 The passage from evidence, affected by that on which it intrudes, to the evidenced as not so limited and more appropriate to their source, introduces a change in perspective, similar to that which is undergone when one goes from evidence of a crime to the evidenced enactment of it. It has a distinctive rhythm, and terminates in a distinctive outcome.

49 The passage from evidence starts with what is mixed with alien factors and subject to alien conditions, and ends with the evidenced as free from these impurities.

50 In the passage from evidence to evidenced there is a shift from an emphasis on the evidence, to the mediating itself, and finally to a production of what is acceptable to a finality.

51 The outcome of an evidencing is a conclusion. That conclusion is not a 'truth' *for*, as long as it is connected with the premiss and the mediating thinker. To make the conclusion be in accord with what is beyond it, one must free it from oneself and from the evidence with which one began.

52 A conclusion is not trued *to* the thinker but *by* him, so as to be acceptable to what is outside him. So far, it is not independent of the process by which it was obtained; it is not yet something to which he has concluded. Not yet freed from a reference to a beginning, it is not at the end of a process of inferring but only an ending for it. The end of a process of inference is a conclusion trued to what is apart from it.

53 The passage from evidence to evidenced brings sharply to the fore an old question: is it necessary that one infer according to a rule; must an inference be guided by what had been paired? It surely is possible to pass from premiss to conclusion without attending to a rule, and to do this without error. Most men think well, but know no rules. Still, if no rule is used, there is no way of knowing that one is concluding to what is justified.

54 A rule used to guide an inference may be deliberately formulated. One can then consciously follow a rule that he has himself provided, and infer within self-set limits. A rule may also reformulate the way realities are objectively related. Often when it is thought that no guide is being followed, account is taken of such objective relations. These are not available as guides when one uses evidence, unless there is some awareness of the limits of a setting within which a source operates.

55 Since in the beginning it is the evidence, at the end of it the evidenced, and throughout the evidencing which achieves prominence, the user must vary his emphasis constantly, with a distinctive rhythm and in a distinctive manner, if he is to be in accord with the kind of limitation that the evidence exhibits and the kind of evidenced with which he is to end.

56 Evidence, evidencing, and evidenced could be heterogeneous. In the paradigmatic case they are homogeneous with one another and their source. There, use is made of evidence that is utilized by the source, of an evidencing that is in consonance with the activity of the source, and of an evidenced that is most completely accommodated by that source.

SOME PERPLEXITIES OVERCOME

1 Eᴀᴄʜ ᴀᴄᴛᴜᴀʟɪᴛʏ is unduplicable, with a center all its own. Whatever it does and whatever it deals with bears the marks of its distinctive individuality. Yet it is related to the things on its left in one way and to the things on its right in another. It will not do to say that on its left side it faces things on its left and that on its right side it faces things on its right. Not only would this require one to break it up into those two parts, but both the right and left parts would have a right and left, and so on without end.

Perhaps all relations are irrelevant, without bearing on what the related actualities are? Were that so, no actuality would be part of an organic whole; none would be able to act or be acted on; none would be located; none could cause or be caused. Each provides a plurality of terms for relations all the while that it itself remains an indivisible private ground for all those terms.

2 A man makes plans, reasons, judges, and assesses. He uses the same grammar again and again to interconnect many different words; he may use the same rules when he infers from many different premises; and he may make the same objective the terminus of different means. His must be a universal mind. But, surely, each individual uses his own personal mind. That mind's functioning is conditioned by his distinctive experiences, memories, expectations, hopes, and beliefs. The two minds must somehow be unified. How? The universal mind is his only because he grounds it in his personal mind.

3 Actualities are alongside one another. When one imposes itself on the others, it prescribes to them, and so far is no longer simply alongside them. If it is inanimate, it provides them with a common referent; if it is alive, it classifies them as well, treating them as of various kinds; if it is human, it is also places them on a footing, as equally objective. The items on which each imposes itself specify and diversify what is imposed.

How could an actuality impose itself on, and be specified and diversified by others which are alongside it? It must be both a universal and a particular. How is that possible?

One answer: In the act of exhibiting themselves, actualities divide themselves into an abstract aspect and a force behind them. As the former, each is a universal but, because of the latter, is imposed in an unduplicable way. This answer allows one to account for the use of minds, plans, rules, but it has difficulty with individuals who seem never to get beyond the expression of distinctive, unduplicable styles. If a style be something abstract, it also has no power to prescribe; if an external force is merely mediated by a style, it allows for no growth and modification of the style.

Another answer: Each actuality instantiates one or more finalities. Though such an instance is individual in relation to the finality, and universal in relation to other actualities, as imposed on others it is an individualized instance of a finality, and therefore can be in accord with what the finality directly prescribes to those others.

The first of these answers could be saved if an individual style be understood to include within it the force lacking to a mere plan or rule. But in order to account for the fact that different actualities affect one another within a common area, the second alternative should be combined with the first. Actualities instance one or more finalities, and express that fact in the ways in which they impose themselves on one another.

Actualities have their exhibitions contextualized, are themselves determined and qualified, and impose themselves on one another in accord with the ways they are prescriptively related in common ways. Since the common prescriptions are imposed on them all, those prescriptions can not be due to any of them.

Each actuality and each exhibition is subject to prescriptions distinct from all in power, status, and career. In order to arrive at the source of the prescriptions, account must be taken of their intrusions on the actualities, both in their severalty, and on them and on their exhibitions as together.

What is universally intruded provides evidence of finalities. Those evidences lead to the finalities once the evidences have been freed, in fact or in thought, from involvement with the actualities; are paired with the evidenced; contribute to processes of evidencing; and help produce claims appropriate to the finalities.

4 Must every actuality and appearance be intruded upon? Must all be controlled or governed? If not, there would be no relating *of* them, but at best only a relating *for* them. But a relation *for* is forever remote from that to which it is referred. Actualities, by being governed and controlled, are related without thereby ceasing to be fully individual and concrete, capable of sustaining terms which are related without being controlled.

5 Both actualities and appearances are at least partly determinate. Were they not determinate to any degree there would be a sheer indeterminateness and that is all. But every plurality has its members in opposition, each with the determination of being 'not that to which they are opposed'. Each is not anything else, and so far is other than whatever else there be.

Both actualities and their appearances are in a relation of opposition to others. Must not that relation vary in accord with the coming to be and passing away of the others? Must not the features of the actualities or the appearances come and go because other actualities or appearances came to be and passed away? Were that horse nonexistent, this book would lack features it now has because of its oppositional status in relation to the horse. It is now 'not this horse'; later, if there is no horse, the book will no longer be 'not this horse'.

Apart from the determination it has because of the other actualities or appearances, each actuality and appearance must have determinations which owe nothing to those others. Without these determinations, a horse and a book would be indistinguishable from one another and, therefore, would not be able to provide distinctive determinate features for one another.

6 Might not fixed features be due to an opposition to 'some actuality or other' or 'some appearance or other'? If so, each feature could be present regardless of what also happened to be in existence at any time. And since these features would be appropriate to a merely generic 'something or other', they would not suffice to make appearances or actualities be determinate oppositional items.

7 Since there must be determinations of actualities and of appearances which depend on an opposition to something which is neither an actuality nor an appearance, and since this must be something specific and not generic, must not each actuality and appearance require for its determinateness a reality which opposes it in a specific way? If so, each actuality and appearance would be faced with a distinctive, presistent opposite. Each, consequently, would have a reciprocal whose only function was to enable it to be determinate apart from all relations to other actualities and appearances. This would be to multiply entities, *ad hoc,* solely for the purpose of accounting for persistent determinations.

8 Each actuality is substantial, with a being, extensions, nature, and unity. Though each is these in a distinctive way, each is these to the same degree. This is possible because each specifies the same intrusions differently, but with the same effectiveness that others do. Does that contention not require that actualities be different from one another before they are subject to common intrusive forces? It does. The fact, though, presents no difficulty once it be recognized that an actuality may be determinately *different* from others at the same time that it is indeterminately *distinct* from the finalities. Indeterminate relative to determinate persistent intrusions, an actuality nevertheless is determinate relative to other actualities.

From the position of a finality, an actuality is distinct from it; from the position of other actualities, an actuality is different from them. From the position of the actuality, a finality is faced as a power which can make what is distinct be determinate; from the position of an actuality, other actualities are faced as opponents which can make what is indeterminate be different.

Actualities are able to act on one another because each has already been made determinate by what is not an actuality. They are able to be determined by a finality because each is already different from every other. The persistent determinations imposed on an actuality are not knowable from the position of other actualities; the difference of an actuality from others is not knowable from the position of a finality.

9 Are persistent determinations not common to a number of actualities? Is not each actuality therefore faced with a plurality of determinate actualities all alike? And does not every actuality give every other the very same determination in the form of a negative of itself, thereby making a persistent intrusion face a plurality of actualities having a multiplicity of transient determinations?

The answer to the first of these questions would be in the affirmative were it not that the difference that an actuality has, because of others, is not a specification of the determinations it obtains because it has been subject to a persistent intrusive force. When an actuality is turned toward other actualities, the determinations it has because of the persistent force are sunk within it. It then, despite its finitude and transience, functions as a self-maintaining, self-centered, self-explanatory, self-limiting, self-determined actuality. It is distinguishable from every other actuality because of its distinctive absorption of what it received from persistent forces.

If a, b, and c were the only actualities, a would face both b and c as 'non-a's', b would face both a and c as 'non-b's', and c would face both a and b as 'non-c's'. B and c as non-a's would present to a common persistent intruder the very same content, did they not face it as distinct entities. As facing this, each actuality is an individual, real, intelligible, distended unit.

10 An actuality is affected independently by other actualities and by common persistent forces. It does not present itself as affected in one way to be affected in another. Instead, it presents itself to each type of reality as that which is relatively incomplete. How could one know such a double fact? What position must one assume to deal with it?

Evidently, one must stand where both are discernible, the one more prominent than the other at one moment, and less prominent at another. A treatment of them as conditioned now on this side and then on that, is necessitated by the need to present analytic results, but the analysis is preceded by an involvement in an actuality as primarily related in one way and secondarily in another. Could an actuality be freed of both kinds of conditions it would be indeterminate as well as indistinguishable from any other actuality. Because it can not be freed from either condition, it is necessarily both distinct and different, an unduplicable irreducible particular.

11 Might not actualities be made determinate by a persistent reality which does not act on them, which exerts no force, and therefore which does not insist on itself against them? If this were possible, actualities would not offer a resistance which had to be overcome. Yet an actuality has to be, before it can be affected; when it is, it specifies what affects it. As a consequence, it necessitates that anything which would alter it be forcefully intrusive, or cease to be present there in contradistinction from its presence elsewhere. Persistent determinations are alien determinations, determinations which are imposed, insisted on, made to belong to that which is in another domain.

Every actuality stands away from all other actualities. When an actuality is subject to an intrusion, it replies to this in a way other actualities do not and, therefore, acquires specific determinations that the other actualities do not.

An intrusion is countered by an actuality. The two, by themselves, though, can not make a single entity; though a persisten*t* intrusion is dominant, this does not enable it to provide a single controlling characterization of the actuality. The result of an interplay of a persistent insistent intrusion and an actual counter-insistence, so far as it reflects the nature of the former only, does not yield a characterized object. Such an object has both interplaying items under a single control.

Were there no power which, in addition to countering the insistence of an actuality with a more persistent and stronger insistence, also encompassed the result, there would be nothing qualified, and therefore nothing which was substantialized or which was made to belong with others to a single cosmos.

12 A complex actuality is subject to a transcendent. This permeates the actuality, overriding the opposition between the insistence the actuality provides as well as the insistence that counters this. It makes the actuality be substantial, have being, be intelligible, extended, and of value.

Might not a transcendent, characterizing the complex of determinate actuality and its countering persistent insistency, just be present there, unrelated to anything else? It is conceivable that its presence might leave nothing over. Might it not be present in all complexes, but be unrelated to anything else? Might it not be an encompassing, permeating feature just present in every complex?

Since a transcendent controls a complex, it is more than merely present there. It exerts power. Since the transcendent controls a complex actuality, it can not get its power to control from the actuality. Nor can that power be intrinsic to the transcendent without making it into a reality which can exist before, after, and apart from the complex, somewhere between the world of actualities and the finalities, powerful and yet unable to exhibit that power anywhere. Were this possible, when the complex escapes its control the transcendent would continue to be, though cut off from its source and from that which it had controlled. Environing the world would be an idle set of discarded transcendents, each with a power of its own, too derivative to be ultimately real, but not strong enough to have been able to prevent what was governed by it from passing from its control.

13 Might the power which a transcendent possesses, though not intrinsic to it, be a fixated part of it, enabling the actuality to use the transcendent independently of its source? If so, actualities would not all be governed by a single power or, if they were, would not be able to slip from the grasp of the transcendent, and pass away. The power a transcendent exercises is part of a greater power into which it is merged when no longer able to control the complex.

14 Contexts and qualifiers all evidence finalities outside the domain of actualities and appearances; all are due to the very finalities that empower the transcendents. Might a context not be the result of an interplay of appearances with a condition? Might these be without any reality outside the product they constitute? Might they not in themselves be more intensive versions of what they were together? Might qualifiers not be just addenda or completions of actualities, needing no references beyond the actualities in order to be understood?

One comes to know that the answers to these questions must be negative, as soon as it is seen that appearances are impotent; that actualities are made to function together; that actualities and finalities persist, able to act again and again; that all appearances are interrelated; that all cosmic entities are interrelated; and that qualifications are intruded on actualities.

15 It is this tree which is substantial, extended, and so on. How could its substantiality, and so forth, provide evidence of some other kind of reality? Does not the presence of insistencies, transcendents, qualifiers, contexts, and cosmic patterns require one to attend to them as integral to what is observed and experienced? If they provide evidence at all must not this be of the actualities and of their exhibitions, and not of finalities?

Use of evidence requires that it be detached from the actuality which sustains it. For this to occur, there must be an end to the effort to penetrate into the actuality. The restraint keeps one at a position where the evidence is faced as directed at the evidenced finality.

16 If an insistence, a transcendent, and so forth, is an expression of a finality, never entirely severed from this, how could it offer evidence of that reality? Will it not be an integral part of the finality? To acknowledge it, is not this already to acknowledge the finality?

The evidences of transcendents, and so on, are involved with actualities and their exhibitions. So far, they are available as evidences. But only when the evidences are detached is one able to get to the finalities which made it possible for the evidences to become involved with the actualities and their exhibitions.

17 To attend to evidence is to pass from it, as merely available, to it as able to be used. But before it can function as evidence, it must be detached from that with which it is involved. Once it is detached, will it not be one with its source? To detach it, is not this already to have what is sought?

Evidence is apart from its source only so far as it is involved with actualities or their exhibitions. But when it is detached it is not yet freed from all taint of that with which it was involved; the detaching of it is not a loosening of it but a fixing on it as that which had been involved. Though it belongs to its source it is not yet entirely possessed by that source, or homogeneous with it. Evidence is always two-faced, doubly tensed. It controls what is alien to it and is limited by this. It gives this a new status but is itself only a factor. The control that it exerts depends on a power not intrinsic to it. It enriches, while still dependent on a finality which sustains and completes it.

18 The detaching of evidence is the work of its user. Does the source of that evidence also detach it from the actualities and exhibitions, and therefore undo the work it engaged in when it initially produced that evidence? Why should it do what it immediately undoes? And if it succeeded in recovering the evidence it produced would it not finish its task immediately ? What then would match a man's focussing on evidence and his subsequent use of it to get him to what it evidences?

Evidence is present because a finality involves itself in actualities and their exhibitions. The actualities sustain and affect the evidence while it controls them. The source, like any user, must detach that evidence, and overcome the difference which an involvement with alien content makes to it, free the evidence from all alien taint and, with the evidenced, take it back into itself. Since its recovery of the evidence via the evidenced is indirect, it cannot return over the same route it originally followed in providing the evidence.

19 A source operates regardless of man; it recovers what it expresses at its own pace and in its own way. How could a man's use of evidence match what a source does?

A match is possible because a mind is no more empirical than a source of the evidence, the evidence itself, or the evidenced. But mind and source need not keep apace. A mind, in its use of evidence, need produce only that which can be assimilated by the source. The result requires a man to acknowledge the very evidence that the source produces. But he can use it at his own pace. At his own pace, also, he can provide an evidenced claim for the source to accommodate. He gives evidence and evidenced roles that they do not have apart from him; and they, apart from him, have a power that they do not have in him.

20 Might not the evidence which a man uses be evidence not of a finality, but of something that he had only imagined? There is no contradiction in such an idea. But it can be eliminated if one can know that what is evidenced is accepted by a finality. A process of evidencing is brought to a close in an evidenced claim. If the claim is sustained, the evidenced (and the evidence assimilated in it) is faced as belonging to a finality. The finality gives the claim a status and career beyond our making.

21 A final source is not observable. How could it be known? A sustained claim has a depth to it, an intensity from which we must abstract in order to have in mind again what we had there initially. Since the source is not alien to the evidenced, but is the evidenced intensified, it is in fact easier to know a finality at the end of a process of evidencing than it is to know the alien actuality or exhibition with which the evidence is involved.

22 The use of evidence requires that its user mediate between the evidence and what this evidences. The mediation begins with an emphasis on the evidence and ends with what is supposed to be in accord with the evidenced with which the evidence is correlate.

Might not a man remain forever in a state of evidencing without arriving at anything? He would, if what he produced was not adopted by the source. It is then that the evidenced becomes more than that which is part of a process of evidencing.

23 How could a man become free of the evidenced if this is what he himself produced?

A source must help a man yield what he had produced, if what he produced is to be made true of the source. What he envisages as a proper characterization of what in fact is, must be accepted by the source as true of it—or he fails to reach what is evidenced.

A man uses evidence to get to what is evidenced. In the course of his progress he makes himself more and more integral to both. His ending is with the evidenced as the limit of a progress of uniting himself with the evidence and evidenced. Did this not occur, there would be no preserving of the evidence in the evidenced. In getting to the evidenced he would lose what defines it to be that which is evidenced; nor would there be anything he was claiming.

By himself, a user of evidence reaches a point corresponding to that which the source attains when it arrives at what is evidenced. The ending of the user's mediation, even when in accord with the end of the process through which the source itself goes in its own use of evidence, still leaves the user waiting further action by the source.

24 A user of evidence helps produce the evidenced. If the result is used to refer to what is outside it and him, it is turned into an evidenced claim about the finality. Might not the user of evidence produce what can not be properly ascribed to a finality? Might not what he was ending with, even when marked off from everything else, not be ascribable to anything? Might not what he produced be an idle idea referring to nothing? Or, if there were something which honors the claim, might not this something be unknowable?

Were one to forge a claim without any base in evidence, these questions would be unanswerable. So long as one proceeds along the lines of a paired evidence and evidenced, the result will be pertinent to a finality. Though pertinent, it may however, be assimilable by the finality only when altered radically. So far as it must be so altered, we do not know the finality; but when it is being assimilated, we can know the finality just so far as we can see how much the evidenced is being altered.

We are now in a position to proceed to a consideration of different types of actuality, and of the finalities which intrude on and interrelate all the actualities and all their exhibitions.

*

SUBSTANCES AND SUBSTANCE

1 Each actuality is a substance. It maintains a hold on whatever it contains, produces, and intrudes upon. It persists and it acts. It has an irreducible, independent core, and receives determinations from insistent, intrusive forces.

If an actuality were not a substance, its parts would not belong to it, and it would disperse itself in the very act of making its presence evident. The very items which it dominates, it would not control; nor would it continue to be despite an involvement in change and motion. It would be inert and solely in itself, or it would be a mere event. In either case, it would not be a source of action.

2 An actuality is not a substance in and of itself. If it were, it would just be different from others, and 'substantiality' would then be only an abstraction. There are many substances because a single substantiality is imposed on and diversified by all actualities.

3 Aristotle, who held that each actuality was a distinct substance, identified their substantiality with a form or essence. That essence, he thought, was not imposed on the actualities but on a passive matter which, together with the essence, constituted the actuality. He knew that an actuality would not be reduced to an event without losing the source of action and, surely, in the case of man, responsibility for what was done. But since Aristotle had no place for an actuality in itself, with its ability to maintain itself against and to interact with whatever insistently intrudes on it, his substances turned out to be just adventitious products of the unnecessary materialization of pure forms.

4 The substantiality of an actuality is a constituent of an actuality by itself. The other constituent of an actuality by itself is the actuality in itself. The first prescribes to and controls the second; this in turn limits and specifies the first. Both are active, but one is stronger than the other.

5 Substantiality is almost entirely sunk within the very complex it helps constitute. Considerable effort must be made to get it free in the form it had before it encountered the other constituent.

6 There is some justification in taking Plotinus and Schopenhauer to be primarily concerned with the insistency of substantiality, Spinoza with the control it exerts, Bonaventure with the qualifica-

tions it introduces, Berkeley with its contextual role, and Bergson with it in the form of a cosmic condition to which it subjects actualities.

Because Hegel supposed that a final reality is somehow involved only with itself, he was faced with the problem of learning how that finality recovers itself by absorbing special cases of itself. Since actualities are irreducible units, and both appearances and actualities are enabled to be together, the problem that must be faced, instead, is that of extricating expressions of final realities from a world of appearances, from individual actualities, and from a cosmos of actualities. Finalities contribute unifying controlling factors to all of these.

These different thinkers are interested primarily in a single, self-centered, powerful finality which, they suppose, alone is real. They are one in holding that an interest in the particular, transient, and empirical should give way to an involvement in a single, more fundamental, overwhelming reality. Observation, practice, discrimination, multiplicity are taken by them to be inferior to intuition, immediate confrontation, or dialectic. More concern for the items on which the substantiality is imposed, and more care in distinguishing other types of goverance to which those items are also subject, the manners in which the governing powers are themselves related to what is more basic, and the ways one must proceed to the latter, would have made patent that actualities have a standing of their own, that they are subject to independent governances, and that these can be traced back to equally irreducible, independent, final realities.

7 The discernment or isolation of the substantiality of actualities is not easy; it is too closely involved with what it interplays with there. It is easier to isolate substantiality in the world of appearances.

8 Though appearances are inert and originate with distinct actualities, they function apart from the actualities to which they are credited. They have affiliations; they clash and contrast within a context of their own which grounds them while it relates them, thereby enabling them to be objective. Once that context is freed from its involvement with them, it is indistinguishable from a substantiality obtainable from any actuality by itself, from any as qualified, or from all of the actualities as within and subject to a cosmic pattern.

9 A context affiliates, possesses, and grounds the appearances of all actualities. But though it provides a single substantiality for them, it is not a substance. It does not exist independently of the particular exhibitions with which it interplays and with which it constitutes an objective world. By itself a context is too limited in range, too completely involved with the exhibitions, and too feeble to act. It needs to be empowered. If it were a substance, it would qualify actualities,

as well as interplay with their exhibitions. But then there would be no unifying areas where the exhibitions of actualities were conditioned together.

10 It would not be correct to deny all power to a context, for it effectively grounds and relates. But the power it has is part of a greater. A context is an attenuated continuation of what empowers it.

11 The power by means of which a context exerts a control is limited. If it were not, the exhibitions of actualities would be overwhelmed, unable to make their presence felt in any appearance. Nor could the control be merely transmitted by the context, for that would mean that the context itself was impotent, unable to be continuous with a more basic, powerful reality. Yet a context can not possess power intrinsically, without thereby being able to exist apart from all exhibitions, and in contradistinction from its own source. It contrasts with this because of its involvement with the exhibitions of actualities; it is able to be so involved because it is continuous with its powerful source. While governing and relating the exhibitions of actualities, it remains connected with what empowers it.

12 A context governs the exhibitions of all actualities, and with these constitutes an objective world of appearances. What produces and empowers it—a finality—consequently has a power greater than that now manifested in the entire world of appearances. Because the nature and power of a context is continuous with a finality, because the finality expresses itself as that context and imposes it on the exhibitions of actualities, the context and the finality have a relation of the less to the more, but a less which has been enabled to have a function of its own. A context substantializes because it has been empowered to do so by Substance.

13 To get from a substantializing context to its empowering source one must free the context from all impurity. This requires a shift from it as grounding appearances to it as itself needing to be grounded, i.e., from itself controlling to it as empowered.

14 Substance grounds a substantializing context and enables it to unite with the exhibitions of actualities so as to constitute an objective world of appearances. The context is Substance attenuated, and provides evidence of this.

15 A substantializing context evidences Substance, because it depends on Substance for its nature, presence, and functioning. Substance, though, it not relative to anything, while the evidence for Substance is correlate with what is evidenced.

16 A substantializing context can take one directly only to evidenced Substance. Substance is evidenced by the evidence, through the mediation of the evidenced which it accommodates.

17 A user of evidence must allow himself to be controlled by what controls the evidence and the evidenced. What he takes to be correlative and relevant will then be correlative and relevant and, therefore, constitute a pair. He is reasonable if he takes that to be a pair which is a pair apart from him.

18 A paired evidence and evidenced should function as a guide for a process of evidencing. For this to occur, the user of evidence must withdraw within himself to a position which is the counterpart of that which Substance has with respect to the evidence and evidenced. That he has done this, he comes to know the more surely he moves to the evidenced and finds the result acceptable to the Substance to which it is referred.

19 Evidence is not usually in focus, and one is not altogether clear as to just what it evidences. It is not neatly separated off, and the relation it has to the evidenced is not often noted. The evidenced, as well, is rarely attended to; an endless number of items could be envisaged as possibly being evidenced by the evidence. One envisages this now and that then to be evidenced, only to find that what was envisaged has little or nothing to do with the evidence. Did one not already have some grasp of what was objectively the case, only by chance would he ever come to know it. When one finds oneself falling short of offering what is assimilable by Substance, one becomes aware that rectifications are to be made in the evidenced until it has the status of a proper claim.

20 A user of evidence is already involved with what is evidenced, but not clearly or steadily. Clarification and control are achieved by his bringing to bear a principle which matches the setting that Substances itself provides. In that setting, the evidence and evidenced are both imbedded. By matching it, the user of evidence keeps the evidence related to the evidenced.

21 Substance moves from evidence to evidenced within a setting in which evidence and evidenced form a pair. If it did not do this, it would have lost the evidence that it had imposed on actualities or their appearances, as well as the evidenced toward which this is directed.

22 Both in a setting and in a principle, evidence and evidenced are relevant and correlative. For a user to attain to the evidenced as pertinent to Substance, there must be a move to the evidenced, consonant with the move by Substance.

23 Evidence, as part of a principle which it constitutes together with the evidenced, should be brought into coincidence with the evidence as in a setting. Were there no coincidence of the evidence as part of a principle and the evidence as part of a setting, the evidence would not necessarily be pertinent to the evidenced as that which is acceptable to Substance.

24 By guiding the movement from evidence by the evidenced, the evidenced is made into a desirable terminus. That evidenced does not, though, become desired until it has become an objective toward which the user of it has already begun to move.

25 Before the evidenced can be made appropriate to Substance (and of the evidence as well) the evidenced must be used to guide a movement ending in itself. If the move is successful, the evidenced grounds the evidence. While still connected with evidence, the evidenced achieves ascendancy, and then acquires the role of a claim directed into Substance.

26 If evidence, by itself, could get to the evidenced, it might have a need for the evidenced, an appetite for it, and an ability to act so as to satisfy this but it would not be evidence which had been extricated. It would be an actuality, able to locate itself in a more remote ground.

27 What is evidenced can not bring the evidence to itself. If it could, the evidenced would be able to bring what needed it into a position where the need was satisfied. The evidenced would be a final ground, rather than a ground which itself needed a grounding.

28 Evidence of Substance is a freed, localized expression of it. This is related to what is evidenced, as the less intensive to the more, as that which was given lodgement elsewhere to that which belongs to a basic, intensive, permanent, powerful ground, the Substance.

29 Apart from a man's use of evidence Substance recovers the evidence of itself, since that evidence is grounded by the evidenced which the Substance grounds. The evidence is brought to the evidenced by the power of Substance. That move is controlled by Substance, but not fully. Where it fully controlled, the movement would be over as soon as it began.

30 The user of evidence, if he is to get to the evidenced, must also bring power to bear. But where Substance makes the evidence more and more grounded, more and more like the evidenced and like itself, both already present, a user adds intensifications to the evidence in the course of a production of the evidenced.

31 The evidenced is produced by Substance when and as it produces the evidence; a user of the evidence, instead, produces the evidenced by working on the evidence. Though guided by the prospect of the evidenced, and though concerned with reaching what in fact is evidenced apart from him, a user of evidence helps constitute what he arrives at. The final stage ends with a claim about Substance. That claim is a created grounding, awaiting a grounding by Substance.

32 Evidence in both cases is adopted by and preserved in that which follows on it. In a single continuous passage what was in focus at first becomes progressively submerged but still preserved. Progress toward the evidenced is in a process in which all the factors are always present, but with changing stresses.

33 By progressively adding intensifications to the evidence, a user of evidence comes closer and closer to the grounding terminus of the act of evidencing. The evidenced a man arrives at is the accumulated product of both the evidence and the process of evidencing. The progress has no assignable limit; there is no end to the additions that can be made to the evidence. But no matter how many additions there are, they fall short, severally and together, of making the evidence be identical with the evidenced.

34 Through the use of evidence a man can get no further than the forging of a claim which is true of Substance. This is not yet to arrive at Substance as it stands apart, but only to it as expressed in evidence as solidified with an evidenced grounding.

35 A user of evidence guides himself by the implied consequent of the principle he is following. His claim is an expression of that consequent as appropriate to a Substance. The claim incorporates the entire series of additions which he introduces in the course of his evidencing. An endless number of specifications can, therefore, be abstracted from the claim with which he terminates the process of evidencing.

36 A user of evidence awaits the acceptance of his claim by Substance on its terms. He may be impatient and may bring the process abruptly to a close. He will then be left with only a hypothesis or suggestion.

37 A user arrives at the end of an evidencing when, through the medium of his claim, he has become subject to an irreducible finality. If he begins with an extricated substantiality he must await Substance's acceptance of his claim in its own way.

38 All the finalities embody themselves more and more as mediators between evidence and evidenced, and thereby bring them closer and closer together. A user is also a mediator. The finalities mediate between what they have already produced; a user mediates between what he had extricated and what he is still to produce. When the finality is Substance it grounds the evidenced and thereby grounds the evidence; the user of the evidence of Substance, in contrast, produces a ground for it and awaits a grounding of the result.

39 A user of evidence does not have a sufficiently adequate grasp of Substance to be able to attend to or to duplicate the evidenced which that Substance sets over against the evidence. If he did, there would be no reason for him to try to get to the evidenced by making use of the evidence; he would be able to attend to it straightaway and come to Substance without having to go through a process of evidencing. By simply surrendering himself to the evidenced he would be taken into the Substance.

Apparently this is how some, who are interested in getting to Substance, envisage the situation. They seem to think that after one has withdrawn from an involvement in daily affairs one is already present in Substance as it is by itself. They therefore neglect the need to master the art of evidencing and the forging of claims. In contrast with the empiricists who are never able to get beyond the possession or confrontation of unacknowledged evidence, and with the process philosophers who are never able to get beyond the process of evidencing, these thinkers reach Substance in a single step. Failing to recognize the thickness of Substance, they consequently overlook the need to progress from evidence of it to it as the source of both the evidence and the evidenced.

40 One is already in contact with Substance when he isolates evidence of it, for the evidence is that finality in a limited guise, affiliating distinct actualities and associating the exhibitions of all of them.

41 There is evidence of Substance because actualities, which otherwise would be indifferent to one another, are in fact affiliated, and because their exhibitions are all in a single context where they have been made to be supplementary, oppositional, and contrastive.

42 Were there no substantializing and affiliating agents produced by Substance, they would not be present at all; or they would be inexplicably adventitious; or they would have no affect on what was alien to them. Evidence of Substance is in the form of grounding conditions which make a difference to that on which they intrude.

43 Evidence of Substance is forced on actualities and their exhibitions. As a consequence, actualities are enabled to possess their parts and their exhibitions; and both actualities and their exhibitions are related by a controlling affiliating ground.

44 The being, structure, extension, or value that an actuality has does not enable it to possess anything or to be affiliated with others. Consequently, we know that actualities have been forcefully conditioned by Substance once we know that those actualities are able to possess whatever they exhibit and whatever actualities they contain, and that they are affiliated in various ways and degrees no matter where they are.

45 Since the force exerted by evidence does not originate with it, when separated from an actuality or its exhibitions the evidence would vanish, were it not sustained by the source of it. The evidence which Substance provides is not only an expression of it; it transmits power originating with Substance.

46 Not until it is finally merged into the evidenced, and then absorbed within Substance, is the evidence of Substance entirely free of that on which it had been intruded, the evidenced with which it is paired, and the man who makes use of it.

47 When evidence of Substance is extricated from an actuality, what is left behind is what had been and, therefore, is capable of being substantially affiliated by that empowered evidence.

This knowledge is at once trivial, illuminating, empirical, and a priori. It is trivial so far as what one knows of the residuum left behind is merely the reciprocal of what one had learned about the evidence, or about the way in which the evidence had in fact functioned with reference to it. The knowledge is illuminating so far as items can be substantially affiliated in other than the present ways, for to learn that they can be otherwise dealt with than they now are is to know that Substance has more power than is expressed in the present evidence. The knowledge is empirical so far as it depends on an acquaintance with substantial entities. The knowledge, nevertheless, is also a priori since it does allow one, by attending to what is present in one domain, to learn about what belongs to another.

48 Evidence requires a grounding in what is grounded by Substance; it may then have a guise which may not be identical with that which it had for man. Evidence of Substance is inseparable from it, but men get to that Substance only by mediating the evidence they extract by the evidenced in which this may be altered.

49 The claims men make about Substance are more or less inadequate, and are to be improved by being changed in the light of the changes to which the finality subjects what it accommodates. They could be idle only if there were something which precluded the claims from having any application. But nothing could make them idle except, paradoxically, the very finality to which such metaphysical claims refer.

50 Men impose conditions which are intended to mesh with the conditions Substance introduces. Their impositions can be viewed as a kind of acceptance of actualities or their exhibitions as being substantialized; as being made appropriate for aesthetic purposes; as being turned into elements in an aesthetic assertion. Or they can be taken to enable men to become involved with what they aesthetically encounter, or as a means by which men assess the aesthetic value of items. But they are best understood to exhibit man's appreciation of the way items are aesthetically harmonized in relation to one another. That appreciation is justified when the conditions he imposes accord with the ways in which items in fact supplement, contrast, or clash with one another.

51 A man's impositions of classifications, structures, actions, and values can be taken to be modes of appreciation. Such appreciations, however, are not identifiable with the pure full appreciation possible to one who is making use of conditions homogeneous with those that Substance provides, since they do not concern the ways in which items are affiliated, but only the ways in which they are coordinated, made intelligible, are dealt with, or assessed, and, therefore, with the items in other than purely qualitative terms.

52 Substance has been given many exalted names: the Way, *élan vital*, the Will, the Unconscious, the Ultimate Ground, Creativity, Nature, God, the Absolute. Any one of these will do, provided it be treated as a proper name coupled with an emotional readiness to be possessed by the terminus of the name. 'Substance' is a preferable name, because it prompts one to keep central its substantializing, possessive power.

53 Pivotal occurrences both elicit and partially satisfy deep-lying emotions. When an involvement with these occurrences is over, the emotions do not as a rule suddenly vanish. Instead, they remain, less well focussed and disturbing, slowly fading away, but still effectively directed toward what is to provide them with terminus and satisfaction.

54 Freed from what elicited and partially satisfied them, deep emotions lead into enveloping depths. The user of evidence also directs himself there by means of his final claimings. He then expresses a different emotion from one that is possible to him when he gets there after having partially satisfied deep emotions in pivotal occurrences. The two emotions differ in degree of intensity. A comparison of them provides one with another check on the accuracy of a claim, in addition to that which is provided by seeing how much the claim must be altered in order to be fully accommodated by a finality.

55 A deep emotion is a vital claiming; it makes no stop with a claim, but instead proceeds directly toward a finality. That emotion is a specialization of an appreciation. Openness, a readiness to be accommodated, is that specialization of appreciation which leads to Substance. When speculative thought comes to an end in a sound claim about Substance, its emotional accompaniment conforms to an appreciative emotional openness.

56 An emotional openness is a form of a surrender to Substance. It can be supplemented not only by speculation but by a communal self-abandonment as well. In festivals, a people come together and reveal the underlying power that keeps them together, and apart from all others. A self-abandonment to a common enterprise is there elicited, spelled out, partly satisfied, and enabled to continue for a while, directed vaguely at an unknown reality. That self-abandonment the user of evidence of Substance matches with an appreciative emotional openness.

57 Communal self-abandonment and individual openness are two sides of one thrust toward Substance, the one expressed through an emotional participation in a common activity, the other as an individual's deep emotional appreciation of what lies beyond him—not at a distance in space or time, but intensively, in depth.

58 We know we have arrived at Substance when a) individual and group emotions are in accord; b) the terminus of the emotions involved in speculation concurs with the termini of deep emotions provoked by crucial occurrences in art or life; c) the claims made about Substance are accommodated by a possessive power beyond them, and thereby enabled to be maintained apart from us; d) the substantializers that are abstracted from what we confront are integrated in what we are successfully claiming; or e) what is abstracted from Substance is identifiable with a claim expressed at the end of a process of evidencing.

59 There are empirical studies which focus on the problem of the harmonies and disharmonies that hold among various colors, sounds, attitudes, and kinds of expressions. In different ways those studies specialize the single discipline of *harmonics*. This, to account for the affiliations of encounterable content, presupposes either a constituting man or a Substance capable of limited expressions.

60 Harmonics has an experiential base and an a priori task. On the basis of what is already known of shapes and sounds, it tries to determine how new shapes and sounds would clash, supplement, enrich, or be indifferent to one another when subject to the kinds of affiliations that characterize the shapes and sounds now present. Its concern with actual cases of affiliation is primarily for the sake of getting a guide for its attempt to understand a pure affiliative power pertinent to any particulars whatsoever.

61 A composer, though he builds on his knowledge of the way known sounds affect one another, is occupied with the expression of a more fundamental power of affiliation, pertinent to all sounds. Harmonics in its pure form is concerned with the very power that interests the composer but as bearing on other kinds of appearances, and actualities as well. No one apparently has come as close to this fact as Schopenhauer in his account of Substance—or as he called it, 'Will'—in relation both to music and the various manifestations of insistencies in the organic world.

62 What is not affiliatable is not governable by Substance, or by a man as an instance of this. The only affiliations that we know to be operative are those which in fact have been produced. All that we can be certain of, therefore, is that men or Substance may be able to operate in that way on what they had not yet operated on—other items still to come or present items in more recalcitrant states.

63 Psychoanalysis depends on the supposition that some items in speech, dreams, actions, or beliefs have been affiliated in undesirable ways. Its account of an affiliating unconscious translates a more fundamental fact, as Jung tried to show; but even he does not deal with what in fact affiliates all appearances and all actualities.

Gestalt psychology tries to show what should be affiliated with a given item, but it does not acknowledge the source of the affiliations. It and psychoanalysis need one another. So far as either fails to recognize the need for the other, its work, or its presence, each remains incomplete. And, since both attend only to living beings, they together fall short of a needed account of what makes all actualities and all appearances be in relations of supplementation, clash, or contrast.

64 We can imagine appearances other than those that are now present. When they are acknowledged to be connected with any or all of the present appearances, an implicit reference is made to the power of Substance, for it is this which connects them.

65 A present appearance can be imaginatively replaced by others, and imagined to change when subject to the power that had been operative before. Disciplines concerned with such knowledge are now being developed under the names of *structuralism* and *depth grammar*. At present these limit themselves to humanistic, linguistic, and anthropomorphical data and, in a Gestalt spirit, concern themselves only with the successful attempts that have been made at affiliating items by means of various limited agents.

Why do men, and perhaps some of the primates, have this ability? Does it enable them to be in accord with what is happening apart from them? To complete themselves? To do justice to what they encounter? Such questions can be affirmatively answered by taking account of the fact that men, in the attempt to find a satisfactory grounding for the evidences which they encounter in experience or which they recognize to be involved in the actualities which that experience presupposes, forge claims that they expect Substance to accommodate. The connections initially acknowledged form the basis for claims directed at Substance, a final power of affiliation.

66 A claim encompasses a series of characterizations of Substance. Moving progressively toward the widest ranging member of the series, one comes closer and closer to determining the nature and extent of the change Substance introduces in accommodating the claim.

67 Together with other finalities, Substance not only provides a context for the exhibitions of actualities, but governs and cosmically relates all actualities. It operates on disparate items, contrasting and fitting them to one another without regard to where they are or how they act.

68 Instead of just attending to the power of Substance as applicable to appearances or to actualities, one might attempt to determine the result of forcing Substance to express itself through narrow channels, and then imagining how the results are affiliated with one another. This shift of emphasis to possible channels allows one to anticipate the form which the expressions of Substance will assume when they intrude on and mesh with alien content. In and of itself, though, Substance has no such channels; the expressions that it intrudes are limited and multiplied by the items with which it meshes. Envisaged channels are anticipations of the limits and multiplicities that actualities provide.

69 What is not yet intruded upon is irreducible, a subject to which all predicates are to be referred and which itself is predicated of nothing. It is an actuality in itself, inseparable from itself as determined by an intruding insistency. When we imagine an intruding insistency separated off, we leave over a counter insistency not yet able to operate.

70 Substantiality is imposed on all actualities. It insistently provides them with determinations, controls the result, qualifies this, provides a context for their exhibitions, and conditions them all as cosmic units.

71 An actuality in itself is affected by the intruding insistency of Substance.

72 An actuality itself interplays with a governing transcendent due to Substance. The actuality itself is already determinate but, together with what it interplays, is subject to Substance's control.

73 A complex actuality by itself results from the interplay of an intruding and a countering insistence; the complexity is not negated or made less substantial when a transcendent or qualifier is imaginatively separated off from it.

74 A transcendent expressing Substance makes what it governs be a substantial actuality. A qualifier expressing Substance makes what it governs be substantial too, but only so far as it remains connected with and dependent on Substance.

75 Every actuality is a substance, for it is substantialized. But it is not a substance simply by being substantialized. This would leave it still possessed by Substance, endowed with substantiality but not on its own terms. An actuality makes use of the substantiality that is thrust on it, internalizing this, taking it within itself, thereby enabling itself to stand away from all else, to express itself, and to possess what it expresses.

76 How could an actuality internalize the substantiality which Substance intrudes on it? Must the actuality not already be independent of Substance, able to function as a distinct, independent individual, regardless of all else? Must it not be irreducible, already a substance?

An actuality in itself interplays with a counter, intruding insistence. The result is encompassed by a transcendent. The intruding insistence and the transcendent both issue from a finality. If that finality is Substance, the transcendent substantializes the product of the interplay of its insistence with the insistence of the actuality. The actuality is qualified by Substance, not at some later time, but at the very same time that it is transcendentally substantialized. Because it is transcendentally substantialized, each actuality internalizes the qualification that Substance imposes; each is therefore able to function in a world of similarly qualified entities.

77 Knowledge of a substance takes its start with evidence of it. This leaves one knowing that which can be substantialized or that which had been substantialized, the first so far as the actuality is treated as being subject to what was isolated, the second so far as it is treated as sustaining this.

78 It takes considerable sophistication and ability to withdraw from the world of practice to the point where one is able to know what an actuality is. One must know how to extricate evidence of Substance and then, instead of using the evidence to take one to what is then evidenced, treat it as able to combine with the actuality to yield a substantialized complex.

79 A knowledge of actualities does not have to await the mastery of special skills. Everyone faces a world of contextualized appearances, and can distinguish distinct appearances there. The distinguishing of one of these appearances requires an emphasis on the contribution which an actuality is making.

80 Had we a sure grasp of Substance and could we distinguish the impact that different actualities have on it, we could use what we distinguished as evidence of those actualities. We could then proceed to extricate the evidence and make use of it to get us to actualities, by following a procedure similar to that which is followed in a process of evidencing Substance. But the knowledge we initially have of Substance is quite thin and not pure. It is mediated by what we ourselves produce in the course of evidencing it, and what we are able to know by reflecting on what we emotionally reach or on what the Substance does to what we claim.

81 The contribution which an actuality makes to its appearance is an exhibition of that actuality. To use the exhibition of the actuality as evidence of the actuality, one must go through the process of extricating, correlating, and mediating the evidence in a manner which proceeds in the opposite direction from the process pursued in getting to Substance, and then await the adoption by the actuality of what is being presented as a claim about it. If the claim is adopted, one can subsequently attend to the result, and abstract from it a characterization which is pertinent to a more remote portion of the actuality than that to which he first addressed himself.

Like Substance, substances are more intensive and concrete than what is evidenced of them, and are able to take over what is being claimed of them.

82 Actualities express themselves because they have been provoked to do so. The qualifications to which they are subject gives them an outside which is discrepant with what they are on the inside. Their internalization of the qualifications, which stem from Substance, allow them to be inwardly what they are being made to be outwardly.

83 The exhibitions of actualities are expressions of internalized qualifications. Since each actuality independently internalizes what qualifies it, its exhibitions and the consequent contextualized appearances will usually fail to be maximally harmonized with the exhibitions of other actualities.

84 Substance honors every claim (in a more or less altered form) which a man forges when he creatively produces a ground for the evidence that he has extricated. The more that the nature of Substance is accurately expressed in the claim, the less does that claim have to be altered in being accommodated by Substance. Most claims, though, must be considerably modified before they are acceptable to Substance.

85 The alteration to which Substance subjects a claim can be known by noting the transformation that the claim undergoes when it ceases to be simply referred to Substance to become integral to Substance as it maintains itself apart from all else. Though it is beyond all particulars and outside the reach of all predications, Substance is knowable and sometimes known.

86 All can have some grasp of Substance at every moment by attending to the affiliative power which connects appearances as well as actualities, and to the substantializing that enables an actuality to possess and ground its exhibitions. The affiliation and substantializing are evidences which are inseparable from, and are to be made integral to Substance through the mediation of accommodated claims. To be aware of that Substance is to be aware of a finality, all-encompassing, harmonizing, and irreducible.

87 If one knows what Substance is, one knows the alteration to which Substance subjects a claim so as to make it be an integral part of itself.

88 We are already involved with both Substance and substances when we focus on evidences for them. Both are discernible beyond the position at which we arrive when we make claims about them, and beyond the position at which we arrive by symbolization.

89 Neither Substance nor substances are objects of observation. But an understanding of what each is apart from the other is needed if one is to understand how there can be a world of affiliated appearances and how there can be a cosmos of affiliated substantial actualities. That understanding is the outcome of a proper use of the evidences provided by an affiliating context, by an affiliating cosmic pattern, or by the qualifications and transcendents intruded on the separate actualities. Apart from such evidences, properly used, one could know appearances, but neither as affiliated nor as possessed by actualities, themselves affiliated in various degrees and ways within a cosmos. One could also know that there were actualities, each maintaining itself apart from all else, but could not know that they were substances, grounding and possessing their exhibitions and the appearances these help constitute; such knowledge is the reciprocal of the knowledge one has of an evidencing Substance.

BEINGS AND BEING

1 Each actuality by itself has a being.

2 The being that one actuality has is no different from the being another has, but its being is its alone and not the being of any other. The two assertions are reconciliable: the being which each has is a common being that it has specialized in a distinctive way.

3 The being each actuality has is not native to it. That being is added to it. Together they constitute a single, complex actuality with a being of its own.

4 If an actuality by itself is not a being, will it not be a nonentity? It would, were it entirely cut off from what it is in itself.

5 One actuality by itself has no more or less being than any other. A mouse has as much being as a mountain, a snowflake has as much being as a rock. Yet these differ in power, promise, career, and value. They are so different in fact that nominalists are prompted to deny that there is anything common to them. Let the nominalist contention be granted; it does not affect the fact that all the actualities are on a footing as having integrities of their own. Indeed, this is exactly what the nominalist insists upon. Yet to hold that all of them are on a footing in this respect simply underscores the fact that there is something common to them after all—their status as individual beings, coordinate with one another.

6 If anything is unreal, it should be those appearances which are the outcome of men's personalized interpretations of what they confront. But these have a core which has at least the status of being available for a human mind. Experienced and remembered, personalized appearances also have relations to other items still to be dealt with by the mind. Minds act on what has some reality apart from them.

7 Personalized appearances are the product of individual interpretations imposed not on actualities but on objective appearances, appearances that do not depend on the action or presence of consciousness. Were there no objective appearances it should be possible to confront actualities and finalities in imagination or in fact simply by removing the veil which interpretations introduce.

8 Objective appearances are unreal in contrast with actualities and finalities. But though no one of these appearances has or is a being, all are together in a single encompassing contextual being.

This color differs from that and the two are different from all the shapes there are. Set apart from other appearances each is without any being, unable to maintain itself in opposition to actualities and finalities. Yet each is in the same context with the others. There together, all stand apart from the actualities and the finalities, open to confrontation, delimitation, use, and interpretation by men.

9 Some existentialists maintain that no actuality other than man has its own being; the beings credited to other actualities are supposedly either given to or transmitted to them by us. After all, they are there for man to use; the natures they present and the status they are acknowledged to have reflect man's interests and concerns. A hammer is a hammer only for man; the components of this and the supposed units out of which the components are built are not found in the world, these existentialists hold, but are only taken to be there by man.

Men do group items together for their own purposes; they classify and thereby coordinate a number of items to constitute a class of things all to be characterized and employed in the same ways. But there are many actualities men have not yet encountered. There were times when men were not, and there are places where they are not now. The very items, which men have made part of an existential scheme, oppose them; their opposition precludes the taking of those items to be wholly dependent on men for their being. It is not even correct to take them to have a mode of being inferior to men's, if that means that they do not oppose men as surely and to the same degree that men oppose them, or that they do not block men, and even challenge, injure, and destroy them.

Sometimes a man's classifications go counter to the groupings various actualities in fact enjoy, and he is forced to alter the ways in which he attends to, organizes, and understands them. In any case, the fact that what is other than man is acknowledged to be there for him, allows things a status for which he can not be the source.

10 The impositions of different conditions by men can all be treated as forms of appreciation, acceptance, structuring, involvement, or evaluation. Each, though, is homogeneous with only part of what occurs apart from the men. Appreciation, we have already seen, is most appropriate to aesthetic dimensions. If appreciation were identified with the use of classifications, rules, practical programs, or evaluations, it would be too acceptive, too formal, too much engaged in changes, or too critical to be able to do justice to what is aesthetically available.

11 Men impose conditions on what is before them. When appropriate, those conditions answer to delimited versions of that most comprehensive, persistent coordination which has its source in Being, applicable to everything, regardless of what men do, and even whether or not they exist.

Because actualities are together under the aegis of a common Being, it is possible for a man to be faced with groupings whose consequences diverge from those he produced and which, therefore, require him to make still other efforts at considering them together.

12 The being of an actuality encompasses it; every part of the actuality is given being by a Being that intrudes on the whole. All the actualities together and all their appearances together are encompassed too, the one by an equalizing cosmic control, the other by an equalizing context.

13 A qualifier, a transcendent, the cosmos, and a context give being to the items they affect. But they are not themselves Being; they are not at once pertinent to all actualities in their severalty, to all actualities together, and to all appearances together. Nor do they have a reality of their own, with sufficient power to intrude on and constrain all particulars. Otherwise, apart from that on which they impinge, they would have the status of finalities instead of being just expressions of them.

14 Since that which is without specificity must be Nothing, Non-Being, is it not Non-Being which endows all else with being, either as it is in itself, or as together with others? One could say this; there is only a verbal opposition between such a contention and one that maintains that Being is the finality by means of which all else is equalized. Relative to other entities, Being is an eternal irreducible in terms of which they, despite their independence, are equatable. Were any particular, or any of the other finalities, taken to be that which alone or which eminently is, Being would be identifiable with 'Nothing'. Attempts to speak of Being as 'Nothing' testify to an overemphasis on the being of particulars or the being of other finalities.

15 All appearances and actualities are also subject to finalities other than Being. Substance affiliates them in various ways and degrees, subjecting them to a common ordering power. Possibility enables them to be intelligibles related by common structures. Each is also locatable in extensions, and possesses extensions of its own continuous with extensions beyond it. Each, too, owes its unity to an ultimate Unity beyond them all.

16 Being itself is characterizable as 'being' from the position of an abstraction or meaning derived from Being. It can also be understood from the perspective of the other finalities as surely as it can provide an understanding of them. It is then characterizable as 'irreducibly substantial', 'intelligible', 'extended', or 'unitary'.

17 To hold that Being is the only finality and that one can get to it only via man, is not only to give Being a priority over all other finalities and make its functioning await the coming of man, but it is to minimize it by denying that it can directly bear on all actualities no matter where they are or what they are like.

In one sense, though, the restriction is harmless. Man differs from all other actualities. One can distinguish him from the rest in somewhat the way in which one distinguishes all appearances from all actualities, as offering a distinctive kind of resistance to and lodgement for Being. But in another sense, the restriction is unfortunate, for it makes Being's power dependent on man's presence. What happens when man is no longer? Will all else cease to be?

18 Evidence of Being is obtainable from any entity whatsoever, and from any place where independent entities are together. That evidence has the guise of qualifiers, transcendents, contexts, and a pattern governing actualities in the cosmos, all equating that which is within their provenance. But the best evidence is given by the transcendents, for these most clearly coordinate and control.

19 'Reality' is commonly used in a number of ways. It refers to what is not a derivative—actualities and finalities; to what is necessary and eternal—the finalities; to what is independent of what any one thinks or what he thinks—actualities, finalities, and objective appearances; and to Being and to what is subject to Being—everything. All these are legitimate.

20 'Being' is a name initially applicable to a finality. It is derivately applicable to actualities precisely because a finality is operative there.

21 The tendency to suppose that 'being' characterizes an actuality apart from Being, is a consequence of the fact that an actuality is real apart from Being, and that the being of an actuality functions with respect to every determination and every part in it in the way in which Being itself functions with respect to the actuality.

22 Being bestows being on an actuality by equating its parts and thereby orienting them toward that actuality. An actuality gives being to everything that is subject to it, because it has a being that it has made its own.

23 An actuality by itself has a being because a being has been given to it. Being enters into it in the form of an alien factor with which it is then intertwined. When that factor is no longer operative there, the actuality no longer has a being.

24 Since an actuality has a being only because of an intruded factor, it is possible for the actuality to cease to be. But if it continues to be real, it will continue to be affected by Being. It can completely escape Being only if it vanishes; well before that time, though, it may continue to be, but fail to internalize the being that intrudes on it.

25 A complex actuality vanishes when its parts defy the controls that had been imposed on it as a single entity. The complex actuality is then distinguishable within the domain of actualities as a merely conceivable reality which had once effectively maintained itself in opposition to the others. An ultimate particle, when it ceases to internalize a qualifying substantiality, will vanish in a similar way;

it will no longer be available for a determination and control by any of the finalities, and will be only conceivably distinguishable in a domain of particles.

26 Were actualities in themselves not independent of one another, they could not separately interplay with the insistence which Being brings to bear on them. And, since each actuality is also a substance, and may have a nature, existence, and a unity as well, independently of its being, it can present further content to be subjected to Being.

27 All actualities are part of a cosmos where they function as distinct items. Each of those actualities there not only has a being, but has that being in relation to other beings.

28 The being that an actuality has, because of the role the actuality plays in a cosmos of actualities governed by Being, is distinct from the being which the actuality has because of its direct subjugation by an expression of Being in the form of an insistent transcendent or qualifier. The one is a term in a cosmic relation of coordination, the other is a functioning constituent of a complex.

29 To obtain evidence of Being one must fixate on some being. But unless this is held apart from the alien actuality or the exhibitions with which it is involved, the being will not be usable as evidence.

30 Though it had initially been involved in and specified by the actuality with which it interplayed, by all the actualities together, or by all their exhibitions, when held away from these, a being is indistinguishable from the being obtainable elsewhere. Still, it is not identifiable with a universal meaning. If it were, it would simply structure what it operated on and would not equalize the items there.

31 An intruded meaning adds rationale, intelligibility, order; an intruded being, instead, enables a number of items to be alongside one another as equals. If the being operates in an actuality, it coordinates what is within this; if it operates on a number of actualities or a number of appearances, it keeps them on a footing as equals, no matter what they are like or how they function. In abstraction from such a being, actualities and their exhibitions would be incomparable. The parts of actualities, too, would not be distinct beings which were coordinated there; they would then not be parts but unit entities which might be affiliated and possessed by actualities but which did not necessarily have the same status. Genuine parts are beings which are equal in reality, all within the compass of an actuality, no more and no less real than they.

32 A being governs that on which it has intruded. Could it be torn away, it would be a governing factor which does not in fact govern.

33 To be available just as evidence, a being must be turned neither toward an actuality nor toward the evidenced. Only so can it be distinct from both; only so can it be something which could be used. Yet to say that a being functions as evidence only so far as it is dealt with apart from its involvement with an actuality, it seems, leaves one with nothing at all, since what enables an actuality to have being is either Being itself or Being as involved with an actuality. When a being is freed from all reference to that actuality, it apparently is already identical with Being.

A mere being, uninvolved with anything, would be identical with Being. But no evidencing being is a mere being; it is affected by that with which it had been involved. Were it entirely freed from all taint of this, and unrelated to what it evidenced, it would be as relevant to one item as to any other.

34 As apart from an involvement with anything, evidence of Being still bears the marks of its involvement. It can be freed from all such marks, but only by being absorbed within what it evidences.

35 A being is attended to by its user. He can picture it as completed by the evidenced so as to become an inseparable part of Being itself. But only so far as there is some grasp of the actuality in which it is, the evidenced toward which it points, and the Being to which it belongs, can the user adequately grasp a being as something faced, distinguished, used, and understood.

36 An isolated evidence of Being, until it is wholly merged into the evidenced and with this into Being itself, continues to bear the marks of the actuality that specified it, and remains directed toward the evidenced as a more complete being. At the same time, Being coordinates it with the evidenced, giving it a status over against the user.

37 What a being evidences is a prospective end for whatever movement one has to go through to satisfy the evidence's need to be completed. The evidence is initially tied down to particulars; it gets free of that limitation to the degree that it is absorbed within what is evidenced.

38 Nothing less than Being could make beings present everywhere. Because those beings are continuous with the finality, they share in its power and thereby enable actualities and appearances to be.

39 Since Being is distinct from and independent of the other finalities, the evidence for Being is necessarily different in nature and role from the evidence for the other finalities. Each of the stages through which one must go in order to use evidence for Being must also be different from the stages through which one must go in order to use evidence for the other finalities, because its different stages are under its distinctive control.

40 It is not possible for appearances or actualities to make the evidence of Being and what is evidenced of Being be relevant to one another. Since they are relevant only so far as they are not turned away from one another, they are so far not involved with what is alien to themselves. Nor can the evidence and evidenced make themselves be relevant to one another, for as correlative they are independent and without the power to overcome that status. Only a finality or a man can make an evidencing being and what it evidences be mutually relevant.

41 Evidence and evidenced are limited in range, and are distinct from Being itself. Neither is primary, independent, or self-sufficient—but for different reasons. Evidence of Being is involved with what is alien to it; the evidenced, instead, is directed toward Being. Each has a side where it is turned away, and another side where it is related to the other. Extricating evidence allows one to turn it toward what is evidenced; in using the evidenced one turns it toward Being.

42 Before it is used, evidence must be identified as that with which one is to begin in order to arrive at the evidenced. Evidence's need to be completed is not satisfied if it is not directed toward the evidenced, for this is what completes it.

43 The evidenced satisfies the evidence. It must be that with which a use of evidence should terminate, an end which is to be attained. Not until it is faced as a desired terminus is one in a position to begin to use the evidence to get to it. But if the evidence is to take one to the evidenced and nowhere else, the evidenced must be able to govern the use of the evidence.

44 A man helps create the evidenced in the course of terminating in it. In using evidence of Being, he engages in a process of producing the evidenced in the form of a claim, forged in the expectation that it will be sustained by Being.

To forge a viable claim, he must get the import of the evidence within the evidenced. The claim ends his use of the evidence.

45 The honoring of a claim about Being depends not on the user but on Being. If the claim is honored, the evidenced that he helped to create coincides with the evidenced that Being sustains. There is no reason to suppose that there is ever an exact fit.

46 A man gets out of the process of evidencing, not by arriving at the evidenced in the form of a claim, but by having that claim taken from him by Being. Until this is done, he is left with a reference to Being which has not been altogether freed from connection with the evidence and, through this, with the actualities or appearances with which the evidence had been involved.

47 The process of evidencing Being begins with a being which was involved with what is outside one. The extrication and use of that being gets no further than evidenced Being in the form of a claim. That claim will be accommodated, more or less altered, by Being itself.

Something similar occurs every day. The judgments we make, the conclusions at which we arrive, the predictions, expectations, and programs in terms of which we live, remain with us and are, therefore, nothing more than phases of ourselves, until accepted in some form by realities outside ourselves. We may not begin our mental processes with material which was obtained from the world, but if we are interested in knowing what occurs outside us, we must end with content which is accepted outside, or which is altered by this until it is acceptable.

48 What is evidenced is correlative with the evidence, and is to be turned toward Being itself in the guise of a claim about it. As so turned, it is made into evidenced-Being, common to and able to complete all beings, and enabling them to be brought to Being itself.

49 Being differs from evidenced-Being as anything differs from a comprehensive characterization of it. The evidence is an abstraction and can take one only to another abstraction, evidenced-Being, in which it is completed. The accommodation of evidenced-Being by Being enables the evidence to become part of Being itself.

50 From the position of anything else, Being is withdrawn; from the position of Being, Being is all-comprehensive. As withdrawn, Being faces a plurality of equally real items. As involved with them, it is faced with tasks of different degrees of difficulty. Since different items have different dignities, Being must operate on them in different ways in order to equate them.

51 Being is involved with both evidence of itself and what is evidenced of itself. Its need to treat evidence and evidenced as equally basic, forces it to emphasize first the one and then the other in a persistent process of accommodation.

52 Being pulsates between the stage where it stands apart from both evidence and evidenced, and the stage where it gives the evidenced the evidence that it needs. To attain the latter stage it deals with the evidenced from the position of the evidence, takes the evidence to the evidenced, and makes the outcome be oriented in itself.

53 Unlike Substance, Being does not accommodate and possess. The evidenced, consequently, has not merely to be submitted to Being but urged. In both cases, though, the finality is the source of the evidence, and enables one to make use of it.

54 A user of evidence forges a claim through its aid. That claim is honored if accommodated by the finality evidenced in that claim. To know whether he has correctly caught the nature of Being, he must see if his claim is adopted by Being without alteration. Being takes charge of what he thrusts toward it, just as Substance takes charge of what he submits to it.

55 A man finds that the evidenced which he claims is subjected by Being to controls and transformations that he is unable to prevent or overcome. As a consequence, he finds himself again and again forced to forge new claims in the attempt to do justice to the nature of Being. Not until he produces an accommodated, unaltered claim about Being can he know what produced the evidence of Being to which he attends.

1 2 8

56 No one can observe Being, face it as an object. But it is possible to penetrate into it beyond any preassignable point. One can also attend to limited situations and see how the process of equalization operates there, and in the light of what is then learned understand how Being could exert a greater, wider-ranging control.

57 Conceiving of possible allocations of areas of equalization through the intrusion of limited forms of Being—the counterpart of a classification and harmonics that can be generated in Substance—permits the formulating of an a priori economics. This looks beyond the production, use, and distribution of resources, to consider the equatable status of groups of entities, and eventually the equatable status of all. One incidental product of such an adventure is the forging of names, more limited than that of 'being', or 'reality', as terms of address to be employed with reference to limited numbers of actualities, each of which requires a specialized approach to make that term singularly appropriate to it.

58 Terms of address appropriate to beings are specializations of 'Being'. They are integral to the evidence that one might use, if one imaginatively divided Being into subordinate beings, each of which controls and thereby equalizes a limited number of items. Classification and other enterprises concerned with the grouping of roles and positions, and applied economics as concerned with the allocation of materials, provide known and empirical illustrations of what has here an a priori ground.

59 Every actuality is substantial. Its substantiality is the inevitable outcome of the internalization of the qualification to which it was subject by Substance. But not every entity is able to internalize all that qualifies it. So far as it fails to internalize the qualification that stems from Being, so far does it remain subject to Being, without enjoying in itself the status of a distinct being. To have that status is one with having native rights.

60 To accept as alone real the lifeless units with which physical science is concerned is to be led to the view that there are no native rights, for those units can not internalize the beings that qualify them. They are beings only so far as they remain dependent on Being.

61 Though some actualities can not internalize a being and are therefore without native rights, all are subject to and involved with Being; their incapacity to internalize what qualifies them does not compromise their status as beings together, under a single governance.

62 Those actualities which are able to internalize a qualifying being are able to function as distinct beings for which all others are coordinate.

63 So far as evidence of Being is separated off from an actuality it is shorn of power. If it were not, there would be a multiplicity of specific beings which continued to exist with their units of power, even apart from the actualities to which they alone were pertinent, and apart from the single Being which the beings instance.

64 Being operates on self-maintained actualities, already substantialized, able to give lodgement to the being that is intruded on them. Being is also able to operate on all the exhibitions of actualities, because these are already sustained by the actualities. Because Being has a status and power of its own, it is able to make every actuality and every appearance be coordinate, the one as members of a single cosmos, the other as within a context.

65 A number of distinguished philosophers, beginning with Parmenides, have taken Being to be the primary or only finality. Other finalities, though, seem more palpable and their effects more obvious. One can readily see that even paltry things are able to provide a ground for their features, and that there could, therefore, be a greater and more basic Substance than they; that the meanings and ordering rules that are employed in language and thought could instance a more basic Possibility; that the smaller regions of extension in which things are and where they confront other things could be limited portions of a more basic Existence; and that there could be a purified, singular Unity relevant to everything, within which the unities that men themselves possess, and other actualities too, might be absorbed. There is an understandable inclination, therefore, for men to suppose that Substance, Possibility, Existence, and Unity are identical with Being. Such identifications result in Being having a number of independent natures and powers. But Being is simple, singular, always the same, producing evidences only in the form of beings. Those evidences lack the powers characteristic of the evidences of Substance, Possibility, Existence, or Unity, just as these lack those evidences' power to coordinate what they govern.

66 Being can be taken to be a substance, for it is affected by Substance, and provides a kind of ground for the beings which give a ground to actualities and their appearances. It can also be said to be intelligible, because it is affected by Possibility, and gives meaning to the actualities and appearances it governs. Similarly, it can be viewed as a kind of existence, for it is affected by Existence, and applies to actualities as well as their appearances as they stand at a distance from one another. Finally, it can be treated as a kind of unity, for it is affected by Unity, and assesses what is within its compass.

Conversely, each of the other finalities can be viewed as a kind of being for each is affected by Being and, like this, takes all actualities and all their appearances to be data for it. But since each of these other finalities grounds, structures, extensionalizes, or evaluates apart from any affect on it by, or reference to, the others, each on its own operates in only one way, to produce only one kind of evidence.

Pure Being, Being as unaffected by any other finality, is not substantial, and so forth, any more than they, in their purity, have being. Yet all are real and irreducible, able to be, just as Being is irreducible and able to be substantialized, and so on, by them.

*

1 DIVERSE THINKERS are agreed on one important issue: men add interpretations, structures, meanings, rules, and order to the content with which they deal. There is considerable disagreement as to whether these conditions, with or without the content, are inside men's minds, and whether or not they are there innately; whether the additions men introduce match what is already present, or are instead something new; whether the men make their additions freely or as mere agents of cosmic forces; whether their additions reflect their experiences, or the structures of their brains or bodies; whether or not they know what they impose; and whether or not they could alter every condition.

The significant oppositions to the common view are provided by a 'searchlight' theory which takes men to encounter what is objectively present without making any addition whatsoever, and by a creationistic view which holds that the content, as well as the conditions applied on them, are produced by men, in one piece. A creationist view has no room for either truth or error; a searchlight, in contrast, yields nothing but truth. Neither, therefore, is acceptable.

2 One could maintain that men produce both the content and the conditions governing them, but do so from different parts of their selves. This is what they seem to do, after all, when they use a language. They then provide the words as well as the grammar governing these words. Though they do not first produce the words and then order them, but speak the words grammatically, nevertheless the grammar prescribes to the words. It issues from a depth in the speakers that the words do not.

Perhaps something similar occurs when one perceives, judges, or explains? Were this the case, here too the conditions would be intruded on content, and with this constitute a new complexity. The obduracy that the content manifests would, though, be a consequence of a man opposing one of his products to the other. But unless he could somehow misconstrue the content, he would then so constitute what he knew that he would not allow any room for truth or error. His, too, would be a searchlight theory which held that he simply illuminated what he was presenting to himself—units of judgment, memories, hopes, sense data, numbers, beliefs.

If a man can misconstrue content—whether he structures it or not—it must have a status apart from him, and so far be indistinguishable from what is available for an independent confrontation and interpretation. If that content were unavoidable, if it were encountered no matter where he turned, if it defied him and escaped from his grasp, it would also be more than anything that he could give to himself.

3 No account can be adequate which stops short with language. Not only are there many languages, precluding the ability of any one to constitute all that there is, but languages presuppose speakers and listeners, not reducible to languages. The fact that a man may be the source of both the rules and units of a language, at least when he is speaking, falls short of showing that he produces everything he confronts, both that which prescribes and that which is prescribed to.

4 It is conceivable that there is a single logic or mathematics that men impose or can impose everywhere, and that it, together with the contents on which the rules operate, is produced by men. Men would then be the sole source of a logical or mathematical universe. That universe would not contain anything which awaited the action of men; it would exist only when they did; it would pass away with them. There would be nothing like prehistoric times, brute particulars, novelties, discoveries; nothing incipient, potential, not yet known in it. And unless one went on to conceive of a finite, limited, personal mind which contrasted with a logically or mathematically constituted one, alike in all, there would be no accounting for error. In any case, only if there were things with natures and rationales that men tried to grasp would allowance be made for actualities existing apart from men.

5 An unerring universal mind is indistinguishable from Possibility, except for the fact that one unnecessarily adds to Possibility a consciousness or ability to think, and a 'cunning' which enables it to face itself with the particulars it is to govern.

6 Might not a primary set of prescriptive rules, logical, mathematical, or scientific, connect a plurality of items whose nature we do not know and perhaps do not need to know, any more than we know or need to know the physical connections that connect the words we speak in order to be able to understand how grammatical rules govern those words? The comparison is faulty. Though the words we speak have their full value only when we speak grammatically, the actualities we attend to already have their careers. It is these we are trying to understand through the agency of the prescriptive principles and which, we trust, will match those that are operative apart from us.

7 Whatever their source, the items which are subject to our orderings—judgmental, grammatical, or conventional—have rela-

tions apart from us and what we bring to bear. At the very least, the items are affiliated, coordinated, located, or evaluated, and thereby sustain evidences of Substance, Being, Existence, or Unity. If to these we added structures of our own making, the content would so far be subject to all the finalities except Possibility. Where men were not or where their ordering was not operative, that content would lack intelligibility; there would be no rationale to it; nothing would guarantee that it might possibily come within men's provenance; and what was not ordered by men would not be predictably convertible into humanly ordered material, for apart from all such ordering, on the hypothesis, it would not be knowable.

8 Some at least of the structures that men introduce when they judge, perceive, and believe, reflect what they themselves are, have experienced, and desire. The grammar to which they subject the words they speak could well issue from their depths, but whether it does so or not, men impose on the words an order those words do not themselves exhibit as so many sounds. A language, with its grammatically used words, may answer to nothing in fact.

Perhaps it is also true that the mathematics, logic, and scientific formulae which one uses when taking account of what one confronts are similar additions, answering to nothing in fact? That on which they were imposed would then be surd, irrational, unintelligible. But if so, we could not know this unless we could look at the content without error.

If we say that content is altered by us, we have already said that we know that it has some status apart from such alteration. We will, so far, have abstracted from the structured material we face, the evidence of ourselves as contributors to it. How could we know that the residue is available for governance by our contributions? Such knowledge would, on the hypothesis, require the use of a mind which alters the content in knowing it.

9 What we confront does not simply stand away from us; it is related to other items and has adventures we can not always anticipate. We know that the suppositions we make are not just internalized forms of structures encountered, because we find that those suppositions are not always in accord with the ways things in fact function. Since these things have some relation to one another to which we try to do justice, and since we do not always know just what the relations are, we are forced to say that if things are prescribed to, conditioned, and made intelligible, this is due to agencies operating in independence of ourselves.

10 We can sometimes impose an order on some things, reflecting the power and interests peculiar to men, reflecting, perhaps, even an a priori ability to organize. Unless this be cut off from all bearing on what occurs apart from human contributions, and therefore does not purport to be true of anything objective, it will be produced in the hope of matching a segment of an objective ordered state of affairs. If it does match, we take ourselves to know what in fact is the case; otherwise, not.

11 Men impose rules, meanings, and other intelligible structures on what they confront. They thereby provide articulations for a plurality of items within a single frame. When emphasis is placed by men on the responsible use of the conditioning structures the result is responsible judgments.

The imposition of structures can be viewed as a form of appreciation, a way of classifying, a practical act, or an assessment. The structures are then faced with what exhibits affiliations, resistances, extensions, and values with which the structures do not entirely mesh. When, instead, one provides structures for what itself has intelligible roles, attention is directed toward what is homogeneous with those structures—formalized actualities or their appearances. If the articulations are appropriate, they answer to segments of all actualities and appearances, so far as these have been given meaning by a single source operating independently of men, and over a wider range than is possible to them.

12 Apart from men, things have natures which are intelligible and from which consequences can be drawn about the functioning and career of the items in which those natures are. The natures are not observable. It is tempting, therefore, to deny that there are natures. In the attempt to account for the supposedly erroneous view, one might maintain that men arbitrarily speak as though there were natures. But then it becomes inexplicable why what occurs is in accord with consequences implied by such supposed natures.

Alternatively, one might appeal to convention and maintain that it is customary for a society to characterize a number of objects in a certain way, and then to refer to them by means of the same terms. If so, why do the objects sometimes behave in defiance of these conventions?

A Wittgensteinean will allow that different items may resemble one another in this or that feature, but he refuses to allow that the resemblance may be transitive. As a consequence, he grants that this may resemble that, and that in turn may resemble something else, but denies that the first need resemble the third. By virtue of what, though, do the items resemble one another? Is it not because they have the same natures? Items a and b resemble one another because they have the same nature; b and c have another nature in common. It is possible for a and c to be unalike, whenever b has two natures.

Many items have a plurality of natures—as the Scotists long ago maintained—each of which is shared with a limited group of entities. Male terriers are allied with other dogs and set in contrast with humans; because of their sex, they are also different from about half of all the dogs there are, and allied with about half of all the cats and half of all the humans, and so on.

This is not yet to go far enough. Despite differences in appearance and behavior, and despite the unobservability of natures, it is proper to speak of male terriers as dogs in the very same sense in which we speak of female greyhounds as dogs. They have the same biological ancestry, and similar structures, organs, and abilities. The fact that from some other position some other common feature might be isolated, does not mean that there are no common features, or even that there are no preferred positions in terms of which one can determine just what natures there are.

13 In contrast with common sense, science cuts beneath resemblances to get to what grounds these. In the course of that endeavor it fastens on common natures which may be partly hidden by differences in appearance. Whales look like fish; biology makes evident that they are not fish at all. We could take them to be fish, stoutly maintaining that whatever lives in water is a fish. But this would overlook the explanatory role that is played by a nature. To acknowledge a whale to be a mammal is to understand, anticipate, and predict something about its gestation, blood, breathing, and movements that could not be done from the base of some feature which just resembled another elsewhere. A nature has explanatory power.

14 A nature is both like and unlike what a Platonist would call an instance of a form. The two are alike in their intelligibility and their explanatory status. Both characterize an entire complex. Both are intruded on what is alien to them. Both provide evidences of a transcendent source. But an instance of a form is set in opposition to what enables it to be located and to function in the world, whereas a nature is involved with this in its full concreteness. An instance of a Platonic form is noble and good, though perhaps sullied by the dross with which it is involved. A nature, in contrast, is a meaning that is enriched by the actuality on which it has been intruded.

A nature is also both like and unlike an Aristotelian essence. The two are alike in intelligibility, objectivity, and explanatory status. Only the essence, though, is identifiable with an Aristotelian sub-stance; it is only the nature that owes its presence to a finality.

15 The traits of an actuality, which it happens to share with any number of others, falls inside the range of its nature without thereby becoming instances of this. Such traits are outcroppings of the interplay of a nature with the actuality on which it has been made to intrude.

16 Empiricists take every identifiable trait to be an irreducible unit, or to be an adventitious addition to it. When the first approach is taken, traits are found to have adventitious features of their own. The first alternative, consequently, leads to the second.

This red and this smell are different. That they are different is something additional to what they severally are. If this addition be taken to be the result of the operation of a mind, that mind will have to be credited with the power of making them different from one another and will, so far, reveal itself to be non-empirically transcending the world they occupy.

17 If all features could be credited to the action of actualities other than those in which those features are resident, the understanding of them would require no transcendence of the world of actualities. For an explanation of the features which characterize one actuality it would be necessary to look only to other actualities. But if there are features which are necessarily present in all actualities, these could not be the product of any or of a number of actualities operating on one another. There are such features. They are terms in relational wholes embracing all actualities.

18 Were one to refuse to do anything more than to acknowledge a plurality of entities, he would leave unanswered the question of why and how those items are present together. Either they are bedrock, and what encompasses them is to be accounted for by referring to some reality which provides relations for them, or the items, too, are produced by some other reality. In either way, one has a relational domain and items related there. The domain encompasses all those particulars, and all those particulars are prescribed to and governed by it as so many terms.

19 Were a plurality of particulars encompassed within a larger particular, the latter would either be final, or would itself be related to other particulars within a still larger particular, itself final, or would be just a domain, and so on. Eventually, we will come to relations which can not be accounted for by attending to particulars, since they bear on all particulars. The relations will themselves be final, with powers of their own, or will depend on what can give them the powers. So long as one knows that actualities, appearances, and features are terms in relations, one knows that something acted on them.

20 Particulars and what makes them be together are not on a footing. The latter is prescriptive, applying to and governing the former. The particulars, in turn, have distinctive careers or implied consequences not explicable by referring to themselves as terms in a relation. If they are actualities, they have their own centers; if they are appearances, they belong to actualities; if they are features they are rooted in the actualities.

An alternative view maintains that there is a single flow, allowing for no distinct items. This requires one to distort the obtrusive characters of experience, which has its rests, distinctions, and independent loci of energy and action. It also requires one to refer to a mind able to convert the supposed flow into a set of distinct items in a common domain where they are so subject to common conditions and controls that they are converted into interrelated terms. This is still to leave unexplained the presence of the particulars, their essential differences, and their independent careers.

Another alternative: A plurality of separate events gives way to itself as unified, only to be followed by a disjunction of new separated events, and so on forever. But not only are the separate events unable to constitute a single plurality without already being somehow together, but there is no reason to suppose that it will always be followed by a unity, or that this will always be followed by a new plurality. If, instead, the plurality and the unity be taken to be inseparable, the unifying relation will be set in contradistinction from those events, just as it is on other, nontemporal views. But the latter alone allow for a unifying relation which converts and governs items that have a reality apart from the relation.

21 If a single item is irreducible, it can still be subject to analysis. The result will be an articulation of it, made intelligible through an act of judgment.

Articulation involves the production of a relation (of which a copula is a special case). If one's judgment is correct, the produced relation is matched by another present in the prearticulated situation, or the produced relation is so solidified by the judger that the result matches an initial unarticulated item.

22 Relations introduced in the course of an articulation provide evidence of a judging mind. That mind is outside the provenance of the items; that is why it can transform them into considered terms relative to one another. To account for the transformation one must take that mind to have a power to enter, via judgment and claim, into the world where the items are. The mind will either be a finality, part of or a specialization of a larger mind, or will reproduce, with more or less fidelity, what a finality in fact does. But it can not be a finality, for it can not of itself govern everything. It might be part of a larger mind. But this one could not know unless one were able to reach that other mind through the agency of the evidence that the first provided. This, some idealists have maintained, is exactly what can be done. Let it be granted. It still is true that the supposed larger mind differs from a finality in nature and power. If it also must have consciousness or intent or judgment or ideas, it will differ because of these as well, for no one of these is necessarily characteristic of a finality. And if it is able to know related particulars truly, it must match the relations and the transformations these impose on actualities, their features, and exhibitions.

23 There are multiple intelligible relations connecting items. All fall within the compass of laws. Even the difference between a sound and a smell is lawlike, relating them in a regular intelligible manner from which consequences can be rationally derived.

Laws do not merely interrelate but prescribe to and therefore encompass, keeping the terms subject indefinitely to the very same connections or to transformations of these. They have various layers. The most general are logical; below these are the mathematical; below these are the scientific; below these are others of more limited scope. All govern actualities in their severalty and as together, their appearances in contexts, and features in their rolls as related terms.

24 All actualities, all exhibitions, and all appearances are necessarily related. Nevertheless, it is also true that the exhibitions, actualities, and appearances are only contingently together with others. The apparent contradiction between these assertions vanishes with the recognition that the entities deny to a necessitation an ascendancy over their comings and goings; at the same time, they are under its domination. They are contingently related because they have limited the scope and power of a necessitation; at the same time, they are necessarily related because they are inescapably subject to conditions operative everywhere.

25 A finality interconnects the exhibitions of an actuality with the exhibitions of other actualities. Limited numbers of exhibitions are also interlinked by each actuality, both contingently and necessarily. When the dominance of an actuality is abstracted from, and its exhibitions dealt with by themselves, their relation to one another will be contingent, to be learned in the course of experience. All the while, in the actuality, the exhibitions will be necessarily connected by the actuality.

26 The factual connections acknowledged in daily experience are the outcome of the neutralizing of an actuality's and of a finality's necessitations by one another. When the two objective necessitations meet in an actuality, a plurality of factually connected aspects of it is produced; when they meet in appearances or a cosmos, a plurality of appearances or actualities, instead, is factually connected. Because it is such connected items to which one initially attends, one is likely to overlook the objective necessitations, and to suppose that all necessitations are due to a mind.

27 To know a final necessitating source one must be able to attend to the formal necessitation which links appearances in limited contexts, use this as evidence of a universal structuralizing context, and end with an evidenced claim about an all-encompassing formal necessity.

28 We are aware that evidence of Possibility can be extricated from a world of appearances, so far as we are aware of a duality there. Appearances fit smoothly within a necessitating context, at the same time that, apart from that context, they make up a single set of exhibitions which are just contingently together because produced by independent actualities.

29 A contingent external relation between items can not exist in the absence of a formal internal necessary relation, for this alone enables the items to be relevant to one another. Nor can there be a necessary relation between items without a contingent one, for a necessary relation's terms are too intimately connected to be able to function as independent units.

30 The idealist thesis that all items are internally linked by a necessity, and the realist thesis that it is independent items that are related, and then contingently, are incomplete but compatible. The one has only relations with nothing to be related; the other has only distinct items with no relations terminating in them. The views are supplementary—another illustration of the fact that everything in experience and in the cosmos is constituted both from the side of actualities and from the side of finalities.

31 Actualities, as not yet subject to necessary linkages, are not contingently connected, any more than a finality in itself has anything which it relates. Actualities, unaffected by finalities, are diffusely together; a finality, unaffected by actualities, is too self-contained, not diversified enough to be relational. The diffuse presence of all actualities is variegated; they become distinct when confronted by a finality. An undiversified finality is flexible; it yields different specifications of itself when met by different actualities.

32 There are no actualities unaffected by finalities. Possibility does not face actualities as diffusely together, but only as already necessarily united by other finalities. The necessity these others provide contrasts with the necessity owed to Possibility. In terms of the latter they, too, can be said to be contingent.

Were one to take one's stand with a causal or some other type of necessity, distinct from that provided by Possibility, actualities connected by Possibility would be faced as only contingently together. The necessities of a causal world face scientific formulae as contingent intelligible connections, even though those formulae link their terms by necessity.

33 To be aware of a law is to be aware of a power able to intrude into a situation to make it law-abiding, at the same time that its items continue to be joined apart from the law. To know the power that imposed a formal necessitation one must first separate off that necessitation and use it as evidence. One then does not affect the governance of the related items by finalities other than Possibility. Indeed, Possibility also continues to govern them, but the fact is ignored.

34 Evidences are distinguished in and by the entities which sustain and are affected by them. Since a wholly dislocated intelligibility is a completely purged intelligibility, it reveals nothing of its previous application. Evidence of intelligibility, when this is held apart from the appearances with which it is involved, is indistinguishable from evidence obtainable and held apart from actualities severally or together.

35 Logicians are inclined to pay no attention to the way in which premisses are obtained. They are satisfied to begin with any premiss and to end with what this entails. They are right to do this, since they are concerned solely with justified movements from accepted premisses to the conclusions at which the movements end. Left over, though, is the problem of how one is able to pass from experience or realities to where inference occurs, and to pass from where the inference ends back again to the world of experience or realities.

There could well come a time when men were so confident about the nature of extricated evidence that they could devote themselves exclusively to the problem of how it could be used to enable them to reach what it evidenced. Something like this is done in the law of evidence and something like this is done in the use of statistics. But metaphysics must attend to the question of extricating evidence before it attends to its use, for it can take nothing for granted.

36 Evidence of Possibility is extricated from the actualities and appearances with which it constitutes intelligible law-abiding compounds, complexities, and items of experience. The extrication is at once a purgation and a detachment, freeing the evidence of modifications that were introduced into it by that on which it intrudes, at the same time that it is held apart from the situation where it was identified.

37 Actualities do not cease to be affected by and to affect the evidence, even after this has been extricated. The brackets men put around the evidence are defied by the actualities. As a consequence, evidence that is used never duplicates the evidence that had in fact been intruded.

38 There is no preassignable degree of impurity that must cling to detached evidence. But whatever impurity remains when evidence is extricated at one time and in one way may conceivably be eliminated by making another effort at detachment at another time and from a different angle.

39 Kant knew that intruded factors were intelligible. He knew, too, that they could be parts of objective situations only so far as they had been enabled to be so. Though he sometimes maintained that one could say nothing more than that a unity accompanied all perception, he occasionally did hold that it was presupposed by and was the source of the more limited unifications that had been intruded into the supposed passive, sensed content that was 'given' to the perceiver.

Kant thought that all metaphysical claims were unwarranted, in part because he ignored his own metaphysical acceptance of the unity which was the source of his unifying categories, and in part because he took metaphysics to be the attempt to use absolutized versions of the categories to characterize what was ultimate. His conclusions are avoidable when his categories are seen to be evidential premises which specialize Possibility.

Kant's transcendental unity of apperception, as was later recognized by some of his successors, is a finality. It was readily identified by some of the idealists with a universal, objective mind, the mind of no man in particular; it is then hardly distinguishable from Possibility, with its power to intrude limited meanings on what is present.

Were one to make a start with the Kantian categories, one would, in order to get to some finality other than Possibility, have to take as evidence those categories as affected by content in four additional ways. To get to Substance those categories have to be grounding controls; Being is to be achieved only if we begin with them as coordinating agents; to get to Existence one must start with the categories in the role of extended powers; and to reach Unity one acknowledges them as enabling what is present to function as unit values belonging together in an ordering irreducible finality. A successful evidencing in all these cases takes one to what is not only more inclusive and general than the evidence, but toward what is more powerful and more self-sufficient.

40 What is evidenced has a role different from the evidence's, and from any generalization of this. Though what is evidenced of Possibility is a more general meaning, it is one which has a greater symbolizing effectiveness than the evidence of it could have, since what is evidenced is directly related to Possibility. Properly used evidence is transformed in the production of the evidenced.

41 If the extrication of evidence proceeded without any guidance, it would be able to move only by happenstance, and could end with what is not wanted. Yet if it were to proceed in accordance with a rule or principle, apparently an act would be required to get that with which one is to begin. Since such an act would itself require the obtaining of a content free from extraneous involvements with matter of fact, we would appear to be caught in an infinite regress. It seems, therefore, as if we have to proceed haphazardly or never be able to begin.

42 We do get to a beginning without presupposing a rule; but if this is possible, why should we not also be able to proceed from there without following a rule? The solution to this problem has a number of different forms, depending on whether we are concerned with the formulation of a rule, the process of evidencing, the identification of evidence and evidenced with an antecedent and consequent, or the presentation of the evidenced to the finality. Each one of these could conceivably be the outcome of a warranted process conforming to some rule and, therefore, could conceivably lead to an infinite regress. Or it could conceivably take place without guidance or control. Fortunately, these are not the only alternatives.

A rule might be followed in order to get to a result efficiently or in order to be able to repeat what one is doing. Such a rule does not justify an outcome; it merely specifies the limits of the process by which an outcome is reached.

It is also possible to follow a rule to get a warranted result. But there is no need to do so; a warranted result can be obtained by meeting other conditions; it can be obtained in a justifiable way without attending to any rule at all. This is what we do when we take a truth of fact and convert it into a premiss.

Evidence can be obtained under the guidance of the prospect of having purified evidence, available for use. Keeping that prospect to the fore, one can be indifferent to the manner in which it is reached. It is sufficient that the purified evidence can be obtained. Did one simply construct or imagine it, or obtain it from a particular situation by unusual means, that would be a matter of indifference.

43 The formulation of a rule involves the pairing of antecedent and consequent. It might be constructed without regard to any matter of fact; and it is constructible without the need even to entertain a prospect. Unlike a premiss, and surely unlike evidence, its constituents need not have any empirical reference. It is assessed by seeing what it makes possible, and is justified just so far as we, in following it, do not end in error or disaster. It is not warranted by its conforming to or realizing some more perfect or ideal rule.

One wants to arrive, from the available evidence, at what is evidenced. On finding that an unsatisfactory result is about to be obtained, one rightly gives up the effort to insist on a particular formulated rule. Rules are desirable. They are to be used, if operating in accord with them could bring one to the desired outcome. Where an attempt is made to lay down the conditions that should be met if a warranted evidencing is to take place, rules are needed to guide one's efforts. Failure to make room for rules enables one to arrive at what one seeks, but if one is not sure that the procedure is valid, one can not know that he had reached a result in a way that others could duplicate and check. Strictly speaking, though, all that is needed is a principle matching the structure of a controlling Possibility.

44 The evidenced with which we pair evidence of Possibility is an indeterminate, without interiority. It lacks depth. In compensation it has a greater breadth than the evidence, and will obtain an even greater depth from the Possibility. But its nature is so dim that we readily misconstrue it. At the very place one might have expected greatest success, when we are dealing with meanings and seeking to reach the intelligible domain of Possibility, we find indeterminateness. This, though, is what should have been expected. What is possible is indeterminate; the more it is freed from specificity and left unarticulated the more indeterminate it is.

45 A process of inference, set over against a rule, moves from premiss to conclusion. It takes time and it takes energy. That is why one tires when one thinks.

46 Evidencing involves a use of evidence, an involvement of oneself with it, and the preservation of it in the evidenced with which one ends. The process is distinctive each time it occurs, and varies in nature, rhythm, and rapidity throughout its course. It may begin poorly. But that is of no moment, for as one moves closer and closer to the end of the process, it becomes more and more what it should be.

47 Evidencing is a self-corrective activity which achieves its proper momentum and direction the closer it gets to its terminus. We are never sure that we are caught up in such a process at the beginning, but we become more and more sure of it as we approach the end. It could benefit by being carried out within the limits of some rule. But it becomes what it should be, whether or not there is such a rule, or whether or not such a rule is followed.

48 Evidencing is progressively self-certifying, so far as it is controlled by the evidenced toward which it progressively moves.

49 The process of evidencing is justified to the degree that it utilizes its beginning fully in the creation of an end acceptable to a finality. Should it end with what is not prefigured in a rule, it will not be a process which is formally justified. But it still may be successful. If it fails, this will not necessarily be because it failed to conform to a rule; it is enough that the appropriate end was not achieved.

50 There are at least eleven different types of inferential process that are well worth distinguishing: a) A *formal,* which proceeds linearly according to a rule guaranteeing that if one starts with truth one can not end with falsehood. b) A *constructional,* constituting the result at which one seeks to terminate—a method used by intuitionistic mathematicians, as well as by artists, particularly those anxious to keep within the confines of some school. c) A *predictive,* where one formulates hypotheses whose consequences are to be assessed in terms of the reports of experience. d) A *social,* where a random result is taken to express a disconnection, and where high frequencies of coincidence are taken to justify causal suppositions. e) An *historical,* in which there is a convergence of many partial, inadequate moves toward a central explanatory fact, to be followed by a narrative which moves in the reverse direction to the initial starting point, in a connected and perhaps dramatic account. f) A *medical,* where observable occurrences are accepted as symptoms, leading to a knowledge of possible causes. g) A *dialectical,* which takes abstract, concrete, or historical occurrences to be necessarily completed by others, themselves requiring further completion. h) A *teaching,* where one so deals with another that he too is prompted to engage in the activity of learning or investigating. i) A *legal,* where 'facts' are supplemented with others, and the whole is subject to an adversary treatment, each giving the result a determinate nature within a legal system—the courts attempting to ascertain which of these determinations is more complete and more consistent with the established law, and accepting it in contrast with its competitor. j) A *symbolic,* in which one begins with an attenuated continuation of some reality and moves into this by intensification and solidification of data. k). A *systematic,* where an attempt is made to be self-critical and probing, so as to arrive at an explanatory account in which irreducible realities are interrelated. Ideally, here one pays attention to all the other ways of proceeding, and indeed makes use of them.

51 The paradigm for a rational movement to any finality from the world of appearances or actualities is a logical inference which begins with some matter of fact from which evidence has to be extracted. If the movement is to enable one to conclude with a claim that will be sustained, it will follow a course governed by an intelligible structure, and end with what is appropriate to a finality.

52 In a movement to a finality, the evidence is absorbed within the evidenced. The fact does not preclude an understanding of the movement as a form of a logically impeccable inference, both because a purely formal relation between premiss and conclusion can express the fact that the former is a part of the latter, and because a valid inference is subject to no other condition but that of beginning with a premiss and ending with the entailed conclusion. Nothing is amiss if the movement is accumulative or not, slow or fast, circuitous or direct, goes through stages or is continuous.

53 A systematic use of evidence moves from a limited situation to a final reality freed from the restrictions characteristic of the limited situation from which the evidence was extricated. One of the tasks of philosophy is to make evident the nature, progress, and terminus of a systematic inference to finalities.

54 Formal inferences with respect to finalities, other than Possibility, must convert actual evidences into usable premisses with intelligible features, so that they can be subject to a formal rule. But the evidence of Possibility already is intelligible; to abstract it from an involvement with actualities or their appearances is to have it in exactly the guise one needs in order for it to be subject to a formal rule.

55 Possibility is reached from intelligible items necessarily and intelligibly linked with intelligible items. It is the source of structures governing the way in which one reaches a satisfactory claim about it.

56 The premisses of an ordinary inference, and those needed to get one to a finality, are not easily obtained. They are initially involved in a dynamic world where they have careers quite unlike what they have when used at the beginning of a formally valid inference.

A movement to Possibility, in accord with that fact, takes its start with an alien intelligible factor which has been extricated from an actuality, from actualities together, or from their appearances together, and related to a possible conclusion by a rule of inference.

57 In a systematic philosophic inference, a rule has the special guise of a formal principle by means of which evidence and evidenced are turned toward one another. A systematic philosophic inferring begins with evidence of a finality and ends with an evidenced claim. The conclusion is what is evidenced, produced through the creative use of the evidence. If the inference is to a claim about Possibility, it is formal, structural, an articulate meaning, a less intensive version of Possibility itself.

58 Claims made about finalities other than Possibility differ from

1 4 5

the finalities in nature, for while the claims are formally expressed, the finalities are different in kind from the outcome of any claim formally arrived at. Alternatively, claims made about finalities, when systematically achieved, are less intensive versions of those finalities, but only in the case of Possibility does a systematically achieved claim also have a formal, articulate structure.

59 Evidence and evidenced refer to the same finality; they are in a relation of the less intensive to the more intensive, of that which is indirectly to what is directly pertinent to a finality. It is as if a premiss had no truth claim of its own, but served only to make possible a truth claim by the conclusion.

60 Evidence of Possibility, which was involved with an alien context, is turned into a beginning of a process of inference to the evidenced; the evidenced at which one arrives at the end of an inference is turned into content more or less accommodated by Possibility. The former act depends on us; the latter on Possibility.

61 When the evidenced has been expressed in the form of a claim, there is nothing more to be done, except to determine if the claim is accepted by Possibility, and how. This is known by seeing if the claim is altered in being accommodated, or if one is able to abstract from Possibility the meaning of what had been offered it.

62 Something of Possibility can be discerned before a claim about it is fully forged. The prospect of a discrepancy between it and the claim can therefore be anticipated, and an attempt made to provide a claim different from that which one was about to present. Usually, though, only the process of evidencing is modified, despite the fact that it then fails to be in consonance with the principle that one had accepted. The priniciple is then treated as so much scaffolding.

63 The extricated evidence for Possibility is a *category*. This had operated on actualities severally, on actualities together, and on appearances together as a rule of organization.

64 An *essence* is a specialized case of a category. A category, in turn, is a specialized case of the evidenced. An essence is to a category what a fact is to a law, and a category is to what is evidenced as a law is to a theory. A fact is a fixated localization of a law; a law is a delimited version of a theory.

There is no sure movement from fact to law or from law to theory. Simple generalization will not do, for a law is fecund, applicable to facts which, though not similar to one another, are enabled by the law to be interconverted. A theory provides a way of relating laws. It may enable one to anticipate the discovery of laws by justifying transformations in a law as it applies under different circumstances.

65 It has been said that God made the natural numbers and that man made the rest of mathematics. It would have been more correct to have said that man makes all of mathematics as specifying a single final Possibility. Possibility is imaginatively expressed in the form of a set of a priori ordering principles or formulae. The natures and interconnections of these are the topic of a formal mathematics.

Logical and mathematical truths are universal and necessary, possibilities which have application to everything that is, and are realized at every moment. A realization at one time or in one place still leaves them available for realization at other times and places.

Both logical and mathematical truths, though sustained by Possibility, exist only so far as they have been carved out of it, constructed in it, or constructed in an imagined domain which is to represent it. The constructions presuppose Possibility itself, and thereby reveal that they themselves can be empirically known only so far as they can be extricated from present situations as evidences of it. Such extrication is of the same order as is the extrication of laws. It is, therefore, as difficult to go from a particular instance of a mathematical or logical truth to the completely general formulation of it, appropriate to the sciences of logic and mathematics, as it is to go from a particular instance of a law of nature to the law as applicable everywhere. The fact is readily overlooked because men, once they have extricated a few logical and mathematical truths, occupy themselves with the creation or derivation of others which are like these in abstractness, formality, and validity.

66 A theoretical cosmological physics anticipates the nature of actualities by imaginatively constructing mathematically expressed laws pertinent to them. The mathematics that it creatively expresses is limited to the actualities that can sustain the mathematics. Because sustaining actualities have an independent status apart from the laws in which they function as terms, they are able to localize and limit the range of the applicable laws.

67 Having once extricated a law of nature, one can follow a procedure similar to that already well utilized in logic and mathematics, and attempt the formulation of related laws. But first it is necessary to extricate some laws, and the involved logical and mathematical truths. One is then in the realm of Possibility.

68 One who is not a scientist can not obtain a knowledge of laws of nature unaided; he is not properly equipped or trained to do this. But he can begin with instances of ethical good, that is, with what ought to be. The Golden Rule, for example, a is to do to b what b should do to a, can be extricated from particular cases. Though this falls short of the sweep of truths in logic, mathematics, or physics, it is within the grasp of any man.

The Golden Rule can be used to deal with unequal items—for example, 'a is to do to b what a should do to a.' The use of 'should' here would normally be thought to restrict the rule's application to responsible beings. But one can also understand the 'should' to refer to an ideal form of action required of every actuality, even inanimate ones. What fails to do what it should in this idealized sense is defective ontologically, falling short of a possible ideal. Possibility is that ideal which all entities are to realize. The ethical good is a special case of it.

69 An ideal excellence can be defied to any preassignable degree, up to but not including complete defiance. It can not include complete defiance, because nothing simply does what ought not to be. This would require it, self-contradictorily, to have various excellencies such as being well-organized, controlled, efficient, and responsible.

To say that something is defective is to measure it in terms of a standard of excellence. To say that it is defective so far as it defies this, is to speak of it relative to that which it defies.

70 The excellence of appearances or actualities is the outcome of the way in which an ideal excellence and that in which it is imbedded insist on themselves together, thereby constituting a single entity in which the excellence itself is enhanced by being specified, and that on which it is imposed is enhanced by being made intelligible.

71 The defiance of what intrudes makes possible the presence of a limited excellence. Actualities compel excellence to have a more specific meaning and career than it could have as a mere continuation and expression of the finality, Possibility. The imposed excellence is itself defective from the perspective of Possibility. But taken on its own terms it is neither good nor bad, defective nor excellent.

72 The prescriptions of ethics are for men to fulfill. They have bearing on all there is, demanding of men that they preserve and enhance values.

73 Ethical prescriptions are directed toward this world. Unlike the future, they have an integrity of their own, and thus provide a base for a progress into a more fundamental reality. But to get to those ethical prescriptions one must start with experience where they are realized or defied. A fully developed ethics exhibits the prescribed good as that which is capable of being specified everywhere and in endless ways. What is now available are only very abstract prescriptions related to a limited number of cases as the more to the less general.

74 Possibility is a finality, no less ultimate and effective than any other. But when one compares it with Substance, Being, Existence, or Unity, it seems so pallid and inert that there is a strong temptation to take it to be something derivative and dependent. For the Platonist, though, Possibility is a primal form governing everything with a power and a glory denied to anything else. From that standpoint, it is the other finalities that seem pallid and inert. To account for their presence and functioning, one must then deal with them under the aegis of a final excellence. Once, though, it is recognized that other finalities are on a footing with Possibility, the insight of the Platonist can be accommodated at the same time that justice is done to the insights of those who diverge from him.

EXISTENCE AND EXISTENTS

1 THE CONDITIONS which men impose on what they judge are of various sorts—aesthetic, taxonomic, structural, extensional, and evaluational. If the content judged is outside the mind, the judgment is experiential; if in the mind, theoretical.

2 If conditions are not only imposed on exterior content, but are presented to it for sustaining there, the imposition is practical. In an experiential judgment, the conditions remain in the individual; in practice, the imposition carries the conditions into exterior content.

3 When conditions that men introduce in experiential judgments are carried further in uninterrupted moves, they constitute practical acts. Though what is practically done is not often judged, a knowledge of what this is, is antecedently exhibited in experiential judgments.

4 An act of imposition intrudes mental content into content outside the mind. The content in both cases is an extended unit extensionally connected with other extensional units.

If a judgment and practice begin with conditions which are themselves not extensional—as is the case when the conditions are aesthetic, taxonomic, structural, or evaluational—they do not enable one to mesh with the existents and, therefore, with the conditions to which those existents are always subject. A structure is an example. It enables one to attend only to the intelligible nature of an existent, not to its existence, and can mesh not with an extension but only with what is meaningfully related to the structure.

5 Both correct experiential judgments and successful practical acts are homogeneous with the existents they condition. They enable a man to bring his own spatial extent, time, and dynamics to bear on what is before him in such a way as to enable this and himself to fit within larger extensions.

6 Content exterior to the mind is confronted as having its own dynamics in space and time. Were the content due to mind, that mind would be distinct from and even oppositional to that which is imposing the conditions. It would also be within a larger extension.

Did men produce the space, time, and dynamics, extending over or extending beyond the content they confront, that content would be without any extensionality or location until man appeared.

Would the men themselves be extended? Could they have a location in a space, a time, or a dynamism? How could they?

Did man produce content on which he imposed extensions or locations, it would have to be produced independently of the extensions or locations. Otherwise it would not be possible to make incorrect impositions at times; the extended world would be entirely man's creation.

7 Practice does not produce a world; it can only attempt to take account of one. That is why practice can be inefficacious, frustrating, and even injurious.

8 The world of actualities is not constituted by experiential judgments; it is not a result of the imposition of the possibility that there might be action by us. Experiential judgments are forced to accord with what has no regard for them. Practice, too, is successful only when it meshes with the ways in which content functions—a functioning that occurs regardless of our interests or our presence.

9 Experiential judgments touch, and practical acts alter what exists apart from us. The experiential judgments, when appropriate, enable us to share in the extensional relations of what is available, thereby allowing us to be interlocked with the very existents that we are conditioning.

10 As standing apart from us and our impositions, judgmental or practical, objective appearances and actualities exist.

11 Practical acts bring conditioning men into extensions in which appearances and actualities are located. But though it is practice that allows one to make contact with existents and thereby with the universal conditions to which the existents are subject, it is only by withdrawing from practice that those conditions can be discerned.

12 'Magnitude', 'quantity', are no less honorific than 'existence' is. No one of these marks a distinctive feature alongside others; all refer to an entire actuality or appearance. There is as much justification in eliminating 'spatial', 'temporal', and 'dynamic' from one's vocabulary as there is in eliminating 'existent' and 'existence'.

13 The spatiality, temporality, dynamism, magnitude, or quantity of an object can not be observed; we know them only because we know in some way other than through the use of the senses. The presence of an extension can not be noted unless we stand away from that with which it is involved. Only then can we extricate the extensional conditions that govern those appearances and actualities.

14 The existence of a particular can be imaginatively subdivided so as to be appropriate to distinguished parts of it. The smallest possible particles known to science provide units for measuring the extent of an existent object as comprising so many units.

15 The existence of an actuality is usually conveyed by means of the copula in an assertion. At the same time that the copula connects a subject and a predicate, it orients them in the object which the subject and predicate together articulate.

16 Kant held that 'a body is extended' is a tautology. It is impossible, he said, for there to be a body that is not extended. The position can not be maintained if one allows for an angelic or other spiritual body. Even remaining with the bodies in this world, there are still issues to be resolved.

Bodies are necessarily extended either because they are located within larger extensions, each subdivision of which is also extended, or because they attain the status of bodies only so far as they are endowed with extension. The first alternative takes what is located to achieve an extension by delimitation from a larger extension. If it is supposed that there are bodies which have to achieve extensions through such delimitation, one obviously has denied the Kantian thesis that a body is necessarily extended. The second alternative, instead, supposes that both bodies and their extensions are the outcome of intrusions on what is neither bodily nor extended. This is perhaps the view that Kant would accept. Since what is being invoked is a transcendent power, the main difference that remains between what is here being urged and the Kantian treatment of the second alternative is that here only is the object recognized to have a reality with a distinctiveness of its own, and the persistent, omnipresent power to which it is subject held not to be dependent on the presence of men or of their knowing.

17 When we speak of an object in quantitative terms, as having such and such a spatial magnitude, time-span, or career, the expression for a quantity, when put in a predicate position, serves to explicate the import of the copula. To say that a man is six feet tall is not to remark on some aspect of him alongside his color, shape, or weight, but to focus on a single extended area where they are displayed. That area is possessed by him; to speak of it is to give an additional specific meaning to the copula which connects the conceived quantity to the designated man, and roots the two in him.

Aristotle took quantity to be a category alongside quality. The scientific revolution, initiated by Galileo, set quantity on a different level, as the truly objective, proper way to characterize what was real. Galileo did not allow the other features, particularly the qualities discernible through the help of the senses, to have an objective status. With him, we should say that quantity and quality are quite different—but for reasons other than those he accepted, since he denuded the world and lost the hold that experience has on it.

18 Quantities are transcendents confined within the limits of actualities. Qualities, instead, are exhibitions of actualities dominating over intrusive insistencies.

19 Quantities, Locke thought, were inherent in actualities, while qualities expressed an individual's external response to them. But both are objective, the one evidencing a finality, the other an actuality.

20 A complex actuality, as already affected by a transcendent, is both qualitative and quantitative; apart from all influence by a finality, it is neither the one nor the other. But since an actuality helps constitute both by exhibitions which continue to fringe the result, it can be known by retracing the exhibitions back to their source.

21 A fat man may still be fat when he loses ten pounds. The fatness characterizes him as a unit, and the poundage characterizes him as a summation of smaller actualities. These observations seem to stand in direct opposition to the view here advanced, to the effect that quantity is transcendent, while a quality is limited in range and located within the extended areas. The conflict is not real.

A quality can spread over the whole of an extension without being transcendent. No matter what its extent, it expresses the actuality. Nor does the fact that a quantity can be understood to be the outcome of the summation of smaller quantities require the denial that a quantity is single, intrusively characterizing a single actuality. Subordinate, demarcated quantities, which a single quantity includes, characterize smaller actualities within the confines of the larger.

It is the single magnitude of a man that makes it right to speak of *him* as fat; it is the distinctive quantities of subordinate particles which provide the means for expressing that magnitude in a sum.

22 The extension of one actuality is at once separated from and continuous with the extension that intrudes on other actualities. The actualities are separated because the extension in each is interlocked with the actualities, to make them single, quantified, and complex. Their separation does not conflict with their connection. If it did, an actuality would be forever involved with a detached bit of extension, or would be absorbed within a cosmic extension. In either case, it would not be able to move, to endure, or to act.

23 If it be one of the higher living beings, an actuality internalizes the extension imposed on it without abrogating the role of that extension as an intruded extension, continuous with an extension beyond. A higher living being, as a result, does not live merely in a location within a larger extension, but lives in an environment—that larger extension dealt with from the position of a privately extended actuality. The extension is here doubly involved with the actuality, once from the outside where it qualifies the actuality and is there contoured and intensified, and again from the inside where it is an integral part of the actuality and as such helps determine what the actuality will do in the larger region that environs it.

The extensions that qualify actualities and are internalized by some of them, are continuous with cosmic extensions, thereby allowing the actualities to be within the cosmic extensions and to function in consonance with environmentalized portions of those cosmic extensions.

24 One becomes aware of the presence of intruded extensions most readily on becoming aware of the difference between what an actuality is as separate and what it is when together with other actualities in an extended cosmos. As the former, it not only has its own spatiality and dynamics, but its own rhythm and pace. As the latter, it is subject to the conditions not only of a cosmic space and dynamics with a geometry and power, but of a time in which the actualities are contemporaries.

25 Apart from qualification by extensions and apart from localization within a single cosmic extension, actualities are distended, symmetrically, asymmetrically, and progressively. Their distensions interlock with limited spatial, temporal, and dynamical extensions, which qualify the different actualities, to make these become the quantified extensions of those actualities.

26 Were actualities not subject to intruded extensions, they would still be distended, but they would not be quantified and distanced from one another. But they are quantified, and they are members of a single spatiotemporal-dynamic cosmos. They pass into the next moment together despite their different paces; they occupy parts of a common space despite their different strengths; and they are involved in causal chains despite their independent activities. These facts can not be explained without making reference to a power controlling them all—any more than one can explain their affiliations, coordination, intelligibility, and values without making reference to other equally intrusive powers.

27 Actualities are affiliated, coordinated, law-abiding, and are in a valuational totality. But, so far, they are not yet contemporaries, not yet in the same space, and not yet subject to the same dynamism. These depend on their being subject to a different distinctive controlling condition, evidencing a distinctive finality. That finality, Existence, makes them be extended severally and together, bounded off, dynamic, and contemporary. Such states of affairs are beyond any man's power to bring about.

28 One of the pivotal contentions of contemporary physics is that there is no one single position in terms of which all actualities could be said to be contemporaneous. It is tempting, therefore, to deny that there is a single common time for all actualities, enabling them to be contemporary in a single cosmos. Putting aside the fact that the conclusions required by physics, since they depend on the acceptance of some unquestioned presuppositions and relate to actualities only so far as these are linked through the agency of light signals, are not philosophical givens, there is the fact that, apart from all light signals, one actuality can be larger than another no matter where this be. That fact can be expressed mathematically as the magnitude of that other plus some additional magnitude. Nothing is here said about the transmission of light signals; it holds regardless of where the actualities are.

Actualities, of course, are not larger or smaller in and of themselves. But to be larger or smaller they must have some magnitude, apart from all others. Because this is possessed by the actuality, it characterizes it; because the magnitude is a delimited portion of a larger extension it can be located in relation to other magnitudes.

29 Were appearances not made to be in a single extensionalized context, they would not be in a common time, space, or dynamic chain. So long as other contexts were operative, of course, there still would be appearances, but those appearances would not, on the hypothesis of the absence of an intrusive extensionalizing context, be extended or located.

30 If, as Augustine held, time is just a distension of the soul, it would not be possible to have a cosmos of temporal actualities or a world of temporal appearances. If everything we know, moreover, is filtered through a time we provide, the object to be known will be atemporal, incapable of change.

31 Though there have been only a few thinkers who have denied the reality or the extension of space—Leibniz, for example—many more have denied the reality or extension of time. McTaggart and Bradley join Eastern thinkers in supposing that time is illusory. Aristotle and Bergson, instead, deny that it is extended, the one identifying it with numbers measuring change and motion, the other taking it to be an accumulative, always present dynamism. The fact that time is usually portrayed by means of a line has prompted still others to take it to be real and extended, but only as a dimension which is simply additional to the three usually credited to space.

That there is more to time than numbers is evident from the fact that it is lived through. Living through is extensive; it separates beginning and end by an interval whose parts are only delimited portions of it. That time is more than a line is also evident from the fact that it is lived through. A line has all its distinguishable parts co-present, but the 'line of time' is constantly being drawn and just as constantly being erased.

Time, like space, as Kant observed, is not a concept, or a universal with a plurality of subordinated specifications. Its conceivable subdivisions are within it, alongside one another, all possessing the same kind of extendedness, and constituting the extendedness of the whole of time.

32 The *now* is an intensive unit in which no part is earlier than another. Environed by a past and future it provides an extended interval between them. Excluding the past as that which is already completed, and excluding the future as that which is not yet, it is vivid and thick. The beginning and ending of it are not the termini of a line, but of an uncontoured indefinite extendedness which, when embodied and intensified, acquires a past and a future, and thereby becomes a limited *present*.

33 A present moment is an extension, at once unmoving and unchanging, within which the known is to be located. Its beginning and ending are co-present, but with one *before* the other. Here it is that the first and last part of a symphony occur; here is the beginning and ending of a war, a sentence, or a conversation.

34 Actualities are distinct, each with its own insistence. But their appearances are impotent and not altogether separable from a context. Green itself is not dynamic, nor is it temporal or spatial. It is the green-of-the-leaf that is temporal and spatial, and gives way to the brown-of-the-leaf. In abstraction from the leaf, the green of the leaf is a constant, just that color. It does not itself become brown. Green is green and brown is brown. But the green color of the leaf is slowly giving way to the brown; the green-of-the-leaf becomes the brown-of-the-leaf due to a change in the composition of the leaf.

35 Appearances do not have a past, present, or future, neighbors, causes or effects. Yet none continues forever; there are distances between them; they predictably give way to others.

36 A context and its source account for what is common to all appearances; differences amongst them can not be due to them since they are impotent, nor to a mind since this has a limited history, power, and scope. Their differences are to be traced back to actualities interacting with a common space, time, and dynamism rooted in a finality.

37 A present moment has no preassignable length, and may encompass any number of smaller presents. As within it, these smaller presents are in an order of before and after one another; outside it they are in an order of earlier and later. A larger-scaled event, such as a culture, though occurring only in a present, embraces a multiplicity of smaller present events, such as changes in culture and language, each in a present of its own.

38 The smallest possible present moment is extended. Otherwise nothing could occur within its confines. It would be just a limit, bounded on one side by an endless past that could not conceivably have occurred, and on the other from an endless future that can never take place.

39 In a present there are two abstractable but actually interlocked facets. One contains what had been inherited from the determinate past, the other what is derived from the possible future. The present unstably unifies the import of the past and the future at the same time that it excludes them.

40 Every spatial, temporal, and dynamic limited region is contained within an all-inclusive, unlimited extension. This can be said to be at once spatial, temporal, and dynamic, or, equally, to be a primitive, ultimate extensionality which expresses itself in these three guises. In the one way it is spoken of in terms of the evidenced at which we arrive through a process of evidencing that started with some limited bit of extension; in the other it is spoken of as in itself, without being identifiable with any one, or with any combination of its basic expressions.

41 An actual leaf by itself is distended. The green-of-the-leaf is an extended delimited region within an indefinitely larger encompassing region. When occupied by the leaf, the region is made integral to the leaf at the same time that the leaf is made a part of the indefinitely larger encompassing extension.

42 The occupation of an extension is inseparable from the delimiting of a larger extension, and a possessing of the result by a particular actuality.

43 An extended occupied region provides evidence of a finality, Existence. The evidence can be used, though, only if freed from its occupant.

44 Extricating evidence of Existence from actualities or appearances is a difficult enterprise, despite the ease with which we speak of the beginning or ending of time, the three dimensions of space, the conservation of energy, and the like. If we could not extricate it we could not know what enabled an actuality or an appearance to be contemporary with others, to be located, or to be part of a single causality. Fortunately, we do not, in order to have evidence of Existence, have to extricate more than a limited, impure portion of a time, space, or dynamics. Nor does it make a difference from where we extricate the extensions. Once they have been obtained, they are as available for use as any extension obtained elsewhere.

45 Evidence of Existence is most readily obtainable from a world of appearances. The recognition that an appearance could be elsewhere, that it could be at another time, and that it could have some other role in a causal process is one with the recognition that the extensions it occupies have a status apart from it.

46 The extrication of evidence of Existence, whether or not this be limited to what is merely spatial, temporal, or dynamic, or to some combination of these, or identified with an existentializing factor in actualities or appearances, and whether or not this be accomplished through analysis or by an actual freeing of intrusive factors from the situation into which they had been intruded, leaves one with a symbol of Existence. Used in a process of evidencing, that symbol leads to what a limited extension evidences, and through this to Existence.

47 Due to the classical Greeks, geometry attained the status of an abstract discipline applicable to a purified form of actual space. As its name indicates, it was once the science which measured the earth. With the advent of non-Euclidean geometries, even the restriction to a purified form of actual space was overcome. But then geometry ceased to provide an account of the properties of actual space filled out and contoured by the earth and other objects.

A pure time is even more difficult to isolate than a pure space.

Clocks and watches are calibrated with the passage of astronomical bodies. The use of such timepieces has stood in the way, not only of the acknowledgment of the times appropriate to music, dance, religion, history, and human transactions, but of the pure time of which all of these are specializations, pertinent to particular enterprises.

Different objects function in different ways. The dynamics of the sea is different from the dynamics of a bird. Yet the only dynamics studied for a long time has been that of inanimate particular things. A sheer pure dynamism subtends these and all other ways of functioning.

The envisagement of a future time, a remote space, and an eventual effect presupposes an isolating of a pure space, time, and dynamism. But instead of attending to these, or even using them as evidence, they are initially accepted as backgrounds on which to project what we imagine might occupy them. It has taken mankind a long time to acknowledge a pure extension because men have been interested primarily, not in knowing it, but in using or imaginatively filling it.

48 To the degree an extension is freed from involvement with actualities, to that degree it loses limitation. The intensive tincture that the occupying actuality gives to the extended region is more and more abstracted from the closer one gets to an evidenced, sheer extension. The evidence still remains distinct from the evidenced. Were this not so, there would be no evidence present and therefore no completing of the evidenced by the evidence.

49 The evidenced is arrived at by using the evidence in a process of evidencing. That process follows on and presupposes an extrication of the evidence. In it there is a beginning with an emphasis on the evidence, and an ending with an emphasis on the evidenced. A single undivided unit present occurrence, its beginning and ending are operative throughout, but with different degrees of effectiveness. At no point in between is one of them without the other.

50 In going through a process of evidencing, a man makes use of evidence to construct the evidenced. He ends with a claim which awaits acceptance by Existence before it can be freed from the process by which it was brought about. When successful, what is claimed will be identical with only an abstractable aspect of Existence; it will still lack that finality's ability to stand apart from us and all particulars.

51 Monists are inclined to give preference to space, process philosophers to dynamics, and existentialists to time. Space seems fixed and present all at once; activity, happenings, events are all dynamic; memory and expectation force what one grasps of space and dynamics to pass through the sieve of time. Each emphasis must be allowed if one is to provide the kind of evidenced that alone is adequate to Existence.

52 Only when evidence and evidenced are themselves dynamic can the process of evidencing be fully homogeneous with its beginning and ending. When beginning and ending are joined, their relationship is to be intensified and concretionalized to the very degree that they are brought into accord.

53 If what is evidenced is to be acceptable to Existence, it can not simply be temporal, spatial, or dynamic. What is needed by Existence is an extensionality of which these are diverse expressions. Each must be supplemented by the others and then, together with these, reduced to the extension that they all specialize.

Space, time, and dynamics stretch out. Each can be occupied. Each can be quantified. All three are involved with one another; when we acknowledge one we also have some acquaintance with the others, and therefore entrench on the extensionality which underlies them all and keeps them together.

54 To know a pure extension one must avoid not only dividing it into a time, space, and dynamics, but must both ignore the limits and intensities which actualities introduce into it, and refuse to fill it imaginatively. But to mark off possible limits within which actualities can be, it helps to have recourse to lines, figures, patterns, structures. This requires the exercise of a mathematical thought unhampered by a concern for facts. The result, though, is still too limited to do justice to a pure extension accommodatable by Existence.

55 A pure extension is continuous with, homogeneous with, and an expression of Existence itself. It is independently but concurrently expressed as time with its earlier and later, as space with its symmetrical relations, and as dynamics with its necessitation. To lay hold of such an extension, one must, in order to produce a claim that is acceptable by Existence, go through a self-corrective process of evidencing which is homogeneous with that extension.

56 It is best to attend to a dynamic situation, extricate a dynamism there, and go through a dynamic process of evidencing; one can then readily arrive at an evidenced dynamic extension. But to be acceptable by Existence without alteration, that extension must be supplemented by space and time, and then, together with these, be reduced to a common extensionality which Existence sustains. More conspicuously than is the case with other finalities, a warranted knowledge of Existence is achieved by going through the process of evidencing not once but many times with a claim that is transformed in being accommodated.

57 The extensions that actualities can occupy can be determined in advance by means of theoretical physical constructions produced in spatial, temporal, and dynamic extensions. If mathematics be understood to concern itself with quantities, numbers, and figures, it therefore makes sense to speak of it as though its constructions were produced in space and time. But the constructions made in pure extension are not those of mathematics. They are the constructions of a theoretical physics.

58 Physics' characterizations of ultimate particles, irreducible unit periods, and transmissions of quanta are the outcome of creative adventures. They mark out the types of region which actualities, severally and together, can occupy. Because the actualities are viewed in terms that the extensions provide, they are spoken of as though they were just units of space, time, and dynamics. But they can be such units only because each by itself already had a threefold distendedness subject to Existence's governance.

59 Existence texturizes, controls, and intensifies what is claimed of it. It thereby overcomes the inadequacies of the claim. There is, therefore, no knowing from a claim just what Existence is like, except so far as an accepting Existence leaves it unchanged. A satisfactory claim presents Existence with a pure extension which is to be concretionalized in what is self-divisive, self-expansive, forever setting part outside of part. How the concretionalization occurs and what it produces can be known only by attending to Existence itself or by seeing what Existence does to what is claimed of it.

UNITIES AND UNITY

1 M<small>EN IMPOSE UNITIES</small> on the items that they confront; they thereby subject the items to evaluations, assessing each item according to the manner and degree to which it can be accommodated by that unity, together with others.

2 Human acts of unification subject items to a common evaluation. If the evaluations are treated as modes of appreciation, classification, articulation, or practice, justice is not done to the need to harmonize the items in accord with the roles that the items have in an objective, unified, final harmony.

3 Evaluations, unlike other ways of dealing with what is confronted, scale items together, in accord with what they are in an objective unity.

4 It is quite common to speak of men as sources of values. It is also common—and sometimes maintained by the very ones who hold that values have a human origin—to claim that items are unified apart from men. Both contentions are correct, though made at cross-purposes. The fact that men introduce values does not entail that there are no values in the objects apart from such an introduction, and the fact that there are unities which are not introduced by men does not mean that there can be no unities introduced by them.

The view that values are the products of men but unities are not, is achieved by contrasting the limited evaluations which men provide (but which should match those that are already present) with the objectively determined unities (that men should try to instance in their assessments). With equal justice one could contrast the objective values that things possess (and which they exhibit in the ways in which they are harmonized with what else there be) with the unities that men introduce (in the attempt to do justice to the ways in which items are made to be together by impersonal powers).

5 We usually do not doubt that men introduce values into what they acknowledge, for we note that different individuals evaluate the same items in different ways. Since men could all be mistaken in their assessments, giving major importance to what is minor, and conversely, there must be values which they should match.

6 We usually do not doubt that men acknowledge unities already present, because we see that they are forced to take account of the

way items function together, regardless of human interest or desire. But if the men did not also introduce unities of their own, it would not be due to them that items were treated as compatible when they in fact were not.

7 Values and unities are global features, encompassing, controlling, not capable of being set alongside the pluralities they determine. Without them, no plurality would be a plurality, a single set of items.

8 Without a number of items, nothing could be said or be known; it is not possible to avoid the acknowledgment of a plurality of some kind. As Plato observed, even to say with Parmenides that a final One alone is, is already to distinguish it from its presence, and thus to have at least two items. But to constitute a plurality, items must be together. Consequently, if there are many items there must be a unity, and if there is a unity there must be many items. Everywhere there always is a plurality and a unity.

9 Might not there be just a plurality of ultimate entities? If so, atomism would be a tenable view. But atomists can not allow for the separation of their atoms in fact or in thought, without thereby allowing the separation, and whatever connections this entails, to have some reality, contrary to the hypothesis that only the atoms are real.

If only atoms were real, there would be nothing real which separates them; if something separates them, there is a reality other than the atoms. If there is no relating of the separate atoms, the atoms will not be together; if the atoms are together, they are under the governance of a unity. For atomists, there can never be more than one unit; no others could be together with this without requiring a unity for the atoms which were together. But with the acknowledgment of a unity for the atoms there is an inevitable denial that there are only atoms.

10 Each finality is a source of a distinct type of unity. Each intrudes its kind of unity on actualities in their severalty. Each enables the actualities to be together in a cosmos. And each helps constitute a context for the exhibitions of the actualities.

By means of the unity that it provides, Substance grounds and affiliates, Being orients and coordinates, Possibility structures and necessitates, and Existence locates and distances what it governs. None of these finalities is a pure unity, a unity *per se,* freed from the influence of an alien diversity. A sheer unity allows for nothing alien, for no divisions, and for no determination by anything other than itself. Such a unity is evaluative—'Unity', I call it.

11 Freed from the controls which different unities impose, actualities would not vanish. Indeed, the cosmos is possible only because actualities are able to be within it. For there to be a multiplicity of distinct actualities in the cosmos, there must be actualities

which can be in the cosmos, and therefore actualities which are not yet subject to cosmic conditions.

12 Starting with the actualities separately, evidence of a finality is found by attending to what intrudes while it unifies. To obtain evidence of Unity, one must isolate an intruder that enobles what it unifies, which gives values to what it encompasses.

13 Were all the finalities, with the exception of Unity, to intrude on actualities and their exhibitions, actualities would be given determinations and be interconnected in a cosmos, while their appearances would all be contained within a complex Context. But included actualities would not yet share in the status of their encompassing actualities. Since appearances, too, would not be assessed, there would be no aesthetic value to the totality of them.

14 The very same physical particles have different values as units in the cosmos, in a man, in an animal, and in a thing, for they are then subject to different limited unities. Within a final Unity they have a single value regardless of where they are or how they function.

15 Mathematical accounts of a cosmological physics refer to a state of affairs that abstracts from the difference that unified actualities make to the nature and functioning of the particles within them. The abstraction is legitimate so far as one is concerned solely with the affiliations, coordination, laws, spatiotemporal-dynamic distances, and status of the particles, no matter where they are or what other relations and roles they might achieve because of the actualities in which they are.

16 Were there nothing but things, parts would be affected only minimally by their encompassing actualities. Only in men can parts be maximally affected, because only men can act in ways which reflect the internalized presence of qualifications originating with all the finalities.

17 Men act in terms of prospects, plans, rights, obligations, beliefs, and truths, and in the course of their acting dictate to their parts where these will be. The dictation, of course, is not complete; particles in particular have their own reality, and continue to function as units within the cosmos.

18 Evidence of Unity is to be found in actualities by themselves, in actualities in a cosmos, and in the world of appearances. We become most aware of it when we attend to a transcendent which keeps a plurality of subordinated parts subject to and enriched by a controlling actuality.

19 A unity makes a complex actuality and a number of smaller actualities constitute a single entity. But now it seems as if we have lost the individual, since the unity which is essential to it is evidently something externally imposed. This consequence would be unavoidable did actualities not reply to the imposed unity and, with it, constitute unit actualities.

20 A unit actuality results when an evaluational unity governs an actuality and its parts. The unit actuality is, therefore, more than the actuality without its parts, more than the parts without the actuality, and more than the unity of the two.

21 A unity, intruded on actuality, raises the parts to a new level by turning them into constituents of an evaluated actuality. To ignore the unity, therefore, is to lose the dignity that the parts have in an evaluated actuality; it is also to lose the unit actuality and, therefore, the fact that the parts are constituents of it.

22 A unity is not usable as evidence until it has been extricated from that on which it had been intruded. To get to the source of the unity, that unity must be freed from what produced distinctions within the unity and thereby made it be less than a sheer unity.

23 The more complete and neat the extrication, the purer is the unity, the more satisfactory is the beginning of a process of evidencing, and the more likely will the evidence be in accord with the evidenced.

24 Unities exert constraints. Did they not, they would not be able to govern the parts of actualities and enhance their status. Were the power of unities not limited, however, the unities would conquer what they intruded on, denying them any status apart from it.

25 Did unities themselves possess the power they exert, with the passing away of that on which they intruded the unities would continue to be, maintaining themselves against all other unities despite the fact that a sheer unity has neither divisions nor duplicates.

26 Logical classes, no less than organic realities, are governed by unities. The various items in a class, despite their many similarities and even close proximity, are unable to be together well enough to make possible the objective exercise of a constraint. Whatever unifying constraining power a class may have is introduced by a mind.

27 The unity that a logical class has is provided by an attentive mind; its members are picked out of various situations where they are subject to distinct unities, and then held together in thought. An *aggregate*, in contrast, has items which are directly acted on by a supervening unity which keeps them together. A *complex actuality*, in contrast with both, is governed by a unity operating on and through the actuality. A logical class has no objective unity; an aggregate has a unity that simply relates; a complex actuality is affected by a unity.

28 The parts within an actuality are directly affected by and governed by unities at the same time that they are indirectly subjected to whatever unities have been imposed on their containing actualities.

That is why the parts are at once distinct units and constituents of wholes.

29 The isolating of a unity does not destroy its power. By using evidence one does not make the evidence any less available than it had been; it continues to intrude.

30 Most of the religions of the world are interested in Unity. Those which speak of a plurality of gods usually remark that those gods are subordinated to some one god, more authoritative or ultimate. Unity, for them, is not only indispensable; it is also prior to and governs a many. Their supreme God is a one for a many, not a one among many.

31 The association of Unity with the God of a religion allows for the use of sacred objects, messages, men, and events as paradigm evidences of Unity. References to such evidences are desirable, even for one who has no interest in religion.

32 The sacred has been the object of study by acute minds over the ages. Without affirming the existence of that of which religious men speak, the distinctions they have acknowledged can still be utilized, if only as a check on what one independently does and finds. What is sacred, of course, is usually thought by religious men to have been deliberately produced by God, but that need make no difference to its nature, involvement, and functioning as evidence.

33 It is possible to remain in accord with religious men so long as it is acknowledged that God is a finality, that he intrudes unities into actualities, and that those unities can lead to him when they are freed from their involvement with actualities.

Used by a secular man, the evidence that the sacred provides is an evaluating unity that can be used as the beginning of an effort to get to Unity itself. That Unity, as so reached, is not conscious, concerned with men; it has neither purposes nor plans. If that Unity be identified with God, it will be God just as a finality, alongside others.

34 A number of arresting arguments have been offered in the past, purporting to demonstrate the existence of God. They have a bearing on the effort to get to Unity. The most famous are the ontological, cosmological, and theological. These, unfortunately, have been encrusted with irrelevancies and have been dealt with in isolation from one another, with the consequence that their import and strengths have been misconstrued. Strictly speaking, they offer fragments of one movement from evidence of Unity to Unity itself. Each is part of a single argument with a distinctive beginning, structure, and outcome.

A teleological argument need not maintain that this world is under the governance of a cosmic purpose; a cosmological need not suppose that actualities have no existence of their own; an ontological need not be taken to try to mentally transform a possibility into a necessity. Such suppositions are dubious at best. Were they granted, moreover, they would not enable one to get to a finality. None of the 'arguments' takes account of the distinctive kind of movement which alone enables one to go from limited and diversified evidencing unities to Unity itself, single, undivided, and all-encompassing.

35 Only the teleological argument begins and ends with an acknowledgment of a value. Without the help of the others, though, it has no way of relating beginning and end, and no way of taking the end to be relevant to God. The ontological and cosmological arguments make use of the teleological; both presuppose prior movements from evidences to an evidenced value sustained by God.

36 The ontological argument maintains that if one grants that God is possible, it follows that He exists. His is the kind of existence, it holds, which both necessarily is, and is coextensive with His possibility. There is a truth asserted here, but it becomes clear only when the object of the argument is taken to be more than a modal term or terminus, for one seeks to reach not just necessity but God, a necessary existent.

37 The God sought by the user of the ontological argument is not merely a necessity. He is also irreducible, centered, intelligible, unlimited, and transcendent, forever engaged in acts of self-maintenance, self-centering, self-expression, self-identification, and self-articulation. This the argument can not reach. One must be able to get beyond the idea or possibility of perfection. But this requires the help of God. Only he can give body to a final evidenced value, for only he can accommodate it.

38 The cosmological argument for God starts with any existent and moves from this to its source. That source is Existence—another finality—not God. To get to God from an existent, one must attend to the value there and then trace that value back to a source capable of acting on existents, directly or indirectly.

39 The traditional cosmological argument can be traced back to Aristotle's argument for a first mover of all movement. It is unnecessarily burdened with the idea that one is in search of a final cause, that this cause produces rather than sustains a cosmos, and that the cause is divine. A stronger argument is obtained when one attends only to the source of an intruded existence, but this is an argument which is not directed toward God.

40 The traditional cosmological argument, beginning with an existence intruded on actualities, can take one only to Existence. If it begins with an existence into which a value has been intruded, the argument will end with Existence as subject to a final value. If one is concerned with tracing that value to its source, one will have to abandon the cosmological argument.

41 The teleological 'argument' for God starts with an intruded value and traces this back to a final excellence. The value with which it takes its start supposedly characterizes the entire spatiotemporal-dynamic universe, unifying and ennobling it; the argument ends with that excellence claimed to be acceptable to God himself. The other two arguments will not be directed at God if they do not incorporate that claim.

42 One can, with considerable justice, take the teleological argument to attend to the kind of evidence that is needed, the cosmological to the relation that the evidence has to the evidenced, and the ontological to the excellence which a final Unity accommodates. By itself, none is a genuine argument, for none offers a logical, formal, abstract proof. All are strengthened when treated as parts of a single intensifying movement which begins with what is partial, intruded, and value-dependent, moves to what turns this into a final excellence, and ends by awaiting acceptance by Unity, complete, self-contained, and final.

43 The God of a religion is arrived at from the position of sacred objects or of sacralized dimensions of the world in acts of faith which stop with what is turned toward the world. But a finality has a reality in and of itself; its relation to the world is only an aspect of it, a result of expressions of itself which find lodgement in actualities, severally and together. Once Unity is freed from its religious tonalities, arguments for it are found to end not with the object of religious worship but with a finality that forever lies beyond its reach.

44 Though, in the end, it is not possible to arrive at any finality without its aid, a man can, on his own, extricate evidence, use it, and arrive at what is evidenced. He cannot, though, make use of a sacred object in this way, for even the extrication and use of this is not possible to him alone. Religion presupposes divine actions beyond the scope of any argument or of the support required by any secular claim.

45 A nonparticipant in a religion can learn which objects the religious take to be divinely affected. This falls short of enabling the nonparticipant to attend to the component which the religious contend has been divinely introduced. A nonparticipant in a religion can not even know that there is a sacred component in what is confronted. But a proper use of unity as evidence will bring him to the point where he can present a claim to Unity for acceptance. If his claim is sustained, he will arrive, through the help of Unity, at the point where the evidenced is adopted by Unity.

46 For a religous philosopher, the sustaining of a secularly forged claim is due to a possibly deliberate divine act. His God, in addition to taking back into Himself what He had intruded as a sacralizing component, ennobles the secular claims a man produces. Since the claim is sacred only so far as it is ennobled by God, and not so far as it is simply accommodated by Him, the religious philosopher can know his God only if he can mystically participate in God and thereby discover what He does when accommodating an evidenced claim.

47 A religious man can pursue philosophy in the very same way that secular philosophers do, differing from them, though, in his acceptance of the supposition that his claim has to do, not with a unity but with what is sacred. Were the religious man to go on and maintain that the evidence he accepts could not have been extricated and used without the help of a religiously accepted God, he would have to allow a) that secular or atheistic philosophers could never make such claims, b) that they could never know if their claims were sustained, or c) that God cooperates even with those philosophers.

a) Claims made by the nonreligious are arrived at through the use of guiding principles that anyone can know and use. b) The knowledge that a claim is sustained can be known by checking the results of evidencing with other ways of encountering the finality, by making the attempt again and again from different positions, and by seeing what can be known of the finality as encountered. And c) if God does cooperate with secular philosophers, those philosophers, despite their disinterest in religion, will be able to arrive at least at the source of the unities that are evidenced everywhere—which is, after all, all that they seek to know.

48 Unity itself, it might be contended, can never be known. This is what Maimonides maintained. Whatever reason one might advance for that contention would also warrant the denial that Substance, Being, Possibility, or Existence could be known. All are finalities. All are irreducible. All are approached through the use of available evidence in a creative process of evidencing. Since the evidence that is used is, through the agency of the evidenced, continuous with and sustained by the finality, the denial requires one to say a) that no such evidence can be obtained, or b) that it is impossible to use it so as to arrive at what it evidences.

a) Evidence of Unity is not observable. No one can know it except by reflecting on the composition of what he confronts and discovering that it is a product of disparate factors, one of which is a valuational unity. Were there no evidence of Unity, actualities severally or together would not have values and would not affect the status of the parts they contain.

A nominalist holds that nothing experienced has been intruded from elsewhere. A nominalistic logician goes further to deny that there are unitary judgments or propositions, and maintains instead that one need acknowledge only sentences; written or spoken. For them there is no evidence of Unity; any identified unity is just the product of arbitrary and usually practical decisions. But a sentence is a unity. Just having a capital letter at the beginning and a dot at the end does not make it one sentence. A capital and a dot, in the absence of a unity which encompasses both and all else between, are distinct items, the one starting a word, the other coming after a word. A sentence provides evidence of Unity.

A sentence has a number of unities. Rules of grammar give the sentence one kind; its presence in space, or time, or living discourse gives it another; the equal status of the words within it as words for that sentence gives it a third; the words clustered in various groups to constitute complex subjects and predicates bearing on one another, gives it a fourth. Unity, in addition, makes them all be the enriched words-of-a-sentence. And what is true of sentences is true of individual words, the individual letters, the parts of the letters, and so on without end.

An act of pointing, decision, or claiming, made on behalf of nominalism, has its own unity. The nominalist is unable to find that unity because he begins his reflections after he separated the unity off, and had it govern his pointing, decision, or claiming.

No evidence of Unity or any other finality can be obtained if the evidence cannot be extricated. But if no unity could be extricated, it would not be possible to approach anything without penetrating it. Knowledge, though, can stop at any point and fixate what is there present. To maintain that no process of extrication is possible or that it cannot have any degree of success, is to deny that abstraction is possible, that distinctions can be made, or that aspects can be fixated in thought or imagination.

Extrication of evidence might be taken to occur in all cases except where finalities, and particularly Unity, had been operative. It might be maintained that these finalities are so powerful as to preclude the distinguishing of that on which they had intruded. But the very fact that one can attend to wholes and parts, shows that it is possible for a unity to remain distinct from the content it governs. It might then be held away only from the content in imagination; it could follow on an act of abstraction; it could be the outcome of an analysis; or it could involve an actual separation of what was confronted into its disparate factors. It makes no difference. In all these cases what will be held apart will be evidence able to function, free from that in which it is present and on which it is operative.

b) It is not possible to isolate evidence but be unable to use it so as to arrive at what it evidences, for this would require it to be self-contradictorily completely resistant to the very agency that had been able to hold it apart.

Conceivably, evidence might not be usable in the very shape which it has when just held apart, and that one could, therefore, use only an aspect of it. Instead of denying that the evidence could be used, this contention requires that one distinguish the evidence as available for use from it as properly used. And that is desirable. It underscores the fact that the use of evidence does not destroy its status as standing in contrast with that with which it is involved; indeed, when used, it becomes more and more a part of the evidenced, richer and purer than it had initially been.

49 Evidence of Unity is available and can be used. No use of the evidence will take one to Unity. A unity is always involved to some degree with an alien element in an actuality, but Unity is final, allowing for nothing foreign. Through the use of evidence of Unity one can arrive, not at Unity itself, but only at Unity as evidenced.

50 Before the evidenced is reached in a process of evidencing, it is faced as a measure of the evidence. To know defects in the evidence is already to have taken account of the evidenced as a measure of the evidence. Since the evidenced lacks the completeness that it will have when it incorporates the evidence at the end of a process of evidencing, the problem of getting to the evidenced reduces to the problem of getting the evidenced in a more complete state than is possible by attending to it as just the prospective end of a process of evidencing.

51 In a process of evidencing, one uses evidence in the creating of an evidenced claim. The evidenced is the evidence completed; to go to the evidenced is to go to a relevant end in which the evidence is purged and its defects made good in thought or in fact.

52 Evidence enriches the evidenced, adding determinations to it as a merely possible outcome. But no matter how much we add, Unity must add still more if the evidenced is to be not only *for* but *of* it.

Evidenced Unity is less than Unity itself, and needs Unity to accept it. When Unity takes the evidenced into itself it may alter it to make it more suitable, and will always add to it in absorbing it.

53 To have evidence of Unity is already to be involved with Unity, for the evidence with which one begins an evidencing process, and the evidenced that is then created through the help of that evidence, are not entirely separable from Unity, their source. But the evidence is accommodated by Unity only as mediated by the evidenced.

54 Just so far as the evidenced is not accommodated by Unity it is inappropriate to it. To know that the evidenced is inappropriate is to know Unity to be that which can correct the evidenced.

55 Might one never be able to forge a satisfactory claim about Unity? Surely that is conceivable. Indeed, this is usually the case. Whatever is claimed about Unity, more likely than not, has to be altered to some degree before it can be integral to it. The extent of that alteration is not known in advance. But it is possible to reduce the degree of needed alteration beyond any appreciable or interesting point.

56 Though evidence never has the form of a claim, it always is acceptable to Unity to some degree, since it belongs to Unity, and has its origin there. Because of its origin in Unity, the evidenced, too, is always acceptable to Unity. If the claim does not fit the Unity, Unity nevertheless has a sufficient grip on it to be able to alter it until it does fit and can be absorbed. A similar state of affairs prevails in connection with the evidence and evidenced used in getting to the other finalities. But the fact becomes most conspicuous in connection with Unity.

57 Unity's acceptance of claims differs from the acceptance which the other finalities provide. Substance accepts and possesses them; Being accepts and distinguishes them from itself; Possibility accepts and subtends them; and Existence accepts and connects them. Unity alone not only accepts the evidence and the evidenced, but transforms them into itself.

58 Unity's acceptance and transformation of the evidence and evidenced is a form of creation. It enriches them, gives them a new import, a new status. This creativeness stands in contrast with the creation usually ascribed to God and to humans, where the emphasis is on the production of what is given a status apart from its producer.

59 Unity is only one of a number of finalities. It and its specificatons are presupposed in all creations of form, content, or both, and in turn presuppose actualities able to sustain what is produced.

60 The actions of all the finalities have their counterparts in creations by men. When men create excellent wholes they most fully instance Unity. Works of art are examples. These are beyond the capacity of machines, animals, children, or copyists.

61 The finalities, other than Unity, are also unities and the source of unities, and this for two reasons: each is affected by Unity (just as Unity is affected by them), and each governs a plurality, though not in the manner characteristic of Unity itself.

62 In addition to the various finalities, there is still another irreducible unity—the unity of all the finalities. Can this be allowed without adding finality to finality infinitely? To have a plurality is to have items together. To have items together is to have them subject to a unity. That unity is an item in addition to the original items, and must itself, apparently, be united with the others by some further unity, and so on without end. If there be a number of finalities, there must be a unity governing them, and that unity, apparently, must be together with the original finalities under the aegis of still another unity, without end. That infinite regress will not occur, though, a) if all the finalities are not together, or b) if, as together, they are subject to a unity which already exists.

a) Each finality enables the other finalities to be together with one another in a distinctive way. From the perspective of each, the others are subordinate to it. But though each imposes itself on the others, since these are just as basic as it is, it cannot subordinate them in fact. The result is a set of four finalities for a fifth.

Sets of four finalities, each unified in a distinctive way, are together. Once again the question arises as to how a plurality can be one plurality without presupposing a one in addition to the plurality, leading to an infinite regress. The answer has been anticipated: the five finalities can be imagined to make a single variegated diffuse whole.

Does not such a contention contravene the fact that the finalities are independent of one another, and can not be blurred together? It would, were the blur anything other than the outcome of an attempt to deal with all the finalities from no position at all.

b) The position from which one can have all five finalities distinct but yet together is provided by an actuality. Each actuality acts as a one for their many, a unity which allows for the beginning of movements to all of them. When we abstract from that unity, we are left, as we are in connection with the actualities from which we had abstracted evidencing unities, only with the imagined variegated presence of them all.

63 There is a difference between a plurality in which items are directed at one another, and a plurality which is governed by a common unity distinct from them all. The first can not be summed; the position assumed precludes it and the rest from being neutrally held together. This is the way in which four or fewer finalities are together—one functions as a unity for the rest. But this is not the way in which *all* of the finalities are together. Such togetherness requires a unity provided by what is distinct from them all.

64 The finalities are independent, separate realities. Each is directed at and affects the others. It can then act as a unity for them. If we speak of all of the finalities when we say this, we do so from the position of an actuality.

65 No actuality, of course, is necessarily forever. It could pass away. Will the finalities not then be deprived of their necessary unity? Not if the passing away of one actuality involves the coming to be of another. There must, in fact, always be at least two actualities, for one alone would be absolutely indeterminate, indistinguishable from nothingness. Each is inseparable from at least one other against which it maintains itself. There need not be more than two. Ours is a contingent world, and that means that there are no two particular actualities that need be, and that there could be two of many kinds, and any number more.

66 For there to be five finalities, there must be an actuality functioning as a one in terms of which they could be together as five. But the need of any one actuality to be with others, entails that there always will be at least two actualities. Just how many actualities there in fact are, how many there will be later, and what their natures are like, though, is a contingent matter, beyond the power of any deducing.

67 If we begin with actualities and end with finalities, we deal

with the actualities as so many 'one's' for all the finalities; if, instead, we begin with finalities and end with actualities, we deal with the finalities as so many 'one's' for all the actualities. There is no single totality of the finalities and the actualities except from the perspective of an ideal unity of them all. But it is not possible to assume, actually or in imagination, the position of that ideal unity and from there encompass all that there is without converting that ideal unity into a matter of fact. At the end of our quest we come to a naming, never to be completed in the forging of a proper name for all there is or for all there ideally might be.

68 Each of the finalities is necessary in itself. Must there be just five? That question can not be answered unless one can show that there must be or need not be exactly five permanent irreducibles.

There is a contradiction in the idea that nothing is intelligible, and also in the idea that one actuality is more real than another, since each is equally a unit for a common intelligibility. There must therefore be a final Possibility and a final Being. But there apparently is no contradiction in the idea that some actualities do not mesh with others, that they are not located, or that they are not constituents in larger unities. Until such contradictions can be shown, the question remains open whether or not there could be a universe with only two finalities. We know that there are five finalities now, for we have been able to isolate evidences of them and to trace these back to their distinctive, irreducible, permanent sources. We know that the finalities enable the actualities to be substantial, intelligible, and extended, with beings and values, for we are able to extricate evidences of Substance, Being, Possibility, Existence, and Unity from those actualities. We know, too, that the finalities enable the appearances of actualities to be in a Context, since these appearances are intermeshed, equalized, rationally connected, located, and harmonized in ways beyond their capacity or the capacity of their actualities to bring about. And we know that the finalities enable the actualities to be together in the cosmos, for they are there affiliated, coordinated, law-abiding, distanced, and assessed in ways beyond the capacity of any or all of the actualities to determine.

69 Each of the finalities and each of the actualities has the role of a one; each is an ultimate reality; together they produce and sustain the appearances that we daily confront. When the finalities act on all the actualities together the result is a cosmos of actualities subject to common governances.

THE COSMOS

1 A COLLECTION is an area where the parts of one compound may be together with the parts of others. It is either unintegrated or integrated. If the former, it is an *aggregate;* if the latter, a *group.* Galaxies, geologic strata, families, congregations, tribes, nations, civilizations, societies, and states are groups, not to be broken down into aggregates without loss.

2 Collections have an identity of their own. They have histories and identities, causes and consequences; they interact with other collections and may themselves be members of still larger ones.

3 A collection may have sufficient integrity to require one to acknowledge that its parts are there together in a way they are not apart from that collection. Nations give additional meaning to the interactions of their members, distinguishing them from similar interactions which those members have with others not of the same nation. Similar things are true of members of a family, of mobs, of galaxies, and of the occupants of a limited territory.

4 There is a singleness to a group because the relation between its members is important to them. Tribal men are connected by custom, language, habit, work, myth, and interest in ways which affect them, keep them together, set them apart from other men, and distinguish them from themselves and others as parts of other integrated collections.

5 Groups are related to one another. That relation need have no affect on their contained compounds or on what these in turn contain. Nations may agree on the way wars are to be declared or on the way they will share archaeological information without affecting the families or the individuals within their particular confines.

6 When compounds form a collection, they become parts of it. What they themselves embrace thereupon is in a new single totality.

7 Some complexes and compounds are not in compounds or collections. Yet they function in considerable harmory. Their concurrence might be by chance. Or they could be kept in consonance deliberately, through the exercise of a limited force used for just that purpose. Or the needs of practice or the particular bias of a theory might lead one to consider a number of them together. At best, they would then be adventitiously kept together for a period in fact or in

thought. Each would be indifferent to another's presence except so far as this imposes itself on it. This is not what occurs in the cosmos.

8 The cosmos contains complexes, compounds, and collections. Actualities there are together subject to common final constraints. These dictate how the actualities are related and how they function with reference to one another.

9 To speak of the soul of the universe, or to treat nature as though it were a single entity, is needlessly to insert a mediator between the powers that affect all the actualities in the cosmos and those actualities themselves. The cosmos is not a compound.

10 Monists know that actualities are turned toward one another, but they deny that this is a result achieved by a power operating on distinct entities. They think that separate actualities or appearances are unrealities, falsely supposed to be distinct by the mind of man. Since such a mind would have to stand away from the monist's only reality so as to be able to make the distinguished items be apart from that reality, the monist is forced to conclude that the mind must be distinct from that reality at the same time that he maintains that the distinguishing is illusory. A distinct mind is not only not allowed by the monistic thesis, it is strong enough to hide the monist's supposed single all-engulfing reality from every one of us.

The opposite emphasis by atomists on a plurality is also in difficulty. The atomists take actualities to be units, altogether independent and separate from one another, but brought together by man's mind. Since that mind can not function in this way unless it can lay hold of a number of atoms, it could not be an atom alongside them. The togetherness of atoms, the atomist must suppose, is illusory. But then so is the plurality of atoms; a plurality is not one plurality unless the atoms are together.

The mind that is appealed to by the monist supposedly sets a multiplicity of particulars in opposition to a single reality. The mind that is appealed to by the atomist supposedly connects a multiplicity. Both attribute to a mind, for which they can not account, a power to create an imaginary state of affairs. Each overlooks a truth about actualities that the other knows—actualities are separate and actualities are together.

Through the supposed working of a mind, the monists and atomists reinstate an ontological situation where all the actualities, in their severalty, are affected by a reality, apart from any mind. And both inevitably take the mind to know that the several actualities thereupon achieve a new status.

11 Cosmic units, be they complexes or compounds, have *relevance*, positive or negative, to one another. What each is and does makes a difference to what others are and do, even though those others are at a great distance, and come, go, and act independently of them. The relevance could conceivably be denied, and it could conceivably be taken to be intrinsic to the actualities themselves. But were there no relevance, there would be no quantum jumps, valency, magnetism, gravitation, and no solidifications and dissolutions which ignore what is proximate to interact directly with what is distant. Were the relevance intrinsic to the actualities themselves, they could not be independent; a theoretical physics of ultimate particles, which took them to be independent units, would either deal with abstractions or provide a distorted account. In any case, the actualities would not be able to exhibit their supposed intrinsic relevance to one another except in certain circumstances. When these circumstances were not forthcoming, the actualities would act as completely independent units. But actualities are relevant to one another even while they independently come and go, move and rest.

12 Were there no power which transformed the independent into the relevant, a theoretical physics of distinct particles and a cosmological physics of interrelated units would deal with realities of quite different kinds. Yet both speak of the very same particles, the one as independent, the other as relevant. The one considers them in their severalty, the other deals with them as belonging together.

13 As members of a cosmos, ultimate particles exhibit a relevance of cosmic reach. Their encompassing compounds, too, are relevant to one another, without compromising the independence of the members. These, consequently, can interact in those compounds as they do outside, at the same time that they are conditioned by the compounds to function in new ways. Chemistry and biology allow for the same truths about ultimate particles but add others of their own, expressive of the bearing that compounds have on those particles.

14 All actualities are in the cosmos on an equal footing, because all have being. A worm has no more and no less a being than an apple; a man has no more and no less a being than an electron. When philosophers of science give a preferential status to some physical particles, when materialists, instead, prefer some supposed common matter or energy, when vitalists take man and mouse to be superior to all else because of the life supposed to be common to both, and when existentialists set men apart from all the others, they face themselves with the insoluble problem of explaining how it is that each of these types is together with the others in one cosmos.

15 Actualities differ. Each, for a while, also maintains itself in itself apart from the others. Yet they are, all together. No one of them can make them all be equal beings, for the equality holds of them all at the same time. If they are made equal it must be by something identifiable with no one of them. Nor can their equality be a function of them all. That would require a dependent product to turn around on itself and make its condition dependent on it.

16 Actualities are in the cosmos at the same time that they are independent of one another. Neither state is a precondition for the other. Their equality is imposed on them and keeps them together; the reality that they individually have is enjoyed apart from the equalized beings that they acquire.

17 Actualities are also ontological intelligibles, incarnations of logical and mathematical formula. These are limited formulations of a single Possibility common to all that can be understood.

18 Laws of nature are logical and mathematical relations specialized and pertinent to the actualities that are being related. The laws are in the cosmos, subjecting actualities there. They are not laws *for* the cosmos, nor conditions which the cosmos imposes on actualities. The cosmos is the totality of actualities related by various powers originating outside the cosmos; one of the ways the actualities are related is as intelligibles subject to intelligible laws.

19 Peirce suggested that actualities had habits which made them function more or less in lawlike ways. That they need not conform strictly to the demands of laws shows that they are not completely under the control of laws, but have a status and an insistence of their own. Their behavior as cosmic entities, though, can not be termed habitual unless there be a habit which they all share and which dictates what they are able to do. If this be admitted, it has been granted that there are laws governing actualities as members of a single cosmos, but the fact is hidden by giving laws the unusual name, 'cosmic habits'. Nothing is gained by that change for a double reason: habits are acquired by practice and lost through disuse; the cosmos does not act and therefore can neither promote nor prevent the presence and operation of cosmic habits.

Peirce wanted to make room for changes in laws over time, and possibly for their evolutionary growth, but this requires no more heroic measure than the acknowledgment that the laws are not constants. Actualities produce deviations in the ways in which the laws are carried out.

20 The laws of nature are intelligible and controlling. They limit the ways actualities act in relation to one another. Their scope is cosmic, allowing for no exceptions. Specified by the actions of actualities in various ways and degrees, the laws are never set aside.

21 Actualities act as distinct entities; they also interact with one another. If their independent action is neglected, they will be taken to be passive particulars, without power or self-centeredness, unable to maintain themselves or to provide a stop for an imposed power. If, instead, their reference to one another is neglected, they will be taken to be without the need to resist, interplay, or respond to one another. Because actualities are at once independent and together in a cosmos, they are able to interact in law-abiding ways.

22 By themselves actualities are both intelligible and law-abiding. Each has the same general nature others have, and all function within the limits set by their natures. The consequences which logically or mathematically follow from their natures in one place are, therefore, in consonance with what follows in another.

23 It has sometimes been held that laws vary in accord with the geometry of the world. If so, this permits one to conclude only that the actual geometry of the world and its laws are in absolute accord. The two could not be identified unless the intelligible actualities, connected by mathematical and logical relations, could be identified with the governed occupants of a cosmos. But the two are independent.

The kind of connections provided by the laws of nature need make no reference to geometry. That both types of connection always and everywhere occur makes evident the ubiquity of the powers responsible for each of them. The geometry, moreover, offers only one type of connection—a spatial. Actualities are temporal and dynamic as well.

24 The extension of an actuality does not reach beyond the limits of that actuality. Yet, unlike a distension which determines the limits of each independently and from within, extensions are imposed on all from without and at the same time, thereby extensionally relating them as delimitations within an extended cosmos.

25 Actualities are spatially, temporally, and dynamically extended. Their extensions are part of a single spatiotemporal-dynamic extension. This the actualities independently fractionate, thereby enabling them to be spatial, temporal, and dynamic occupants, extensionally connected with one another.

26 All actualities are locatable in a single time, in a single space, and in a single dynamics which together constitute the extension of a single cosmos. Each actuality, with its extension, is located within that cosmos.

27 The extension of each actuality, because continuous with an extension outside it, is continuous with the extension of every other actuality.

28 Actualities are compelled to be extended, are compelled to be extended in comparable ways, and are compelled to be within larger extensions.

29 Actualities can change their positions in space, time, and in the casual process, because they, and the extensions which they limit, have integrities of their own. If the actualities were not independent of the cosmic extensions they would not be able to persist, act, and move. If the extensions were not independent of the actualities, there would be no place in those extensions into which the actualities could enter.

30 Time, space, and dynamics function independently of one another. It is conceivable, therefore, that one of them might be present and the others absent.

31 Each actuality exists apart from all the others. Each fills out a present of the same kind and duration, but in its own distinctive way, to make this its own present, having nothing to do with any other.

32 A number of actualities are together not only in the same present, but in a succeeding present. That they may be individually sluggish or fast makes no difference; despite the fact that each has its own present, a number are not only in a common present but in a series of common presents. Since they have different rhythms, durations, and careers which need not, and sometimes do not, mesh, their continued copresence can not be due to them in their severalty. They are and remain contemporaries because they are subject to a time which encompasses them.

33 Some actualities pass away and some originate at different moments, but when they in fact exist, actualities are together in a single cosmic present. Still, time has no power of its own. Present actualities must be made to be contemporaries in time by powers outside both them and time.

34 Within the embrace of their compounds, parts are symmetrically related to one another over a distance. Each is spatially extended, and spatially related in its compound.

35 One can imagine a distance which is only a fraction of that over which a part in fact spatially extends. Magnitudes are always mathematically divisible. But if there be ultimate particles, their magnitudes will not be factually divisible. The actual magnitude of an ultimate particle can be no smaller than the particle itself. But compounds can conceivably be factually divided—though at the price of destroying that compound.

36 All actualities are located in a single cosmic space. That space, can not be produced by them severally. Nor can it be accounted for by reference to something unextended, or by space itself. Actualities, in nonspatial relations, must be made to be together spatially by a power outside them and space.

37 No matter where actualities are, they have some magnitude. One of the magnitudes is then and there smaller or equal to some other, not because a signal or energy has been transmitted from one to the other, but prior to this. Its magnitude is either mathematically identical with or a part of the other, no matter what the distance between them. A mathematical relation between magnitudes holds regardless of the spatial relations between the items compared.

38 The relation between equal magnitudes of actualities or between the magnitudes of smaller and larger actualities is not between mathematical entities, but between magnitudes-of-actualities. These are at a distance from one another in the same cosmos. To account for them, reference is to be made to a power able to have the distensions of distinct actualities coincide with delimited spatial regions within a common space. Only what is not an actuality could allow the actualities in their severalty have spatial extensions continuous with a space outside them.

39 Causality occurs in time and involves spatial objects; it also has its own extensional range and units. It operates between subgroups of contemporaneous, spatially related actualities, where it is specialized in the form of limited causal links, each with its characteristic antecedents, processes, and outcomes. That causality is no supposition or rule introduced into the cosmos by human minds. Such an introduction would itself be a causal act, requiring that causality be presupposed in order that it be produced. Also, if a mind is to bring causality into the cosmos, it must be a mind with a cosmic reach, powerful enough to change separate actualities, each with its own career, into a constituent of a single causal process, and powerful enough to make subsequent occurrences be the necessary outcome of what preceded them.

40 Distinct actualities can not themselves constrain and direct groups of themselves; they are subject to the causal dynamics of these groups. The groups, in turn, can not be entirely separate from one another, without thereby making them be completely isolated causal systems. They would then act as though they were separated by perfect ontological vacua. In effect this would deny them places within the same cosmos.

41 Causality is a single necessitation exhibited in specialized groups and chains. It requires for its presence the action of a power capable of transforming distinct actualities into components in various causes, processes, and effects, all specializations of a cosmic dynamics. If the exercise of that power is said to be causal, it is causal in a different sense from that which characterizes groups and chains. It acts vertically and not horizontally; it is unspecialized and not broken up into small causal situations; it operates on separate actualities to make them part of a cosmos, and does not relate them in various groups to what takes place subsequently. It functions somewhat in the way in which a God is sometimes said to sustain the cosmos He supposedly created.

42 If there were a creating God who made actualities be in a dynamic cosmos, He would inevitably do three distinct things: make actualities in themselves; make each dynamic; and make them dynamic together. Since the last two require only the action of a power able to introduce a dynamism into things already in the cosmos, they require a power quite different from that used in creating. In effect one would have added to the power of a God, who supposedly created actualities in themselves, another power which worked on these.

43 Once it be granted that actualities have an integrity of their own, one allows that they are able to maintain themselves even against God. It is odd to suppose that they had been made to defy their maker. In any case, created or not, they would then be the proper objects, not for a supposed God, unextended and simple, but for an Existence with the modalities, space, time, and dynamics.

44 Causally connected actualities remain distinct while they are made to be dynamically together. A single, persistent power evidently operates on all from a position outside them, converting them into cosmic terms in cosmic extensions. The actualities would have to be re-created or sustained anew at every moment, were it not that they continue to remain independent while they are related.

45 Finally, actualities are unit values. Did a unity not govern an actuality, this would fall apart, or it would remain variegated and boundless. Did an actuality not ultilize the unity, the actuality would forever disperse itself.

46 In an actuality unity functions centripetally and thereby counteracts the actuality's centrifugal expressiveness. The result is a unitary reality, at once insistent and self-maintaining.

47 Some actualities exhibit little variety, others much more. In some—the organic—a multiplicity of items is distinguishable only with effort and at rather arbitrary points; in others—collections—distinct items exist apart from and act in some independence of one another.

There are no perfect organic units where genuine diversity is entirely lost; there are no perfect aggregates having no unity at all. An organic unit without a multiplicity of parts would be a limited diffuseness with nothing to organize and enhance; an aggregate not governed by a unity would not even be one aggregate. Organic units without genuine parts are units filled out; ungoverned aggregates are abstractions which have been brought under one concept.

48 A governing unity dominates a multiplicity and makes it one. If cannot, therefore, just be alongside the multiplicity. The power of a unity may be so slight that it does no more than enable the multiplicity to be a single set of items; it may be so great that all the items are made to be mutually supportive. In both cases an insistent power is transmitted through the unity, but in the second some power is also fixated in the unity, enabling it to possess the multiplicity, and thereby have some affect on how the items there will function.

49 A unity acts on actualities as separate and as together. It enables them to be evaluated units independent of one another as well as to be members of a single unified cosmos, or nature. The separate units exhibit different unities; each unity is concretionalized by the actualities on which it operates. Interrelated units are the concretionalized separated unities transformed into termini by a single cosmic power. Were there no such power, different unities would not belong together. Did it not convert the separate unities into termini, the cosmos would encompass only facets of the actualities and not the actualities themselves.

50 Because it is inseparable from a diversity, the unity of the cosmos can not be identified with a final, absolute Unity. Such a Unity allows for no diversity. Nor can Unity be itself one of many unities; if there are many unities they must be held apart from Unity itself, as so many unifying agencies.

51 Actualities as together in the cosmos are relevant, coordinated, law-abiding, located, as well as evaluationally united. These different ways in which the actualities are together are due to the presence and functioning of the different finalities, together producing a single cosmic pattern.

52 Ultimate physical particles are interrelated in the cosmos. They are together under the aegis of common laws and, this regardless of the existence of men, their interests or products, or even of any macroscopic entities. The acknowledgment of this fact allows for the recognition of that impersonal mathematically mastered universe which is of interest to rationalists. The price paid for this is very high if one goes on to say that everything else is just the outcome of some complication of this original set. Who could so complicate it? What warrant is there for reducing the reality of men and their distinctive lives and works to just particles in a cosmos?

Still, no matter where one turns, the same physical laws of nature are operative—in living things, in works of art, in political activities. What the physicist knows are not only invariants to be found in every domain, but what occurs no matter what the domain. If his units are taken to be the product or terminus of men's interests and the undetachable objects of their distinctive inquiries, one joins the idealists and existentialists in making the units pivot about men and their activities. The physical domain will then be set within the actual cosmos in which all actualities, no matter what the grade, are together, itself set in contradistinction with that part of the cosmos in which men, as more than physical, themselves are.

53 Surely, the physical world existed before there were men, and continues to exist apart from them and their concerns? Yes, but this does not entail that the only irreducible realities are physical particles subject to cosmic laws, and that everything else is the outcome of some combination of these, for, apart from men, the physical particles are clustered together in various limited groups within the confines of unified macroscopic things.

54 Each thing is a self-bounded actuality in which a cosmic unity is limited by and solidified with a cluster of particles. Each thrusts beyond itself to produce a distinctive stretch terminating at other actualities.

Physical particles are either clustered or are in the gaps between clusters. They are all encompassed in the cosmos where they are subject to the same laws while they continue to function in bounded clusters, between which are separately functioning particles.

55 When we move into the world where men are, or into the even more restricted world occupied by works of art, we pass, not from a world of mere particles, but from one in which bounded things with their particles are interlocked at the same time that their particles are together with all others within a single cosmic domain.

56 Inside the worlds of men and of art, things function in relation to what men introduce in ways similar to the ways in which the particles function in relation to the things—they are encompassed within new unities at the same time that they continue to be interrelated with one another as they had been before.

57 The physical cosmos of clustered and unclustered particles is not a function of man's interests or presence. Even more evidently, the actual cosmos of which the physical is a part is independent of man. When we speak of the physical cosmos as existing apart from men we are on the firmest ground, if we do not take it to be separated from the actual cosmos.

58 The actual cosmos is inseparable from an ideal cosmos embracing the possible unrealized ways in which actualities and finalities could have been together. That ideal cosmos is the actualities and finalities as maximally together, together as they ought to be.

59 The actual and ideal cosmos together leave over no alternative from whose position it could be marked off, established, or fixated. It can not be named. 'A universe' does not name it, but instead refers to the actual cosmos as needing but not possessing the ideal. The two do not constitute a single entity, able to sustain a single name.

60 The actual cosmos falls short of the ideal cosmos. One cannot hold it apart from that to which it is inseparably attached; to grasp it, one must share in its effort, participate in its perpetual and never successful effort to become one with the ideal cosmos which it needs.

61 A name, if directed at what is unstable, incomplete, dispersed, misnames it in the very act of being brought to bear. It should then be replaced by a naming. Though there is no name for the totality embracing both the actual and the ideal cosmos, each in its full integrity, there can be a naming of it, a reaching toward what never is unified enough to have a name.

62 The ideal cosmos is not absolutely perfect, complete, lacking nothing. It is no *causa sui*, able to actualize itself, for this would require it, at the very least, not to need the inadequate actual cosmos. It needs this though it can never fully master it.

63 It is not possible to take a final stand with the very effort to have the actual and the ideal cosmos united. This would not only require one to suppose a reality beyond both, but would also end with an activity of reconciliation. Either this never would be completed, or it would have already brought about a perfecting of the actual cosmos and a realization of the ideal cosmos.

64 The actual cosmos is not all that it could or ought to be. But it has an integrity of its own, maintaining itself in the face of any other alternative. The ideal cosmos, too, has an integrity of its own, maintaining itself in the face of the inadequate, partly disharmonious actual cosmos. If there be a power beyond both, it will be one which allows each its integrity. But since each needs and reaches to the other, that power could never complete its task of holding them completely apart.

65 Whether it be supposed that the actual cosmos perpetually strives to realize the ideal, the ideal perpetually strives to master the actual, that there is a reality which perpetually tries to unite them or perpetually tries to hold them apart, or finally, that beyond all these there is a power which perpetually tries to keep the different efforts in equipoise, there is not yet anything sufficiently real to be named. A name would bring the termini of each of these efforts within its encompassment. Consequently, it would either complete what was essentially incomplete, or it would leave termini outside its range and therefore would fail to be the name for all that there was.

66 When incompletable processes are acknowledged to be confined within a single domain, there is a shift from a consideration of realities vainly endeavoring to master others, to what can be clearly marked off. This can be both known and named—'the actual cosmos' for example.

In the actual cosmos incompletable efforts by actualities and finalities are kept in balance. Each of the processes, as confined within it, is then also available for knowledge, and can be named. The actual cosmos itself, though, as caught up in the process of realizing an ideal, is itself available only for a naming, since there is no domain within which it and the ideal cosmos are confined.

2 / COMMENTS ON

First Considerations

ABNER SHIMONY

SOME COMMENTS ON PHILOSOPHICAL METHOD

THERE IS MUCH that I am sympathetic with in the first two sections of your new book. I agree with your general program of how to move from appearances to reality and how to reconcile the fact that one's own point of view is particular with one's aim at universality. Nor is this agreement accidental, since much of my own general philosophical program was learned from you. I also like the prescription which you state in "The Task of Philosophy," paragraph 12: "A statisfactory method for reaching what is universal, constant, and real attends to what intrudes on actualities or interlocks with their exhibitions. It then extricates the intruded or interlocked factor, moves to what this evidences, and ends with a claim that holds of the source of the intrusions." The difference between our ways of philosophizing may lie in the different ways that we construe this passage.

To me the passage suggests that there is much overlap between the method of the natural sciences and that of philosophy. Without excluding other philosophic methods—introspection, examination of presuppositions, analysis of concepts, and dialectic—I claim that the hypothetico-deductive method is indispensable for philosophy. Even if the aim of philosophy is to discover truths which are not contingent, it remains appropriate for philosophers to use the hypothetico-deductive method, since human beings may not have direct insight into some necessary truths and may not have the intellectual power to disentangle necessities from contingencies in any direct way. Consequently, we may be able to do no better than to consider all the evidence available to us and to judge as best we can which of the hypotheses so far formulated best accounts for the evidence. If so, then an attitude of fallibilism is called for, since even if one hypothesis accounts for the evidence better than any clearly formulated rival hypothesis, there is always the possibility that an ingenious hypothesis of the future will do even better. A great virtue of the hypothetico-deductive method is that it permits us to deploy in a controlled manner conceptions which are far removed from common sense, and in this way to escape from the limitations of an anthropocentric view of the world. It also follows that the results of the natural sciences should be taken very seriously in philosophical investigations. I do not mean to say that the status quo in the natural sciences should be unchallenged and that metaphysical conclusions should merely be drawn from it as corollaries; indeed, the warning in favor of fallibilism is a sufficient caution against such an uncritical conclusion. But I do mean to say that scientific results which prima facie concern the nature of space, time, matter, cause, chance, organism, and other fundamental concepts should not be dismissed as mere instruments for organizing our sensations, but should be given serious weight in philosophical examinations of these concepts. For example, I believe that relativity theory has taught us something very profound about the nature of space and time, and your dismissal of it in "Evidences" indicates a failure to give detailed attention to the evidence.

You evidently interpret your own passage on philosophical method in a very different way, and wish to distinguish quite sharply between the methods of science and philosophy, and also between the degrees of certitude to which the two disciplines can properly aspire. You say, for example, in "Tentative Probings," paragraph 49, that "Mathematics, logic, and science have a greater range than my daily outlook. They seem to show what things are in fact and not what they have been made to be for a society of men. The existence of a plurality of geometries, alternative logics, and conflicting scientific interpretations of the same facts, however, closes out this possibility for me." Your dismissal of the philosophical significance of these disciplines is hasty, since there are other interpretations of the plurality than that they are unreliable: for example, one may be better than all the others and show itself to be better upon close security; or the alternative theories may actually be talking about different things; or there may be less discrepancy than seems at first, because there are equivalences that may be discerned if one sees through the accidents of formulation. In any case, the argument concerning plurality of doctrines can all too easily be turned against you, in view of the multiplicity of philosophical schools and the difficulty of obtaining canonical settlements of philosophical disputes. It should be added that the fallibilist attitude which I adopt in both science and philosophy is not tantamount to skepticism, for there can be progress toward the truth even if the goal is not fully attained.

A good passage for exhibiting the differences between our philosophical approaches is where you make a number of assertions about actualities. I think that I might be able to give these assertions appropriate interpretations that I would agree with, and in fact I think that they are very good as phenomenology. Whether or not you like the compliment, I feel that you are a remarkable phenomenologist, and that is where you have made your greatest contribution to philosophy. But I am not at all satisfied with what you offer as explanations of your phenomenological reports. I want to know how it is that there is "cosmic control to which all actualities are subject," and in what way they are "self-centered realities," and with what qualifications they are "together in cosmos." The answers which you offer throughout your book to these requests for explanation are not as illuminating as you intend them to be. For example, you say at the beginning of "Substances and Substance" "Each actuality is a substance. It maintains a hold on whatever it contains, produces, and intrudes upon. It persists and and it acts. It has an irreducible, independent core, and receives determinations from insistent, intrusive forces." I am able to understand these lines in one of three ways: as more phenomenology; as an extrapolation to all concrete entities of certain concepts which are known to be appropriate to human phenomena; or as a sketch of an explanation of great generality. The third is the most interesting way to construe the lines, but it is also the most problematic, for one should not mistake a sketch for the detailed realization of an explanation.

If there is an impasse between us, it is perhaps this: that each thinks the other is too much engaged in abstractions. Or perhaps the point should be amended: I know that you are vividly aware of the concrete, and you are also aware that a philosophical system inevitably uses abstractions in characterizing the concrete. (As I recall, you are critical of Hegel on this matter.) The issue is then whether the abstractions which you employ are as general, as rich, as interesting, as revelatory of structure, and as free from anthropocentrism as you believe. I think not, and I believe that attention to the natural sciences would at least partly help to correct the defects of your account.

Let me say once again that I have no intention to defend the scientific status quo. Much of my own work has been devoted to examining conceptual anomalies in quantum mechanics and to arguing that they can not be solved without going on to a deeper physical theory than we now possess. Furthermore, the state of the mind-body problem is enough to indicate that natural science is still far from its maturity. But these statements do not contradict my thesis that philosophical and scientific investigations should go hand in hand.

Science and Philosophy: A Reply

THE WILLINGNESS OF A PHILOSOPHER, who is at home in modern physics, to accept the general program of this work, makes me want to treat our disagreements as minor or incidental. This, though, would not only do injustice to the seriousness of the present questions, but would slight the truth that differences in method can produce great divergencies in direction, pace, and result. The challenges must be met full-face.

1 There are a number of basic disciplines—biology, chemistry, and physics; logic and mathematics; history, anthropology, psychology, and sociology. Each is pursued by many independent inquirers, making use of concepts and methods, criteria, checks, and tests in subtle, sophisticated, and illuminating ways. Some analyze, investigate, open up areas, and achieve what the rest can not even imaginatively envisage. All challenge and rectify the established views, not only of their predecessors but of ordinary men. Civilization progresses as a result of the almost unconscious interweaving of the activities of a host of different investigators persistently and honestly seeking to attain as much of final truth as they possibly can.

There is no investigation, no branch of knowledge, and no established method that a philosophic study can set aside a priori, or safely ignore. All studies have joints, connections, dimensions, and procedures no philosopher, sitting in his study, could possibly know. The vigor, clarity, effectiveness, mutual support, and criticism of the physical scientists, in particular, demand respect. Their achievements are so impressive that almost everyone is tempted to imitate them, to build on their discoveries, and to accept their speculations. It is not surprising to find that even historians, theologians, and philosophers have taken them as models, guides, teachers, and sources. The scientific outlook is so pervasive that the most romantic and anti-intellectualistic, the most anthropocentric and personalistic of men is inevitably affected by what the sciences affirm, and even by what they suggest.

Are the assumptions, procedures, and achievements of the sciences superior to those characteristic of other special disciplines? Do they enjoy a privileged status? Must every account follow their methods, use their checks, adopt their conclusions? To answer such questions in the affirmative is to overlook the less well-known but equally insistent, differently grounded claims made on behalf of history, linguistics, sociology, psychology—and metaphysics.

A pyramid is a whirling mass of particles. It is also a monument. It was set in place decades ago, may be marked with strange hieroglyphics, and has already yielded considerable knowledge of the past. It is beautiful and it is sacred. Its shape allows for multiple mathematical calculations. Any one of these facts can be and sometimes has been taken to be more basic than the others. But it will be so only in terms of some purpose, some presupposition, some standard which itself needs justification. It is conceivable that one of them may be more important or more relevatory than all the rest. This, though, will not be known unless it is possible to stand outside them all and assess them from a neutral position. One of the objectives of a systematic philosophic inquiry is the achievement of such a neutral position; but it can reach this only if it does not insist on giving preferential status to some particular, limited outlook.

All inquirers are initially interested in following out the clues discerned in what is daily confronted. But because each discipline attends to only some of those clues, because each makes use of a special method in order to obtain certain kinds of results, and because each ends with accounts that do not in fact and never did intend to speak of what the others had mastered by their use of different evidences, procedures, presuppositions, tests, and assessments, none can be taken to be basic to all the others.

The claim that science, mathematics, logic, linguistics, and history—to take some of the more conspicuous enterprises of the day—are in no need of supplementation by other special disciplines or need not be overarched by one all-encompassing view is rarely made by those who contribute to them. It is usually urged by a philosopher, making evident his special predilections and his willingness to ignore other areas of knowledge.

If philosophy did not have its own subject matter and its own methods of procedure and certification, it would have to resort to the tested agencies used by others. A good case could then be made out for it to use the constructive method of a mathematics, the analytic method of a logic, the convergent method of a history, the creative method of an art—or the hypothetic-deductive method of some branch of science. A desire to have coherent, precise formulations, to arrive at what is certain, to produce a preponderance of evidence, to allow full play to creativity, or to provide wide-ranging, fruitful, verifiable explanations, will make a choice of one of them be at once palatable and satisfying. But philosophy does not depend on them nor they on it for rules or guidance. None need borrow the methods or use the tests that have proved effective in the course of other inquiries.

Philosophy is concerned with providing a comprehensive account of whatever there be, and understanding the conditions for knowing this. Alert to what the special disciplines can and can not achieve, it seeks a systematic, justified formulation of those irreducible realities which explain and ground all else and, therefore, what is both assumed and affirmed in other inquiries. It does not compete with these; it does not repeat, depend on, or adopt what these suppose, affirm, or claim, not because it is disdainful of them, but because it has its own tasks, its own objectives, and its own checks. Neither it nor the others should be made to stay within the limits which characterize endeavors distinct from its own. The broad sweep of philosophy makes it an inappropriate guide to empirical discoveries, just as its concern with the past denies history a good basis for prediction, and the emotionally toned creative work of art keeps it outside the meshes of a mathematical rule. None knows what the others can and do know; what each discovers can be made one's own only by participating in it. That is true of philosophy no less than it is true of any other enterprise.

2 A philosophy, if successful, should arrive at outcomes which govern, interrelate, and are specialized by everything. To engage in it properly, one attends to a distinctive kind of evidence—that which can be found anywhere. Only this grounds a move to what is either native to or conditions everything, a permanent stage where all other transactions take place. If it finds what has been intruded on every particular, it has evidence enough to warrant a bold yet cautious move toward that which produced the evidence. The rationale of the method can be partly expressed in terms sanctioned by logicians, mathematicians, and scientists. But not without change, addition, and subtraction, since it seeks to arrive at a different point and to justify its practice and outcome in a distinctive way (see following "The Philosophic Enterprise: A Reply," paragraph 1).

3 The work of finite, confused, blundering men, philosophy is unbelievably pretentious, since it seeks final answers. At the same time, it is radically modest, always trying to expose its own weaknesses, to make evident to all where it may have failed. It is not reasonable to suppose that any man will ever successfully attend to all the evidence that is available and relevant, that he will extricate it properly in every case, or that he will always be completely objective and self-controlled, without conceit, prejudice, or sudden lapses in insight and even from good sense. The necessities at which he arrives are inevitably streaked with contingencies, and distorted by carelessness, unexamined assumptions, irrelevancies, and downright errors. Every step needs justification, criticism and, often enough, correction.

Every philosophic work must be done over, again and again; every one must be rewritten and rewritten. Each forward move invites a backward look. Sooner or later there comes a time when all the different parts are to be brought together in order to see if they make a single, self-sustained whole. It is then that its author, no less than others, is best able to see where and how he went astray—a privilege denied to those who attend only to selected topics, thrown up perhaps by current controversy.

Again and again a systematic thinker is held up, baffled, at odds with himself. The suggestions of other philosophers, scientists, ordinary men, the settled wisdom of the race, and the insights of dramatists and poets may then prove most helpful, but only if sifted, reinterpreted, and perhaps radically altered. Science and the hypothetic-deductive method may seem to be more promising at one juncture than at others. If so, there should be no hesitation in making use of it under the aegis of other procedures more directly related to what is of primary concern.

A philosopher adventures alone in somewhat the way a painter or poet does. His aim, like theirs, is to produce a perfect whole. Unlike them, he seeks to forge a single, intelligible account, grounded in what is irreducibly real, and capable of explaining and being explained by evidence found everywhere and always. He has no recourse but to struggle honestly, self-critically, imaginatively toward the outcome which the evidence demands, correcting himself in the light of the deviations he finds between what he is saying and what intelligibility, coherence, and explanation require, and experience reveals. His adventure is doomed to failure, inevitably flawed. The defects, though, will be discovered in good part because of what has been achieved. Usually, the most that he can do is again and again to check what he has done; look at it from different angles; criticize it as sharply as possible; and search for what he and perhaps everyone else at the time is taking for granted, but which may not be able to withstand persistent questioning. Other and better views will surely follow on his if he has done his job well. Neither he nor anyone else should be satisfied until the pivotal facts of daily life— the existence of a plurality of resistant, active items: men, animals, things; language, society, ethics, art, history, and religion; science, logic, and mathematics; stability and change; the one and the many, the private and the public; rights, responsibilities, value, work, play, hope, faith, birth, death, tragedy, and comedy—are all able to find a place where they cohere with and perhaps illuminate and supplement one another. There is no end to the need to clarify, check, justify, confirm, re-articulate, and to make use of whatever promotes the formulation of a comprehensive, clear account of what is ultimately real, how it can be known, and how it can explain and be explained by what can now be fastened on.

4 Physical science attends to the nature of space, time, and matter. So do other disciplines.

The spaces connecting men in a milieu and an environment, in a society, in games; the spaces of paintings, buildings, sculptures; the spaces between friends and enemies, lovers, parents and children, all differ in contour and tension from the space in which physical particles are together. The different spaces buckle and flatten out in different ways and under different circumstances.

History has a distinctive time; it slows down at one moment and hurries on at another; that time is different from the time of a symphony, a play, a dance, and the healing of wounds—and the time which is pertinent to the movement of the stars and the planets.

There is one kind of causation in nature and another in history; one kind of causation in a drama and another in a society. If only one of these is allowed or is taken to be a paradigm, strong claims and vast areas of knowledge will be rather cavalierly ignored. The refusal to attend with equal seriousness to all the ways in which not only space, time, and causality, but inference, conditioning, and activity take place has too long stood in the way of an adequate account of the world in which we live and which we seek to understand. We must try to do justice to them all, to account for their existence, and to try to show how they could fit together. But to do that we must look beyond them all, making use of a method, vocabulary, and checks appropriate to what is sought and not to what other enterprises deal with quite well on their own.

5 There are, to be sure, many ways in which different geometries, logics, scientific theories, spaces, times, and so on can be assessed and finally interrelated. One may be preferred to others for any one of a number of reasons—simplicity, familiarity, accord with common speech, practice, analysis, usefulness for science, and so on. But these reasons themselves need justification. In the end, the justification will have to be that it promotes, better than any other, the learning and mastering of what is irreducible and final, and what results from the interplay of this with whatever particulars there be.

Primary preferences are justified by what they enable one to know; what is ultimately real sanctions some decisions more than others at different places and times. Realities are reached by making the right decisions; what we know indicates what we are to choose. Once again, where we begin will have to be justified by where we end, and where we end will have to begin a way of understanding better than ever before what it was with which we began. A choice of this geometry over that, if made in abstraction from what is primary and all-encompassing, may answer to some good purpose, but surely this will not be the purpose which sustains the philosophic quest.

6 There is no canonical way to settle philosophic disputes. But if one can reach a final explanatory account of what there is and can be

known, one will also make evident the principles in terms of which every philosophy is to be assessed, including that which claimed to be all-encompassing.

7 A philosopher should be a phenomenologist, which is to say, he should attend carefully to the nuances and subtleties of what is present, and describe it with care and fidelity. If he stops here, though, he stops at the beginning of philosophy, for he then stops with an acknowledgment of evidence but does not make use of it.

8 There is a difference, I think, between a scientific and a philosophic cosmology. The one is necessarily grounded in particular scientific discoveries, and sets the outermost boundaries of what is scientifically significant. A philosophic cosmology, instead, attends to the ways in which independent types of reality interplay. The one seeks a frame, the other is concerned with a product. Ideally, the two supplement one another, expressing the same truths from different positions. Neither is helped by being tailored to fit the other, for this requires a neglecting of what is presupposed in fact and theory and an acceptance of what has only a tentative and limited import, or a forcing of controlled inquiries and well-established results inside an account having no scientific sanction. The consonance between the two that all desire requires each to be independently pursued.

9 The conclusions of philosophy have wide generality. That does not mean that they are proportionately problematic. If they are grounded in what is found everywhere, if the philosophy pursues a careful course of evidencing, if its claims are about what conditions all else, if what it says at the end of one line of inquiry is independently used to begin another, ending where the first began, if the whole is coherent, comprehensive, and illuminating, and if it converges toward the point where the major arts and sciences are apparently moving, a philosophy has about all the power and range and the kind of objectivity and certitude that it is possible to have at that time.

10 The outcome of philosophic speculation is not the product of generalization or abstraction. These are ways of losing the world in formulae, detached categories, and promises. Universality is not generality; comprehensiveness is not the prerogative of the abstract.

11 Are the philosophic conclusions anthropocentric; do they lack objectivity, richness; are they willful, arbitrary? If so, there are errors somewhere. No appeal to other disciplines will enable one to eradicate those errors or to benefit from their discovery. I see no other recourse but to go over the ground again from different positions, modifying, adding, and subtracting. Other disciplines and investigators may make one aware that something is amiss. But only within the bounds of a philosophy will it be possible to understand what those errors mean to it, and how they are to be corrected.

Philosophy and other inquiries help one another most when each does all it can in its own way and on its own terms. Each, it seems reasonable to say, will benefit from the rest maximally only if it successfully avoids adopting their ways and underwriting their results.

RICHARD T. DE GEORGE

SOME COMMENTS AND QUESTIONS ON
METHOD AND THE FINALITIES

In the comments that follow I have tried to consider Weiss's book in the light of his past works. He has set himself an awesome philosophical task and the results are imposing. In reading through the text I found some sections—such as his discussion of space and time—especially illuminating and original. Yet there is much in the work that I found puzzling.

Weiss argues from everyday experience to his metaphysical observations and conclusions. He goes beyond appearances. He defines his terms and gives some ordinary philosophic terms special meanings. Within the framework of his system he uses his terms consistently. But consistency alone does not compel acceptance.

How does Weiss know so much about what is beyond appearances, and how can we test whether or not what he says is in fact the case? The answer to these questions is not clear because the method he uses is not clear to a reader of this work. Weiss is neither a traditional empiricist nor a traditional rationalist; he is an adherent of neither ideal nor ordinary language, though he makes use of both. A dialectician, he moves beyond appearances by arguing that the alternatives he presents to his own position are unacceptable. But he does not show that the alternatives he rejects are the only possible alternatives. Unless he can clarify more precisely what his method is, his system runs the danger, even if it is true or correct, of not being believed, accepted, or developed further by other philosophers. A consideration of four aspects of his system illustrates the difficulty.

Starting from appearances, Weiss gets to actualities and to finalities. The actualities are reminiscent of Leibniz's monads, though they seem to have windows and to interact with one another. If, as Weiss claims (see "Actualities," paragraph 8), "an actuality in itself . . . is neither real nor unreal, independent nor dependent, present nor absent, neither this nor not this, not unique, not duplicable" how can he speak intelligibly about *it* and say, for instance, that a trancendent makes *it* a determinate actuality? How does he know that the categories we apply to appearances apply also to actualities?

Weiss gives prominence in his system to actualities and finalities. Yet in his analysis he speaks of appearances, conditions, factors, relations, and contexts. These are neither actualities nor finalities, though they are presumably real. Since they are neither substances nor dependent upon substances in the way qualities are, several questions arise about their status. Do they exist, and if so, how do they exist? Are they unities? How in general do they relate to finalities? Similarly, reality seems to include them as well as actualities and finalities. Yet reality as a whole does not seem to be a unity and does not seem to exist in Weiss's meaning of 'unity' and 'existence'. How all the components of reality are together and the mutual relations among many of the components remains puzzling.

Weiss argues to five and only five finalities: Being, Substance, Possibility, Existence, and Unity. His position is original but not convincing. The kind of argument by which he arrives at these five finalities seems to lead as well to other finalities, such as Power and Good. However many finalities there are, what is the status of finalities and what is their relation to each other? What sense can we make of Possibility which is not a being, substance, unity, and does not exist? What does it mean to speak of Unity which does not exist, is not substantial, and so on? The status of finalities would be clearer if they together formed a substantial, unified, existing Being, capable of actualizing possibilities and realizing the Good. Weiss argues against a traditional, infinite, unchanging God; but even if these arguments are valid, they do not show why the finalities must be (nor how they can be) as distinct as he makes them.

Finally, since Weiss's method is not entirely clear, it is difficult to know within his system how to resolve problems—such as the mind-body problem or the problem of universals—which he does not raise in their usual form. Alternatively, if these problems do not arise in his system, it is difficult to know why they do not, since they seem to arise from the kind of evidence from which Weiss starts out.

*

The Philosophic Enterprise: A Reply

No MATTER HOW GREAT THE WISH to work on fundamental issues freely and independently, one is inevitably affected by what is currently thought. The very language one uses, the concepts that come readily to the fore, the way one proceeds make evident that a common past and contemporary events are having their effect. A respect for the sincerity and intelligence of one's fellows requires a consideration of the views they have so carefully wrought.

It is right to be disturbed by any account which fails to attend to alternatives. I thought I was constantly alert to them, though I did not always always remark on the fact. Every assertion was forged in the light of reflections on other positions, classical and contemporary, and often on some merely envisaged. Such autobiographical remarks, however, can not weaken the effect of warranted criticisms directed to the presented work. This, though, has a right to be considered apart from the demands of contemporary fashion or the reigning schools. A direct answer to the questions raised may make a little more evident the legitimacy and value of the present adventure.

1 Every method is unclear when just read about and not used. Only in use do its distinctive parts have distinctive roles, clearly separated from one another. Every method, too, is unclear, because necessarily explicated in other terms. There is no remedy for the first except a willingness to attend to the appearances, to note how they are together, and to seek for an explanation of the fact that universal, controlling conditions alone will enable them all to be together. A remedy for the second is provided by offering various characterizations of the same items.

The account I have given here has a logical cast. It emphasizes the nature of the evidence—omnipresent and not altogether accountable by the items which it governs; a process of evidencing—involving the completion of the evidence by the evidenced, and conversely; a termination in claims—symbols of the realities one seeks to reach; and an assessment of the claims—based on an awareness of the way in which they are corrected in being accepted by the realities at which they are directed. Alternative characterizations of the same procedures and outcomes attend to the fact that one begins with the most attenuated aspects of realities and moves to those realities by a process of intensification; that metaphysical evidences reach their final termini through the help of what is irreducibly real; and that appearances are products, dependent for their presence on the interplay of actualities and finalities.

2 The results of a philosophic inquiry are tested in a number of independent ways (see following "Process and Substance: A Reply," paragraph 18). Is the claimed outcome altered when it is accommodated by the finality into which it leads? If one has forged the claim properly, it will be accommodated without modification. Does the outcome provide an explanation for that with which one began? The right outcome shows what is explained to explain what explains it. Are the same results achieved when one goes over the same route, sometimes in the old and sometimes in new ways? If one has arrived where one ought, different and independent efforts will be found to sustain one another. Are there additions, irrelevancies, unwarranted claims? If not, the evidence should take one directly to its source. Does it enable one to see the seriousness and the value of the achievements characteristic of logic, mathematics, and science; religion, art, education, history, politics, and sport? One of the fruits of philosophy is the way in which it enables one to understand why one might want to devote a lifetime to any of these and other widely appreciated pursuits. If one attends to them as well as to the evidences provided by appearances and by actualities severally and together, a good beginning will be made in producing a systematic account of the universe in which all of us are and with which we never wholly lose contact. A consideration of alternative views is one of the things that must be done along the way. (See also following "Process and Substance: A Reply," paragraph 28.)

3 Each step in a philosophic inquiry deserves to be examined critically and often, and from many angles. Throughout one must ask oneself root questions and not rest until they are answered in better ways than they had been, or in ways that cohere better with the answers that had already been well-justified. Repeatedly one must ask: Do the results so far attained mesh with other conclusions independently arrived at? Do they cohere with what we daily know? If not, can they make evident where and why and how daily acceptances are to be modified? Does what is learned about actualities fit with what has been claimed about the finalities? Does the interplay of the finalities and actualities clarify the nature and presence of appearances? Have the various ways in which particulars are together been properly distinguished, related, and justified? Does the account of actualities and finalities, and of their interplay, provide adequate foundations for a cosmology which is at once coherent and adequate enough to enable one to understand how men could be distinctive, live in societies, have a history, and still be able to be together with things and animals?

Such questions have been selected from a larger group. Indeed, there is no one set of questions that must be asked. It is often better to see which come to the fore at different stages of the inquiry. At no one moment are all the questions well-focussed or the answers entirely clear; there can be no assurance that further questions about what seemed final will not have to be faced. Philosophic work is never done. But there comes a time when the parts and the whole seem to make more sense than what had been previously said by oneself and others. It is then right to expose the work for public examination. One of the examiners, sooner or later, should be its author. If he is, he will find himself driven to consider facets, dimensions, issues, positions, and characterizations he had not noted before.

4 One can surely begin where I did not, proceed in a different way, and arrive at different results. But this does not mean that all alternative procedures and formulations are on a footing. Not all are equally good. Some must be discarded because of their narrowness, arbitrariness, incoherence, or their incompatibility with other, better certified claims. None, of course, is to be dismissed a priori, but only those deserve to be taken seriously which are as well-grounded, as justified, and as explanatory as those already examined, elaborated, and sustained. As a system comes into clearer focus, what once had seemed promising is sometimes found to be incompatible with what is already justified, and with the attempt to achieve an organized, intelligible study of whatever there be and can be known.

Alternative views must tell us why there are appearances, how one can reach their sources, how the appearances are able to be together. If they meet that elementary requirement, they can help one avoid overlooking or wrongly stressing or undervaluing vital junctures and factors. Nothing less than constant vigilance, radical self-criticism, fresh and honest persistent thinking will allow one to escape making serious blunders. But there is no way that one can be certain that the best of answers has been obtained. The most that can be done is to try to offer the best possible answer that can be obtained today. When such answers are presented elsewhere, backed by facts, evidence, descriptions, and arguments, I hope that I will be honest and flexible enough to accept them in place of those I have urged. It was some such attitude that forced me to give up views central to earlier works. For the present I do not see what is amiss in what has now been set down. The presented criticisms, I am sorry to say, do not make evident where and how I have gone astray.

5 Why not adopt other views which have been long established or are more popular? After all, they have withstood considerable scrutiny from many sides; they deal with issues that interest many; they proceed and speak in ways which have met with considerable approval. Why entertain another view, particularly when its author confesses that he might be wrong, partial, confused, and at almost every crucial point and on every vital issue? One reason is that it begins where everyone must, in what is now present to unreflective experience, possible to every man. Those who take their start with sensa, sensations, ideas, language, intentions, or with the results or methods of science or history, officially start at some remove from where all inquiry begins; they presuppose what they themselves can not acknowledge. Another reason is that it attends to what warrants a move beyond that beginning. Unlike commonsense philosophies, which accept the dogmatism, unclarity, arbitrariness, and indurated beliefs of ordinary men, it also joins science, logic, mathematics, and other muscular disciplines in a search for what is better grounded, more stable, and yields a better explanation than what is daily unreflectingly accepted and acted on. But instead of abandoning what had been initially acknowledged, it seeks there for the evidences that will enable one to move with justification to what made such a beginning possible.

The most obvious of evidences is that provided by the conjoint presence of a number of appearances. No one of these could account for their togetherness. To take the more obvious cases, all are spatially and temporally conditioned; all are equally appearances; and all are affiliated in various degrees and ways. No man has a mind or a power broad and strong enough to encompass and govern all of them in all these ways. Since the governances are independent of one another, they evidence different all-comprehensive effective finalities operating on a multiplicity of actualities and their exhibitions. Once those finalities are known, one can go on to inquire whether or not it is these that act on the actualities in their severalty and on the actualities together. The answers do not come as readily nor with the clarity that one had managed to achieve before. But they too, are in the affirmative.

6 Were philosophy the property of a federation of clubs, each with its own rules and demands, one could describe some men—a Kierkegaard, a Frege, a Peirce, or a Whitehead—as too eccentric or idiosyncratic to be worth attending to. But all that one has a right to ask of a philosopher is that he be honest, resolute, free, and creative; that he be aware of what had been already achieved by pivotal figures; that he be sensitive to the nature of the perennial problems; and that he be alert to the difficulties his approach and efforts must overcome. Philosophy is too radical an enterprise, too probing, too self-critical and independent to allow it to be the privileged possession of any establishment.

As a matter of fact, today's most dominant, influential thinkers—Wittgenstein, Heidegger, and Whitehead—are quite unsystematic, without clear beginning, method, or end; they move and conclude more or less as their spirits dictate. An advance is made on them, at least in principle, if one makes an effort to show just where a start must be made, how one might best move on, and what it is that must be finally affirmed. One question surely ought not to disturb: Do one's contemporaries take one seriously? They are not philosophy's primary or only audience; that audience, one hopes, is the generations to come, and eventually civilized mankind.

7 One might wish to say what an actuality is like from the position of a finality or of some other actuality. When an actuality is characterized as intelligible, unified, and the like, it is dealt with in terms that reflect the fact that it is being approached from an outside position. Surely, this is legitimate. But if one wishes to say what the actuality is like apart from everything else, one can do no more than identify it as an irreducible individual in which a difference from all other actualities and a distinctness from all the finalities are solidified.

8 The same categories do not apply to appearances and to the actualities which provide constituents for those appearances. Appearances are inert, contextualized, and dependent; actualities, in contrast, are active, independent of one another, and cosmically together under common effective conditions.

The exhibitions of actualities and the expressions of the finalities, no less than the outcome of the interplay of actualities and finalities are not to be characterized in the same ways as are the actualities and the finalities as these stand apart, independent, self-maintained, self-bounded, irreducible. What depends on these is comparatively unreal, unable to act, insist, or resist. One can, of course, assert that whatever is, whether dependent or independent, derivative or primary, is real. But then one takes the universe to contain a miscellany of different kinds of reality. There is, in one sense, only a verbal difference between such a view and the present, since they apparently differ only in the range they allow to the term 'reality'. But in another sense there is a profound difference between them. To end with a miscellany is to end with a collection, without having any clue as to how the members are related. If, instead, one distinguishes the more from the less fundamental, and explains the latter in terms of the former, one leaves everything as it has been before, but now explained and clarified, with the derivative and dependent given grounding.

9 The names I have used in connection with the different finalities were intended to be in some accord with traditional uses. Unfortunately, the tradition is neither clear nor steady. Still, it does not seem to endorse a reference of a 'primal power' to a distinct finality, but rather to what is common to and diversely expressed by different ultimates. The Good, in contrast, does have a long and honorable tradition. On other occasions I have used the term to refer to an Ideal as having pertinence to obligated beings. Today it seems to me that it

is better to use it to refer to what is common to but diversely present in Possibility and Unity, and not as the name of a finality.

10 It is conceivable that there might be more than five finalities. But none is to be set alongside the others unless independent evidence for its presence is found.

There was a time when I acknowledged no finality at all. Later I found it necessary to take account of Possibility in order to explain how it is that distinct actualities, each living through its own time, move into the next moment together, and together coordinately divide and give determination to a common future. Only after a long struggle was I able to free myself from that restricted point of view. Nothing less than four finalities, it seemed to me, had to be acknowledged if one were to do justice to the primary ways in which particulars are together. Later, I discovered that one of the supposed finalities, 'Actuality', confusedly joined together two, independently functioning, irreducible realities. Subsequent experiences, reflections, and difficulties might well make evident the need to acknowledge still others, or to see that what was thought to be one was in fact a number of finalities with independent natures, modes of operating, and effects. Nothing in what I have said precludes discoveries of that kind. They might be found as a result of reflections on the nature and relationships of known finalities, through the agency of better procedures, or by using new evidences, independent of those that had been already noted. I will have no hesitancy in accepting what is reached in any of these ways. In the present work, I have paid particular attention to what has been intruded everywhere, thereby making all appearances as well as all actualities be together, and qualifying every actuality in the same way. These intruders, because not conceivably attributable to any particular—since they act to all—and not traceable to the mind of man—since they pertain to what exists apart from him—point to and are explained by what has sufficient power and range to produce effective particularized and cosmic unities, otherwise not possible.

11 Each finality affects all else. Each must, therefore, affect every other. From the perspective of the others, Possibility is a being, substance, existent, and an evaluating unity; Being is a possibility, substance, existent, and unity, and so on. If we attend to only one finality, and from that position characterize appearances or actualities, our terms should reflect the fact that we have, for the moment, neglected other conditions. If no account is taken of any of the finalities, of course, appearances and actualities are to be spoken of only in the limited, empirical terms that are appropriate to the transient or the derivative.

12 When one submerges the different finalities in a supposed more primal reality, important distinctions are lost, or one transports the distinctions and their accompanying independent operations into the body of the supposed primal entity. In what sense is a God one if he acts in multiple, independent ways? If he acts in only one way, how account for the presence and independent functioning of actualities and of appearances, and for the different governances to which they are all subject? I know that some of the greatest thinkers in the world have affirmed that there is only one finality, and that many of them have identified it with God. But it is also true they have been plagued by an inability to make sense of the presence and action of actualities, the diverse ways in which these are qualified, and the different ways in which actualities as well as appearances are together.

13 The mind-body problem and the problem of universals do not arise here in their usual, unresolved form. That is to be expected. It surely is desirable. Those problems are not primary ones. Not only do they have limited scope, but they arise in only some parts of the universe. There is no mind-body problem until there are beings which have both minds and bodies. Nor does the problem of universals, in its familiar troubling guise, make an appearance except for one who accepts certain theories of definition, conceptualization, language, and logic. Both, though, can be identified as epitomizing the perennial problem of the One and the Many. They are then able to be dealt with along the lines laid down in understanding of how omnipresent powers control and interconnect a multiplicity of particulars, and the ways in which each actuality provides a one for all the finalities. The mind-body problem, the problem of universals, and similar issues must be properly located and identified before we can hope to find their resolutions.

A mind is a one for the body's many, and the two are together in the individual substances of men and animals. Universals are unities with different degrees of power, from a minimal characteristic of aggregates, to a maximum characteristic of organisms. It is also true that what is known is an object of and perhaps tinged by a mind, and that in every part of the universe there are distinct, acting bodies. Mind and body in these cosmic guises are localized, together with distinctive constitutive densities, rights, intents, identities, and merits, in irreducible individuals. The unification of all of these affects the limited forms which transcendents assume when they are specified by those individuals.

RICHARD RORTY

QUESTIONS ON PHILOSOPHIC STYL

THE ATTEMPT AT COMPLETENESS which you have offered in successive books is the sort, roughly, which one finds in Hegel's *Logic* rather than in his *Phenomenology*. Under the spur of such critics of Hegel as Kierkegaard and Marx, many people think that if one is to have a sense of completeness in one's view of how things hang together, it is going to have to be by an account of concrete history rather than by providing a permanent neutral matrix for all possible inquiry. Do you have any sympathy with this preference for the *Phenomenology*, and with such attempts as the later Heidegger's to "overcome the tradition" through commentary, as opposed to synthesizing the tradition by further abstraction?

Your search for completeness and unity sometimes seems to reflect an insistence that every relation between entities must have something to do with the constitution of those entities. Throughout your work, this insistence on some form of internal relatedness seems a major theme, and is perhaps the greatest single difference between you and Hegel on the one hand and most of your contemporaries on the other. The insistence seems more a methodological than a metaphysical thesis—to illustrate an ideal of what a complete account consists in rather than a view of how objects are. What do you think of the various attacks on the necessary-contingent distinction itself in, for example, Quine and Wittgenstein, and of their attempt, reminiscent of Dewey, to soften all such distinctions as that between necessary and contingent, internal and external? They seem to want to do this by denying distinctions, and by denying part of what you want to do in putting forward new kinds of unities. Is there anything general that can be said about their "dissolving" strategy as opposed to your "constructive" one? The aim seems the same, but the means radically different.

In an attempt to make Hegel's point about the need to bring together subject and substance, some recent writers (like Derrida) have tried to criticize the whole notion of writing as representation of reality, and to view the use of abstractions by philosophers in the same terms as the use of images by poets, without the use of the universal-particular distinction, and without the use of the distinction between symbols for the general and symbols for the specific (because without the use of the concept of "symbol" at all). In your attempt to do philosophy in as general terms as possible, do you need the notion of a philosophical system as a symbol of, a description of, some sort of representation of, reality? Or can your view assimilate this latest attack on the subject-object distinction?

History, Commentary, and Discourse: A Repl

THE PRESUPPOSITIONS OF PHILOSOPHIC THINKING and writing have been so rarely examined that almost any probing in that direction is bound to open up unsuspected vistas. It is good to have before us clear and neat questions directed at present and established philosophic customs. They illuminate the nature of the enterprise; but they neither promote it, I think, nor bring it to a halt.

1 History is one of the basic disciplines, with distinctive objects, methods, problems, and outcomes. It does not replace other inquiries, nor turn these into subdivisions of itself. Nor do other inquiries replace it, or turn it into special cases of themselves. Anthropology, psychology, economics, and other humanistic disciplines, the sciences, and the arts, need not give way to it, nor it to them. Each can deal with the occupants of the same world that the others do. But each will do so in its own distinctive way. Ideally, they should supplement one another within the frame of a single well-grounded outlook.

2 History, history plain, secular history, is distinct from philosophic history. The first is a long-established discipline. The other is a late development, reinterpreting, recategorizing, and abstracting from the first in terms of philosophically grounded ideas of change, progress, value, purpose, and causation. I have yet to see a warrant for it, or for its claims.

Neither the discipline of history nor philosophic history makes an objective, systematic account unnecessary. Not only are there fixities in logic and mathematics, and prescriptions in ethics and law, but history itself occurs within a universe which it obviously does not and can not account for. That universe is grounded in nonhistorical realities. The ongoing, accumulative course of history, though, does make evident that some things once thought to be basic are in fact derivative, doubtful, or false, and that the most persistent concern with what is eternal is time-bound. The fact must be kept in mind, even when one affirms what is true always and necessarily. It does not compromise this. But it does make one hesitate and question.

3 A commentary enjoys a triple advantage: it assumes a single position from which a diversity of views can be understood and assessed; it attends to great, completed works; it may stand so far away from the views it examines that it can escape much of their bias. But it is also parasitical on the very kind of work it itself eschews. It depends on others to engage in basic philosophic inquiry but refuses to engage in it itself.

Perhaps what is being supposed is that the days of creative philosophic thinking are over? How could such a halting of a primary type of inquiry be justified? Surely, it is not enough to show that it has never fully succeeded. On such grounds one can get rid of all sculptures, painting, symphonies, poems, and plays. No one of them is without flaw. How could one show that from now on philosophy must be without value or promise? Does this not require an insight into the future that is beyond the capacity of everyone? Even if one were to decide that the entire past of philosophy was a series of dismal failures, that it was on the wrong track, that it was confused and misdirected, this still would not show that there was nothing further to do except to comment on what had been done. A reasonable man, of course, will eventually abandon a project that has proved to be unfruitful when carried out by men of genius. But I have not found any demonstration of that failure. I do not know the evidence that reveals philosophy to be a futile pursuit.

A retreat to commentary may also be due to a failure of nerve. This, I think, explains Heidegger's move. His stopping with a half-completed *Sein and Zeit,* his joining up with the Nazis, his treatment of Husserl, his unwillingness to admit that he committed grave moral errors, his boastings about his originality, his fraudulent philology are of a piece with his taking his commentaries on major figures to be major philosophic adventures. One does not overcome tradition by writing commentaries; rather, one then accepts it as a datum.

4 Progress in philosophy surely is not achieved by engaging in continued abstractings and synthesizings. Philosophic thinking hews close to what is always known and to what this makes available. Each significant effort starts near the place where others did; it moves along routes not too alien to those traversed in the past; it constantly arrives at what was discerned before. It progresses by inches. Given sufficient time that may add up to a great distance.

5 Relations are internal to their termini, for these are the termini of just those relations. The bigger is in a relation of larger to smaller. Termini, though, are but aspects of items which have standings of their own, and are, therefore, able to provide those termini for those relations. It is objects with such and such magnitudes that are related as larger to smaller.

6 Wittgenstein and Quine rightly question the dogmas that empiricists unreflectingly adopt from rationalists. They know that there are no hard and fast divisions in experience. Just as daylight merges

into twilight, and twilight into night without break or juncture points, so necessity and contingency; the private and the public; interpretation, perception, and action; universal, particular, and individual; reason and passion; certainty, confidence, belief, dubiety, hesitancy, and misconception slide one into the other imperceptibly. Each of them, too, seems to have endless degrees. The fact does not compromise the sharp distinctions which formal inquiry knows and uses. Nor does it affect the independent, oppositional status of ultimate realities. It surely would be a mistake to carry unchanged everything that is true of the world of appearances into what is real beyond all appearances. The greater the success, the more would one duplicate the world which one was trying to understand. Getting rid of arbitrary distinctions introduced into accounts about experience makes more, not less, evident the nature of the distinctions which characterize the realities that experience presupposes.

7 A 'dissolving' strategy approaches philosophic issues with the presupposition that philosophic paradoxes, perennial questions, and speculative accounts are willful and perverse, always to be avoided. It tries to translate them into logical, linguistic, scientific, or commensensical forms, or to avoid the areas where they are persistently and obtrusively present. All the while the original situations remain. The problem of mind and body can be dissolved by treating it as though it concerned two sets of occurrences, needing only to be correlated. But the grounds for those occurrences, the place from where the correlations are imposed, the question as to whether one has done full justice to the initial data are then not dealt with. And there will still be the problem of understanding the area where the questions originally arose.

A 'constructive' approach confronts rather than avoids, and tries to face the issues where and when they arise rather than taking off for some other realm where presumably they can not be formulated. It is acutely aware that there have been no satisfactory answers given to many crucial questions, and that it is conceivable that these have been misconstrued and improperly handled. Without losing the problems, it therefore seeks to deal with them from new angles, within a more rather than within a less comprehensive view of the nature of things and knowledge. One can pick up a golf ball and put it in a hole. It is more difficult but also more satisfying to solve the problem of how arm, club, and ball can be brought together so as to drive the ball into the hole. Philosophic inquiry is voluntarily undertaken. It gets in its own way when it deprives itself of the tasks it has set itself to master.

8 Derrida is right, I think, to look at philosophical writing as a type of literature, involving the use of images, metaphors, and other agencies by means of which basic visions and insights are portrayed and communicated. The distinctions that are pertinent to recording,

reporting, dialectic, argument, and systematization are then rightly neglected or minimized; but that does not mean that they are not present, unchanged in role and import. Poets can report, judge, and claim, at the same time that they attend to the weight and affiliations of their words. Philosophic discourse, though not a type of poetry, resonates in multiple ways at the same time that it represents, refers, humanizes, socializes, and austerely formulates the nature of what is true everywhere and always. It is, to be sure, also symptomatic, symbolic, and expressive of individual thinkers and of their time, background, and history These facts are interesting only because philosophy itself has something important to communicate. If it did not, the Derridas would turn from it to other writings.

9 Were a philosophic system a symbol of the universe, it would enable one to penetrate into it in depth. Were it to provide just a description, it would have neither beginning nor ending. Did it represent the universe, it would be able to act as its surrogate. Instead, philosophy attends to its joints, limits, and constant, common factors in an effort to articulate and communicate the nature of what there is and how it could be known. Were one to treat philosophy simply as the expression of some individual, one would minimize its referential, objective side; if, instead, one took it to be a set of detached truths, one would cut it away from its roots. Private and public emphases must be held together in equipoise at one moment for one purpose, and given different emphases for other purposes at other times.

A philosophic system asks that it be judged as a set of interlocked claims purporting to do justice to what all must presuppose and what all in fact encounter. It makes use of addressive terms, transcendentals, and other expressions which are pertinent to what lies outside, though reachable from the position of daily life. It can not be deprived of these, or allow for their translation into others, without being turned into a different enterprise.

10 Philosophy is engaged in voluntarily. Ideally, it refuses to accept any basic claim without assessing it; it then tries to forge others that are free of the defects that marred previous accounts, but without introducing further, more serious ones. The exploration of new prospects, if it is wide-ranging enough and sufficiently well-grounded, should make possible the discovery where it itself is deficient, thereupon prompting another effort, not altogether unmindful of what had already been done or achieved.

IN DEFENSE OF PROCESS

FIRST CONSIDERATIONS, together with *Beyond All Appearances*, is a thorough-going metaphysical system. Although I have some questions about what this enterprise consists in, I have no reservations about the legitimacy of the attempt to frame a metaphysical vision of the world and am concerned only with whether your vision is the best one, magnificent as it is.

1. ACTUALITIES

In "Substances and Substance," you say:

> Each actuality is a substance. It maintains a hold on whatever it contains, produces, and intrudes upon. It persists and it acts. It has an irreducible, independent core, and receives determinations from insistent, intrusive forces.
>
> If an actuality were not a substance, its parts would not belong to it, and it would disperse itself in the very act of making its presence evident. The very items which it dominates it would not control; nor would it continue to be despite an involvement in change and motion. It would be inert and solely in itself, or it would be a mere event. In either case, it would not be a source of action.

What kind of argument is this to a philosopher like myself (and some process philosophers, various kinds of Platonists, and a few billion Buddhists) who believes that events are the basic units of existence? It has the appearance of a *reductio ad absurdum* argument. But what you represent as absurd (not contradictory, perhaps, but implausible enough to warrant rejecting what entails it) is just what I regard as hard-won truths. Let me underline how much I reflectively believe to be true what you regard as absurd.

1 An event, on my view, has a harmonious structure; there are many kinds and degrees of harmony. Some events are merely coherent; you would call these "mere" events. Others are harmonized so that certain parts dominate others, determining the overall structure in a greater degree than those others. For instance, the focal points of a painting determine the background limitations; the brain of an animal determines his bodily movements. Events with a high degree of "dominance" organization might be called "centered." But this sense of centering does not entail that an event has a "core," independent and irreducible. Rather, the center is dependent on the harmony containing it. The experiences of centeredness, such as intense self-reflection, or feelings of self-possession associated with meditation or dance, can be accounted for as specialized kinds of harmony. Why is not the event-theory of actuality good enough for centeredness?

2 "Its parts would not belong to it." Of course, an event's parts would belong to it according to their roles in its harmony. And insofar as they play roles in other harmonies, they also are parts of other events. In itself a "part" simply is what it is (a harmony in its own right). But since it is part of other harmonies it is *not simply* in itself; some of its nature is to be relative, because of its participation in many events.

But is there not a stronger belongingness of parts to things? There are two kinds of real belongingness of parts in events. *First*, things can be considered as parts of events by the boundaries people impose on them; your discussion of the imposition of boundaries on appearances is splendid, particularly if you stress that it refers to experienced realities as well as appearances. If the boundaries are objectively valid, that means that the events really harmonize together into inclusive events in the ways the boundaries project. The carving up of the continuum is conventional, but valid. *Second*, parts belong to some events because they *ought* to. Some harmonies are ideal or obligatory for putting together given sets of potential components; events usually called "enduring things" are those whose patterns are normative for the *recurring* collections of potential components.

To hold to a stronger, substantialist, doctrine of belonging leads to the mischievous result that components must a priori and by nature belong to actualities. It is simpler to say they belong empirically when the containing harmonies are right. The substance theory suggests a *kind* of belonging is necessary by nature, whereas the event theory allows any assertion as to *kind* of belonging to be a cosmological generalization.

3 "It would disperse itself in the very act of making its presence evident." Setting aside the special connotations of that sentence deriving from your discussion of "evidence" throughout the book, I agree that an account must be given for action, but do not believe a substance is needed for such an account. An action would take place when an event comports itself according to some basic value, an ideal for its dominant part, for instance, and when natural laws carry

the effects of that comportment over into other events. A person, say, comports himself intentionally, raising his hand on purpose; the result of this is that the ball is caught and his team wins the game. Of course, the effects of the way an event comports itself do not all stem from dominant values in the event; perhaps the event is a mere harmonious aggregation; there is no "action" here, only causation. On the other hand, an "effect" is the result of a great many conditions, not only those provided by the agent-cause; perhaps there is no dominant variable in the causal conditions, no actor. This means that responsibility in this case could be traced to no single agent. Why is not the best philosophical strategy an event theory allowing highly focussed intentional action as a special case and also allowing more dispersed contours of causation?

4 "The very items which it dominates it would not control." An event controls its consequences only partially; domination is hardly ever complete. But an event may control its dominated items in the *important* respects, as the brain dominates the rest of the body. Even on your view, where a substance would dominate the features it has resulting from alien impingements, the control cannot be complete; the very relation of dominance requires other finalities, on your view, to contribute the required diversity.

5 "Nor would it remain over time despite change and motion." Indeed one of the reasons for rejecting the doctrine of substance is that it implies an embarrassing number of things that would have to hang around until annihilated. In experience the coherence of most things as enduring objects is much looser than a substance view would lead us to expect. Of course, under certain causal conditions the same harmony tends to be instantiated again and again, leading to the legitimacy of saying "the same thing is still here." This is a translation, preferable for practical purposes, of "this event is in a string of antecedent events." "Thing," in the phrase, "the same thing," refers to the pattern of the harmony, not to some underlying substratum undergoing changes. One of the important practical purposes for referring to enduring objects is when there is an ideal for the string of events in which later events are responsible for the effects of earlier events. This is the root of a valid doctrine of moral responsibility; but it also holds for any causal situation in which we hold a later event responsible for consequences flowing from an earlier event (the events are connected by a common ideal so as to be the same agent). As to moral responsibility, the philosophic problem is to show how a person at a given date is responsible for actions performed by him at a previous date; he must inherit special obligations. Why does an account with continuity of substance help here? Substantial continuity would be necessary, not obligatory. An event philosophy where continuity is a matter of inheriting patterns at least suggests the inheritance of a pattern of obligation.

6 "It would be inert." Although your adjective is meant to be derogatory, there is a sense in which I would insist upon it. The vitality in an event, both to itself and by which it effects consequences, is in its happening, its coming-to-be. Its coming-to-be is a process of rendering partially indeterminate possibilities determinate. But once it has come to be, it is a completed past fact; past facts are inert. Inert past facts determine subsequent effects because those later events must take them into account, not because facts continue to act when past. Since events still coming to be are not yet definitely existent, they can not then be causing effects outside themselves. Now you might say that this means that actualities-as-events do not act in the world. But I say that action in the world is a matter of process *connecting events,* not of events alone. Actualities-as-substances performing their essential actions (insisting on themselves) in a contingent and alien environment are only special cases of process.

My objections so far have been less to your position than to your argument. You defend your view by showing that its denial leads to undesired consequences. But I and some others desire just those consequences, and there are respectable cosmologies and long traditions integrating them into a more or less coherent view. You may be right that we are mistaken; but by and large you have not argued that we are. There are precious few metaphysicians these days, and if you directly engage even one more position you will have made a high percentage increase in serious readership!

2. SUBSTANCE

Let me now argue briefly but directly against your position that actualities are substances. For the sake of argument, let us temporarily set aside the considerations deriving from the motive of giving an account consistent with your theory of five interacting finalities and deal just with the account of substance.

It should be pointed out first that your criticisms of Aristotle are significant not only for what they say about Aristotle but also because they disengage your own view from the usual criticisms of Aristotle. You have the novel theory that particular actualities are the results of the interaction of Substance with the other finalities. Substance by itself is relative to nothing—not internally differentiated, not knowable from the outside or from the inside either. This is similar to what Whitehead's creativity would be were it not for the further differentiation of many and one in the category of the ultimate; it is also similar to Aristotle's prime matter. The other finalities, however, lend differentiation to Substance by giving it an internally complex intelligible nature, with existential power

215

distributed to various parts consonant with the nature of those parts, each part having "being" equal to every other part, and all parts unified so as to be valuable relative to each other from a single point of view. Your account, of course, is more complex than this, with each finality providing a special nuance to the context in which the parts of the universe are together, and also providing means for transcending any part to the other parts or to the finalities themselves. But let me try to understand the relation between Substance and the various actualities with substantiality in as simple a way as possible.

What surprises me in your account is the move from something like what I have just said to the characterization of actualities as having irreducible, independent cores. It appears that you have slipped Aristotle in through the back door. The general account of Substance interacting with the other finalities might equally well allow that its differentiations are of equal weight, that Substance merely particularizes an even-textured intelligibility, that the distribution of existential power is nearly homogeneous throughout the universe with geometrical truths being quite conventional, and so on. It is possible, in other words, for Substance to be differentiated without the reproduction of actual substances with cores and thick divisions between inner insistent characters and outer resistant surfaces. Or to put the matter another way, it is an empirical matter whether, where, and in what degree the universe is divided into individualized substances best described with Aristotelian metaphors, or events of varying integration and intensity best described with process metaphors, or a dull homogeneity perhaps best called "ether." Your general account of Substance-getting-differentiated allows any of these interpretations, and the importation of the solid-core view seems unwarranted. The event view fits just as well.

You might argue that the proper movement of thought is from experience to the interaction of the finalities, rather than the other way around. So, we find substances in experience and need to uncover finalities that account for them, although the finalities conceivably could have interacted to produce a process world instead. But typically you do not argue this way. Instead, you say we begin with appearances, not actualities. By reflecting on the stresses in appearances you say we find our way back to actualities. But when Whitehead, for instance, in his analysis of vector forces, followed the stresses behind appearances he found events, not actualities; many Buddhists, similarly, in their doctrine of dependent origination, find Emptiness. Are our experiences really different? Or do our experiences include the leading strings of different metaphysical theories so that we beg the question for each other?

Suppose the above objection is not serious. I need more clarification of the sense in which a substantial actuality has depth and inwardness. Your use of the notions of affinity and harmonics is intriguing. It conveys the sense that the inner stirrings of your heart set up a sympathetic vibration in my own, that depth calls unto depth, that the motive for adumbrating a thing beyond its surface stems in part from a resonance of its privacy with our own. But why can we not say simply that this is just a special kind of harmony, of structural pattern? Spatial fitting together is not the only metaphor for harmony; resonating responsiveness is another. But why need we say there are substantial actualities with inward cores independent from each other? Is it not simpler to say some harmonies are structured with highly dominant orders, so that their edges are buffer zones against neighboring collections of events, and such that their denser dominant parts harmoniously resonate with similarly dense and dominant parts of other harmonies?

A potential answer to this question is that substantial inwardness is needed to account for the feeling of subjectivity. It is one thing to encounter or contemplate a harmony, it is another to *be* one and feel what it is like. To call actual things events with harmony is to speak of them as objects, when they are also subjects. In my view the subjective feeling of any event is in its coming-to-be, whereas its objective character is what it comes to be, including the existential fact it exists. Your view has subjective inwardness and objective publicity at once. Yet it has the disadvantage of needing alien entities to unify the inward and outward parts. If you would cite subjectivity as a phenomenon that needs a doctrine of substance, it would be good if you could say why the coming-to-be of an event is not an equally good explanation.

3. EVIDENCE

The objections in the above two sections have supposed that philosophical argument is some kind of dialogue. That is, your conclusions should be established by showing them to be better than other people's (particularly those I take seriously). Obviously you believe the same thing or you would not have invited people to write you objections. But for the most part the dialogue is only in the "Comments on First Considerations," and the body of your text mainly rings the changes on how metaphysically interesting things "evidence" each other.

Your theory of evidence itself is ingenious and helpful. I appreciate the view that the line of direction pursuing evidence is congruent to but opposite of the line of causation producing evidence. This departure from Kant's view that the conditions of intelligibility are logically prior to those of causation is a healthy one, to my way of thinking.

The main plausibility of your theory of evidence, however, is that the theory is what you would expect if the cosmological scheme of interacting finalities with contexts and appearances is true. The theory of evidence is a subtle epistemological version of the metaphysics of finalities in which the order of knowing is opposite to the order of being. If this interpretation of your strategy is right, what do you mean by it? Do you claim that the theory of evidence is true because the metaphysics of finalities it so neatly complements is true? Do you claim the metaphysics is more plausible itself because it can be complemented by an effective epistemology?

A standard complaint about Husserl is that he says much about describing but himself hardly ever describes; his arguments are unfoldings of the inner dialectic of transcendental philosophy. In a parallel complaint, I wish you had given more evidence, not just assertions about the logic of evidencing. You talk about philosophy with metaphors of investigative activity, "probings"; the suggestion implied is that you will uncover the goods for us. What you show me, however, is not evidence of finalities or even an uncovering of them, but the special logic of interacting finalities.

In connection with my previous objections, it seems to me your theory of evidencing is a special case of a more general philosophical view and applies only so far as your theory of substances applies. Its basic logic is that complex things are the result of interaction of two or more other things, and that by tracing the contribution of each interactor we can move from the complex to the things that interact apart from their interactions, with due attention paid to the contexts containing the route of tracing evidence and to the risk of disengagement at the end of the trip. But this supposes that the metaphors of substances can be applied universally to the final components of the evidential world. For instance, Possibility and Unity are not the same as Substance; yet for you they have inner cores of their own and features received from other things (else there would be no evidence of them); they have needs and "act" so as to make contributions to others, not only providing passive contexts but making things intelligible and worthy that would not be so otherwise.

Suppose, however, that the basic components of complexes or harmonies are not all to be described according to substantialist metaphors, that the substantialist model is only a special case. Strictly speaking, all that is required for a thing to enter into a harmony is that it be partially determinate; whether it has an independent existence depends on what kind of determinate nature it has. Why may not there be some components of appearances, for instance, that do not evidence anything beyond the appearance? I suspect that you believe that evidence-tracing has a special goal, that of finding an entity that is self-sufficient and explains itself; if so, this view needs defense. The alternative is to believe that the goal of inquiry is to make things intelligible and, perhaps, necessary; the external causal roots of some component of a harmony may be absurd and hence uninteresting to the search for intelligibility except as providing occasion for a discussion of chance or spontaneity. At any rate, it seems to me a different cosmology would give rise to a different logic of evidence.

4. Finalities

At any risk of merely adding wrinkles to old disputes, certain questions should be raised concerning the finalities. Each finality is a complex of its essential character and the characters it needs to receive from the others. By virtue of what are these two kinds of components united? Unity itself is only one of the finalities and thus can bear only a conditional relation to the others; the unity of, say, Substance's essential character with its conditional unity can not be itself the conditional unity. Even to say that the finalities are in fact not independent and self-sufficient but rather actually interdependent is only to point out that they are complexes, not to explain them.

Some critics of *Modes of Being* had urged you to give more weight to the being of which the modes were modes; the suggestion there was that such being would account for the integrity needed for the finalities, each for itself. You now have included Being as a finality, contributing equality of mutual presence to each of the other finalities and their conjoint products. But this only multiplies the problem. How do we account for the integrity of the other finalities with their being?

What is the epistemological status of your proposals regarding the finalities? Several answers come to mind; but each has its difficulties and I am unclear which if any you would embrace.

1 The metaphysics of finalities is an empirioreflective *discovery* about entities brought into our experience. But then I think you need to give evidence for them directly, over and above arguing that they are what one would expect on conceptual grounds.

2 The metaphysics of finalities is a descriptive generalization of experience, providing categories that contain necessary relations between them, but that itself is only a hypothesis. But then you have not pursued philosophic questioning far enough because you have not commented on why there are these finalities rather than some others or none at all. On this interpretation you would be doing cosmology but not ontology. If this is the extent of your philosophic scheme, it shares the shortcoming of Whitehead's categoreal scheme, namely that of being plausible but arbitrary in shutting off the question "why?"

3 The metaphysics of finalities is a necessary hypothesis in the sense it is the only scheme that can make sense of our world. But then

you would have to argue even harder than I have urged above to show that this scheme is superior to alternatives.

As you know, I believe that the first principles of a cosmology are empirical generalizations (whether they are your finalities, Whitehead's categories, or whatever). As such they are arbitrary and contingent in the sense the world could be different though in fact is not. But precisely because the first principles are complex and allow of alternatives, the question "why these" can be asked. You believe that "ultimate" questions like this are to be answered by reference to simpler constituents that individually do not need further explanation and that together explain the original complex. But as you so well point out, such constituents or finalities must themselves be complex if they are to be together, and the question is thereby merely transposed. My sense is that complexes contain a contingency over and above any question of available components; that contingency is the product of *decision*. You admit that decisive element in describing processes that have antecedent components ready to be decisively combined. I would go so far as to claim that the decisiveness is the more important part of intelligibility, and believe it makes sense to say the basic elements of the universe are what they are rather than some other because they were created that way *ex nihilo*. Why is that not acceptable?

Of course, if one believed a decision requires a substantial decider rather than merely a decisive event, then the theory of ontological creation would require a theistic God with all the troubles of unity and relation your finalities have, one who would have to be explained by something higher, and so forth. But this is just one more reason for making substantial activity a special case of event activity.

One could also object to the creation theory by saying that a decision simply explains nothing; at best the motives in a decision can explain the decision made, and creation *ex nihilo* has no antecedent motives. But this objection supposes that explanation is only by deduction from what is known to be logically or causally prior, and the prior logical and causal premises are the very things to be explained. Explanations also can be by *pointing to* decisive acts. Is it not an advance upon the claim, "the world is arbitrarily such and so," to say "the world was arbitrarily created to be such and so"? The former explains what might only be a possibility; the latter explains why what is actual is indeed actual.

My reference to ontological creation is not merely to advertise my own view but to suggest that, if there are problems of unwanted mystery with one creative act producing the first principles, your theory has those problems five times over. Each of your finalities acts so as to make its contributions to the others. Apart from those others, its potential actions are just as arbitrary and unprincipled as divine

creation; since the finalities are determinate only in mutual conjunction, the *structure* of each contribution results from the conjunction
that contribution establishes. Because the essential contributions of
each (providing substantiality, being, intelligibility, etc.) are the
results of the acts of contributing, you have five miraculously creating gods. One is enough, really, and in fact preferable in light of the
problem of coordinating five. It makes good sense to allow the one
creative act to bestow whatever inwardness, being, intelligibility,
existence, and unity the world exhibits.

5. Experience and dialectic

My last set of considerations ia a theme that has run throughout
these comments; why am I so hard to convince? In private you can
cite my dullness and devotion to prejudice. But in public it is necessary to raise the question of the context of philosophizing.

First Considerations deals with this issue in the opening chapters
with a Cartesian autobiographical account of the development of
philosophical knowledge and then with an account of what is known
so that the development of such knowledge is what you would
expect. Aside from too much emphasis on beginning with your
private self and having to learn about distant things (a Cartesian
consequence of too strong a belief in substances with cores, I think),
there is no difficulty empathizing with the autobiography and taking it to be the story of Everyman. But the autobiography fails to
make your philosophical conclusions public precisely because it is
an idealized, fictionalized account. Paradoxically, a real autobiography, for instance, of what you thought about Peirce when editing
his papers, would be more convincing in justifying your disagreements with him.

What is the difficulty with an Everyman account of the development of knowledge? The problem is that it must assume that it
hangs on no issues other than those focussing the development. But
of course we all know there are other issues. Your initial depiction of
childhood as a process of learning to cope with uncertainties, a
process not complete seventy years later, is not an innocent beginning; Descartes would be overly fond of it.

There is no such thing as common neutral experience, unsullied
by philosophic biases; that you tell your story the way you do reflects
the conclusions you defend in later chapters. On the other hand,
mere debate between philosophic positions does not provide a
common public world either. The positions can be debated only in
the context of shared experienced activity. But because my experience is tinged with my philosophical theories, you can not address
my experience so as to share it without addressing my theories too:
your experience tinged by your theory is not my experience from

which I start. (Of course, there is no need to address *my* experience or theories in particular, except insofar as they present live philosophical options to your own. Throughout these objections of course I have not offered my views as the truth or as the only alternative, but rather as *typical* options your arguments should address.) To make your view public it should be defended more dialectically, I believe. By "dialectic" I do not mean completing what we already know partially, but rather showing the advantage of one's view from the perspectives of others, uncovering suppositions, and creating intellectual experiences that build a common world.

A rejoinder to this complaint is that a philosophy is genuinely a new view of things, appropriately with a new language; it must be entered into to be appreciated, and when appreciated it testifies to itself by its richness and coherence. Most philosophers can think in Aristotlese and Kantese; those who have read this far here can think in Weissese. Despite the richness of your language and vision, however, I am not persuaded that your problems are really my problems so that I should see things your way in order to solve them. From our historical vantage point, it might seem that Aristotle, for instance, was merely talking to himself and in such a magnificent way that his soliloquies have become our cultural context. But, in fact, his soliloquies were dialogues with the philosophic problems of his existential culture, particularly Plato, Eudoxis, et al. More than most contemporary philosophers, I probably share much of your sense of what our own philosophic problems are. But sometimes I find it difficult even so, despite effort and sympathy, to see that your soliloquies are really dialogues to which I am party.

But I would love to be shown!

*

Process and Substance: A Reply

A LEADING, ORIGINAL THINKER of a dominant school of thought performs a service when he sets out its main contentions in sharp opposition to the claims of others. Lines are clearly drawn, hidden implications on both sides become evident, and the dialogue that one conducts with oneself is given an objective and often a better form. But it can also tempt both sides to become more rigid and to sound more belligerent than they in fact are. I hope that my deep appreciation of the care and thought that has been spent by Neville on his defense of process will not be obscured by my attempt to deal with the issues sharply and directly.

1 Ongoing, change, process, coming to be, passing away are omnipresent. Their neglect in Wittgenstein's *Tractatus* reveals that work to be fatally flawed; their transformation into formal structures betrays the truncated and biased character of classical rationalism; their division into episodic bits by Descartes, Hume, and Whitehead ends with an incapacity to take proper account of organic life, action, causality, and history; the conversion of them into root irrationalities by Bergson obscures the very truths he wished to emphasize. No philosophic view can hope to stand if it does not take them seriously, neither exaggerating nor minimizing their roles or importance.

Nevertheless, there is much to be gained by remaining with such a pivotal item, provided that it not be forgotten that there are a number of others—for example, language, concept, substance, intention—which are also pivotal. By giving maximum value to any one of them, the exploration of its range and power is promoted, and considerable justice is done to the fact that it has an important role. Much, too, can be learned by seeing what must be done to accommodate the truths on which others have concentrated.

There is perhaps no better way for a young person to start on the lifelong adventure of philosophic inquiry than to enroll in a school which urges the claim of some favored item; some method that has proved fruitful in some other field, or seems flexible and novel enough to be able to avoid the errors of the past and make possible new advances; and some thoroughgoing way of assessing established contentions. His school allows him to increase his technical vocabulary; to master new techniques; to cover quickly wide ranges of data; to maintain a steady outlook; and to get ready answers to difficult questions that otherwise might keep him struggling for an indefinite time. The school of process philosophy stands out among most of the others for the high degree of ingenuity that its leaders have displayed in tucking inside their scheme the distinctions, facts, principles, discoveries, and problems that concern other thinkers. They are very skillful in patching up breaks and leaks, and in thinking of new agencies and devices by which to lay hold of the dimensions of God and the world that are constantly eluding their grasp. And, when all else fails, they so engagingly express a willingness to give up interest in obvious features of perception, causality, discourse, time, possibility, ethics, action, art, and history, that one tends to overlook the recklessness behind it. No one else seems to have mastered the art of candidly confessing failure so well that it sounds like success. Taken as offering a fresh perspective and as a halfway measure it has much to commend it. But because process philosophy insistently operates from a narrow base and is so occupied with protecting its flanks, the exhibition of its virtues makes all the more evident how badly these need supplementation.

The nature of experience, practice, and inquiry; responsibility, dedication, planning, action, and work; love and hate; growth and maturation; possessions and rights all require references both to what is transitive and to what is steady, to process and to substance, to what does not and to what does maintain itself. The task of philosophy is not to replace either or to produce a pale copy of one of them inside the folds of the other, but to do justice to the obtrusive presence, independence, and interplay of both—and much else.

1 One reason for referring to a center is to account for a multiplicity of expressions having various degrees of opacity and a common origin. Another is to try to make sense of identity over time, and the different ways the same entity may act to accomplish the same results in different circumstances. A core cut off from all expressions would not be their center.

It is the same cat that hungers and thirsts, crouches and springs, that was once a kitten, and is now resting in the sun. The cat is not independent of these exhibitions; it is not a pattern overlaying unit pulsations replacing one another in sequence; it is not devoid of power, persistence, and an involvement with what is present to and with it. Is there a good reason in fact or theory for denying that it is present for quite awhile, diversely and partly exhibited in ways which tell us something of what is at the base of all of them?

2 A harmony is a product within which one can often distinguish dominant and recessive strands. But this is not yet to remark on the origin of the strands, on what produced the harmony, on what remains identical amidst change and thereby gives the harmony

support and a career for a considerable period. An event-theory can perhaps allow for something centered, but it has no room for what expresses itself in many ways at the same time, and in similar and different ways over a stretch of time.

Harmonies are the successful outcomes of the fitting together of constituents. Unless that fitting is controlled by the constituents—which is the reverse of what is found—a harmony will be accidental, or will be traceable to an overarching power. A Cartesian world of atomic moments is brought into harmony with the facts by identifying conservation with creation; a Humean gets rid of that creating God and then either gives the power to habit or thought, or stands astonished before the fact that the future is relevant to and produced through the help of what preceded it; a Whiteheadean returns to the Cartesian frame but with a God who helps make the world better and better.

One must acknowledge more than a sequence of events if one wishes to make provision for concerted action, the carrying out of a decision, or the persistence of a responsible agent with his guilt, tasks, and promise. Patterns are too inert, God's ways are too unknown, a retention of the past too much a passive condition to allow one to rest with them if one seeks a satisfactory account of what is, what is happening, and why. I do not see how the thesis of atomic moments is made more plausible by enrolling a billion Buddhists in the school—granted, which I do not, that they belong to it.

3 Organic beings attend to what is gross and palpable. The lion pursues the elephant; it knows nothing of the particles rushing about within the elephant's confines. Is there a primordial continuum which the lion unknowingly carves out? Why should one believe that? Let it be granted. Must not the lion have to stand outside that continuum to work on it? And when the elephant turns about in terror must it not also have to stand outside the continuum? How clever of both to carve out of the continuum the very units that already exist apart from it.

4 If a harmony is normative, it is prescriptive, conditioning, and perhaps controlling. If it is also acknowledged to be persistent, distinctive, intelligible, extended, and of value, there is apparently little to distinguish it from a juncture of a number of finalities. One would still have need to refer to actualities. They punctuate, resist, and interact with the expressions of the finalities.

Were there just a single global, complex, final unity there would be nothing it could prescribe to. There would not be a number of harmonies; we would have no reason to expect disharmonies; there would be no reason why one harmony should follow on some other, or on some disharmony; we would have nothing that was harmonized, and nothing which made use of a harmony in a distinctive, limited way.

It may be 'simpler'—though that is surely not obvious, and if true is not necessarily compelling—to claim that when a man says what he intends, all that is involved is a number of harmonies fitting together. And if it be added that he spoke responsibly, that he wrote it down, and that he continues to affirm it, it still might be simpler to speak of nothing more than a succession of harmonies. Since one will not yet have acknowledged a particular possessor of the different harmonies, one would have no warrant for saying that the succession occurs within or for a single being, striving to survive and prosper in the face of recalcitrant and injurious things. Common sense is not enough, but surely it is not to be abandoned lightly, wholesale, without regard for what it says and points toward.

Occasionally various strands happen to fit together. Some sounds supplement others heard at the same time. In other cases, it is necessary to act in order to make items harmonize. In still others, one begins with disorder and ends with what is more or less well-ordered. All the while a self-identical, productive, and sometimes a responsible being is at work.

If a man's hands and eyes did not function in harmony, must we content ourselves with recording the fact, and that is all? And when he trains himself to act in a less fumbling, self-frustrating way, must we stop short with the comment that somehow a disharmony gave way to a harmony, perhaps with the help of God?

5 It is not possible for a reflective man to accept the world of everyday without making some changes. It is too disjointed and incoherent to satisfy one who would know what is present and why. Science, mathematics, logic, history, art, as well as philosophy, move away from it in order to better understand what is objective, real, steady, and basic, and what is not. But one should move away from it only if and so far as one must. Its distinctions, components, courses, and lessons should be accepted until the presence of borderline and difficult cases, error, ambiguity, superstition, prejudice, contradictions, incompleteness, and new discoveries force one to modify, supplement, and sometimes to reject what is commonly held. I suggest that what then be done is to see if there are steady, controlling, intruded factors there, use of which will allow one to reach what clarifies, rectifies, and extends what had been originally accepted.

It is not the objective of philosophy to portray a new world, no matter how neat, noble, simple, or arresting. One of its tasks is to hold on as much as possible to what is daily known while making its grounds evident, thereby giving one a better hold on most of it than one had had before.

What warrant is there for denying that it is the same man who began and ended a day-long fast, or who clung for a while to the idea that there were persistent realities? Such a warrant would have to be so strongly entrenched, so well backed by what has been already learned, so badly needed in order that everything be clarified, explained, and understood, that one was compelled to accept it. Even then it would be wise to suspect that one had blundered somewhere.

Common sense is not sacrosanct, but its primary claims—for example, that there are things, animals, and men, with short- and long-ranged careers, that they act and suffer, and that there is more to them than they are now exhibiting, inheriting, aiming at, or synthesizing—have been sufficiently well-sustained over the course of time as to make it desirable to proceed slowly and cautiously with any radical alteration, translation, abandonment, or denial of what it persistently maintains. Ideally, the crude and confused reports of unreflective experience are to be replaced by others more broadly based and which are capable, in the end, of explaining what is reliable and unreliable, and what is primary and secondary in the everyday world. At the same time, provision has to be made for the pursuit and achievements of history, art, religion, mathematics, logic, psychology, sociology, anthropology, linguistics, geography, and other disciplines that are being pursued with rigor by dedicated men. The radical reformation of daily views which an 'event theory' demands needs much more justification than it has so far received. To just assume it and abide with the consequences, no matter how odd and contrary to experience, may show fine character perhaps, but not the wisdom or insight one wants from a philosopher.

To be sure, a cosmology has a much larger range than common-sense thought; it is aware of laws and conditions which govern the activities of ultimate particles. But I, too, am in the cosmos, and so are cats and dogs. To allow our particles to be there alone is to do injustice both to us and to the cosmos.

6 Individuals act. Rather than allow this, it is being maintained that 'natural laws carry the effects of one event into other events'. The work of individuals is here attributed to universal, fixed structures, or to universal powers. Not only are individuals then denied efficacy, but laws—properly expressed in universal terms—are required to dirempt and specialize themselves so as to be appropriate to different events. If there is anything wrong with the outcome of the operation, the fault evidently will have to ascribed to the laws which carry into the future what it would have been better to have left in the past.

There can be little question but that what I do is inescapably limited by what the structure and dynamism of the world allows. But it is still I who act, I who am accountable for the consequences. It is I who began a chain of events so as to bring about a desired result which I am to enjoy weeks later. When I make something I employ energy to convert an indeterminate prospect into a determinate result. The outcome depends on conditions and material—and on what I intended and therefore did, sometimes for quite a long time.

It may take weeks for a composer to write a symphony. Is there a gain in understanding his activity and achievement if one ignores the fact that he has been working day after day, doggedly advancing and retreating, irritable and elated in turn? At each moment his decisions are affected by what he has done. He remembers and he retains—but he also forgets and discards. All the while he remains selfsame, an individual determined to finish the symphony. To admit this is not to suppose that there is a substratum underlying all changes. The composer is not hidden; the landlord can find him; his wife will speak to him. But he is more than he is exhibiting at any one moment. That more is what he is making manifest, but more intensive, more concentrated, more persistent and undivided.

7 The question to be answered is not whether an event controls anything fully, but whether an event can control at all. An event is an ongoing which exhausts itself in its coming to be. Distinguishable factors there achieve dominance at different portions of its indivisible career and can, so far, be said to dominate. But an event can not use its components to bring about anything else. It can not act, interact, or make. The control that an actuality exerts enables an event to make its parts and constituents function on behalf of some work or result which the actuality is bringing about outside itself— not necessarily at a later time, but then and there. When the Humean temporal atom is identified with a Leibnizian monad one adds to the difficulty of a present, which has no genuine past or future of which it is an integral part, that of a present that has nothing alongside which can be perceived or with which it can interplay.

8 I can see that a son might assume his father's debts. I can see that a man might later admit that he had to make good a failure of an earlier date. What is hard to see is how a later event can be responsible for what is essential to the being of a prior event. I must be missing something here. What is wrong with the usual observation that there are obligations to which a man is subject over the course of his career, and that a failure to satisfy those obligations makes him guilty from then on, someone who failed to do what he ought?

Is everything remembered? Is nothing forgotten? Does it make no difference if it be retained in the form in which it had occurred or in some radically transmuted guise? On what does the type of inheritance depend?

9 The present, I agree, is where the indeterminate future is being made determinate. The past, I agree, is a domain of determinate, inert items. Is action then only "a matter of process connecting events"? If so, there is no one who acts and thereby turns indeterminate prospects into determinate results. Are all actions merely temporally aggregated items, all equal in length, each replacing a previous one which exhausted itself in its coming to be? Why deny that it may take hours, days even, to complete some act? From the outside one could separate off early portions of that act from later portions. But as part of the act they are all within its undivided present.

10 I do not maintain that actualities are "the results of the interaction of Substance with the other finalities." I take them to be independent realities which are affected by all the conditions that hold everywhere. Nor would I identify Substance with Whitehead's creativity or with Aristotle's prime matter. The one is too temporalized, and somehow set behind all other powers; the other is over-spatialized and supposed to be intrinsically unintelligible. As I see it, Substance relates all actualities in terms of their ability to supplement or contrast with one another. It is differentiated in the course of its application. Like the other finalities, it is knowable from the 'outside' since it is reached from evidence intruded on actualities. Like the other finalities, it is knowable on the 'inside' as well, since the evidence is a continuation of it, and it is moved into further, at the outcome of a process of evidencing.

11 Actualities are centered in intensive unities where all their possessions converge. One is forced to acknowledge the presence of those actualities for many reasons—for example, to account for expressions, rights, actions, responsibilities, and appearances.

Pertinent to the discussion of Substance is the fact that actualities resist, interact with, and act on one another and the finalities. Were there no actualities one would have to say that Substance is differentiated by the other finalities, or that it pluralizes itself. In neither way would one account for self-maintaining individuals, their appearances, and the ability on the part of some of them to discover what is final.

12 Were it true that Whitehead traced appearances back to their sources and found events where I find actualities, you, I, and others should try to go over the ground again and see what we then find. I am not aware, though, of any effort made by Whitehead to trace appearances back to their sources. Had he been interested in doing this, he would not have adopted Hume's view of sense data and Leibniz's view of contemporaries, and contented himself with a descriptive cosmology. I have learned many things from him, both when and after I was his student. I must confess I find it hard to identify him as one of the process philosophers. To be sure, his self-designated followers may have made considerable improvements on the original scheme; the changes they have made, though, seem to me to involve a loss of many of the fixed items on which he insisted, with a consequent denuding of the cosmos he tried to understand. Since his account already required the sacrifice of a great deal without a compensatory gain in understanding, it seems evident that these followers are moving in the wrong direction.

13 Were one to speak of particulars as determinate, specific, multiple, differentiated, and the like, and were one then to take what is ultimately real to be the very antithesis of such particulars, it would be proper to refer to that reality as indeterminate, general, unitary, undifferentiated, empty, and so on. All the while, one may be intending to refer to the latter as fecund, rich beyond expression. The Emptiness of the Buddhists, as I read them, is taken to have such richness, to be full, irreducible, final, forever, and enhancing. Apart from their supposition that there is only one finality, their comparative neglect of the actualities that are subject to it, and their difficulty in affirming that there are men who seek to reach it, I do not find a great difference between what I say about Being and what the Buddhists say. If there is a difference of any magnitude, one ought to look at what is before one and see if evidences can be extricated there which will lead to what is everywhere and always. One might also see what a finality does to the claim that one has expressed about it. I readily grant that I may have misconstrued or misdescribed Being. But if so, I do not know where or how.

14 Resonance is only one type of occurrence. Were it alone, it might be possible and even 'simpler' to say that 'some harmonies are structured with highly dominant orders . . . and such that their denser dominant parts harmoniously resonate'. Actualities, though, are also coordinate; they are intelligibly connected; they are dynamically interrelated in a cosmic space and time; and they have comparable values. Each is governed, individually and cosmically. An example: an actuality occupies a limited portion of space and does so in a distinctive way; that space is continuous with an independently existing and contoured cosmic space. The actuality's affiliations with others are not neatly calibrated to the size of the region it occupies or to the distances it has to other occupants of space.

15 Since there is no good warrant for supposing that 'a feeling of subjectivity' is characteristic of things or plants, one must find other grounds for holding that they have a substantial inwardness. I am led to affirm it when I try to explain their diverse expressions, their persistence over indefinite periods, their ability to act, their resistance, and their punctuation of what otherwise would be undifferentiated universal contexts and governances.

Were there no self-maintained actualities, you, the tree, physical particles, and chemical compounds would not act on one another, or make a difference to the ways in which common conditions function locally. If these consequences did not disturb or if they were desired and congenial, we would then have to ask again what the purpose of a philosophic inquiry was. In part, at least, I think it is to hold as tight as we can to what we already daily know while going as far as we must in order to understand how that beginning was possible. There are other ways of characterizing the philosophic enterprise—to understand actualities, to produce a viable cosmology, to understand necessities, to ground the different disciplines. I see no need at the moment to give up any of them. None, so far as I see, rests on an attempt to justify 'a feeling of subjectivity' or takes it to be fundamental. Provision for this must be made, of course; a failure to do so would show that something had been misconstrued.

16 Some subjective feelings are transient; others persist, pervading the entire body. Both—the latter most evidently—presuppose actualities, and can not be identified with the coming to be of a momentary occurrence. When I am self-conscious, or when I attend to an injury, I counter my externally approached body with a privately expressed feeling. The two are experienced together. Neither my 'outside' nor 'inside' is a domain, neatly bounded off from all else. The two are always together. Yet they are distinct; their contents and rhythms are not always in accord. What I suffer from without sometimes requires changes from within; and what I am from within sometimes demands changes in what I am from without.

17 A reference to 'strategies' has overtones of war, winning over opponents, ingenious solutions, cleverness, all of which do violence to the spirit of philosophic inquiry. It divides investigators into camps, ignoring the objective which should be common to all. Perhaps nothing of this is intended, and all that is meant is that knowledge is advanced by going in one direction rather than in another. I will assume that this is what is meant.

18 Dialectical difficulties discovered in the course of an attempt to develop a comprehensive naturalism almost forty years ago made me aware of the presence of a condition that was pertinent to all actualities. Other dialectical difficulties and attention to the claims of various thinkers made me see the need to acknowledge still others. I then turned toward common experience for confirmation, and from there moved back to the finalities. The circuit was made many times, with many rectifications, hesitations, and checks, backwards and forwards. The result was, on the whole, a clarification of what was daily encountered, of actualities, and of the omnipresent effective conditions which governed them all. It is, therefore, true to say that a knowledge of the finalities (and actualities) grounds my understanding of what is confronted; it is also true to say that what is confronted provides a beginning for a progress toward and into the finalities (and actualities). It is the latter half that is being emphasized in the present work. Its unclarities and mistakes should make evident the need to follow it by better efforts.

Of course, one moves in a logical circle if conclusions are used to warrant that with which one began. Yet, if the circle is all-encompassing and if each beginning is independently made, the result will not only be without logical flaw—which is true, of course, of every circular argument—but will have the merit of being well-grounded a number of times. A beginning with actualities and finalities ends with appearances, their product; a beginning with the appearances ends with actualities and finalities, their sources. The first is synthetic, constructive, requiring a consideration of the way in which thrust is met by counterthrust, condition by condition, the one by the many; the second involves analysis, a process of symbolization, and a refined form of the classical cosmological and teleological arguments.

By engaging in each effort independently, one is able to provide a check on the outcome of the other. Still, the understanding of the appearances should be guided by what one knows of actualities and finalities—and conversely. Such guidance is both unavoidable and desirable, provided that each move ends a fresh beginning, and that clues are willingly but carefully pursued, no matter where they lead. One thing is certain: the procedure is to be repeated again and again until one is reasonably sure that no important steps have been taken arbitrarily. Care must be taken not to yield to the temptation to make one's account neat and finished no matter what the facts or warrant. It would not be surprising to find that I have more than once gone further—and in some cases not far enough—than the evidences, checks, and explanations justify. There is no remedy for this but vigilance, repetition, self-criticism, backed by a willingness to alter, substract, and abandon what can not be sustained.

What is sought is a complete, well-articulated, justified account of the nature of knowledge and reality. That no finite man can reasonably suppose he alone can achieve. He must be content to have come a little closer to that ideal goal than he, and perhaps others, managed before. Other concerned and competent inquirers may help him in many ways. But he will not get what he needs if he stays inside some school, for there other approaches, diversely specializing a common enterprise, are deliberately rejected. Instead, the philosophic project should be kept in focus while past as well as present successes and failures are used as objective tests and guides.

19 Evidences of finalities are to be found by attending to appearances and to actualities, and noting what is present in and for, but not native to them. It is a fact, is it not, that you, I, the cat, and the shoe are equally real, that we constrast with one another in various ways and degrees, that we are intelligibly linked, that we are together spatially, temporally, and dynamically, and that we have comparable values? Do not these all point up factors which no one of us could have provided? Are not these factors beyond the power of a mind to produce, sustain, make present everywhere?

It is not true that all this is only "a special case of a more general philosophical view and applies only so far as [my] theory of substance applies." Kant remarked on some of the evidences; so did Hegel, and earlier, Plato, Aristotle, and Aquinas; yet they differ considerably on what they understand Substance and substances to be. I think we can find some of the evidences, too, at the base of the cosmologies of Newton and Einstein, though they make use of them for different purposes and proceed along different routes than the philosophers do. The scientists and the philosophers are not competitors; nor are they in a rigid order of first and second. Their independent investigations promise a better common conclusion than one in which either remains within the limits characteristic of the other.

If the present account forces method and results within a prejudged supposition that Substance or substances are ultimate, it suffers from a serious defect. The supposition can provide a beginning for an approach to appearances, but this will not suffice to show how all the appearances are together in space, for example. Such a result requires one to turn in a different direction.

20 Each finality provides a base in terms of which all else can be described. Possibility and Unity can, therefore, be characterized in substantialistic terms. It is equally true that Substance can be characterized in terms expressive of the fact that Existence, with its dynamism, or Possibility, or Unity, or Being has been used as a base. Substance can be correctly characterized as unifying and assessive—to adopt the position of Unity; it can also be correctly described as extended, pulsational, in process—to adopt the position of Existence.

21 I agree that "[a] goal of inquiry is to make things intelligible." I do not add to this the special task of "finding an entity that is self-sufficient and explains itself." If I did I would join with those who rest with an all-creating God, if this idea could be made intelligible.

22 What appears to be absurd should provide a challenge, not a resting point. Difficulties in the way of understanding rightly provoke new attempts to understand. Seen rails converge. It is absurd to say that the train and the passengers shrink as they recede into the distance. The refusal to rest here is what grounds controlled inquiries into perception, optics, perspective, and the like. Similar motives prompt the formulation of a philosophical cosmology and a metaphysics. Once achieved, these, too, ground ways of grasping what before was obscure, confused, inexplicable, and apparently absurd.

23 The features which a finality acquires from the others are made integral to it by that finality. Each internalizes what impinges on it to make it one with itself. We all do something like this on a smaller scale all the time, adopting what is intruded on us, more or less modified.

24 Is there an overarching One for all the finalities? Again and again, I have been urged to acknowledge it. There are serious difficulties in the way.

a) Would I not have to acknowledge another One which encompasses the first and the finalities, and so on without end? b) How could the One allow the finalities to be distinct? c) How could the One allow them to function independently? d) How could a single, final One, allowing no diversity within it, engage in a multiplicity of actions? e) If there be a multiplicity anywhere, does this not stand opposed to that One? f) Were there just one finality, how could it account for the fact that actualities have natures, for example, that are independent of their extensions?

For there to be a plurality of finalities, the finalities must, of course, be together. There must be a one for them. Is it not enough to observe that each actuality provides a one for all the finalities at the same time that each finality provides a one for all the actualities? If there are reasons for moving beyond such a result, I hope they will soon be stated.

25 Every philosophic system shows severe strains, omissions, and confusions. A system must eventually be abandoned when it is unable to acknowledge or enable us to understand the presence of existing interacting things, living beings, and man's sympathy, emotions, art, society, self-consciousness, creativity, appearances, as well as the togetherness of men and other actualities.

26 The evidences for the finalities are not simply what 'one expects on conceptual grounds'. Such a statement ignores both the fact that one begins in experience and is there led to acknowledge universal governing conditions, and that one can proceed by symbolization and intensification as well as by argument. One conceptualizes, articulates, systematizes to communicate, to judge, to provide clear bases for inferences. But this does not preclude the concepts being rooted in what is itself not conceptualized, and yet not irrational or absurd.

27 'A descriptive generalization of experience', I agree, yields at best a plausible account which arbitrarily terminates inquiry. A cosmology must be grounded, explained, justified. This is exactly what an account of the finalities and the actualities, each real but affecting the other, is intended to provide. I have always objected to 'descriptivism' as not being sufficiently systematic, controlled, or testable to be able to provide a satisfactory method for philosophy.

28 Once again it is said that alternatives should be seriously considered. It is good advice, but most unclear. a) What are those alternatives? Are they specific claims made by others yesterday and/or today? Or are they, instead, logical alternatives? Are the first not too few, and the second too many? Are not the pertinent ones raised in the course of a radical self-criticism? b) Where does one stand when one considers the alternatives? If one remains within some narrow alien frame, they surely will be distorted. If one just adopts the frame of some particular school, one will surely miss the subtleties that its members so well know. I think there are two answers to the difficulty, and they belong together: one properly envisages alternatives from the position where every man is daily, and one envisages them from the position of the philosophic enterprise. In both ways one is able to view them impartially, biased neither toward a view where some are neglected or minimized, nor toward one where some are favored and perhaps exaggerated. By taking both positions one escapes some of the limitations characteristic of the established commonsense outlook and the emptiness of a completely general outline.

If it be held that a man is a series of unit events, each inheriting from its predecessors, all overlaid by a single pattern, one very clearly rejects what even its defenders live by. The view that a man has a self-identity and individuality, that he has rights and duties, that he acts and makes, and that he is guilty for what he did sometime ago, does not have this defect. But other views are also compatible with what is daily known—that he is a social unit, that he is a sinner, and so on. All can benefit from the insights expressed by the others, and even from those incorporated in alternatives that are discarded because of their implausibility or ultimate incoherence (like the theory which allows for no minds in which theories are forged). But one will not be able to decide amongst them until it is seen how they support and are supported by what else is daily known, rightly inferred, reached into, and claimed. One then begins to find that, as part of a comprehensive system, most of the supposed alternatives are isolated aspects, momentarily focused on.

Ideally, there are no alternatives, only different stresses within a single whole. Though the whole is no continuum, there is, one can say, a continuum of variant formulations of it. One good measure of the tenability of a view, therefore, is its ability to allow, by limitation or a shift of emphasis, justice to be done to what is claimed from other positions.

If someone had produced a complete and perfect account there would then be little more for the rest to do but, for various purposes, to stress different portions at different times. Because there is no such perfect account, other attempts must be made to produce it. Each outcome, instead of setting itself alongside others, should offer itself as a matrix from which these are to be abstracted. Short of that, what is there but the incomparable contentions of obstinately partial views?

29 The universe could conceivably contain more than five finalities. Conceivably, one or more of these will eventually be seen by me or others to bundle together a number, or to have mistakenly broken up what is in fact one. In the meantime, no great harm is done, so long as one remains in touch with what is beyond all appearances and actualities, and which enables each to be together with other appearances and other actualities.

30 What further knowledge or insight is achieved, what is illuminated or justified if one holds that what is ultimately the case was 'created that way *ex nihilo*'? Would one not just double supposed brute ultimates, and that unnecessarily? Why must there be a prior decision? By whom and by what will this be made? Since it is brute, will it itself not require a prior decision? If not, why is it all right to stop with an inexplicable decision rather than with a supposed inexplicable universe?

Are these questions answered if instead of allowing for a being who decides, one just holds that there is a deciding event? Putting aside the problem of understanding what a deciding event could be and how one might be able to know that there is one, is anything more being done than to remove the entire problem to another location?

31 Might the entire universe be only a possibility? If it could be, does that not show that its presence is due to some decisive event or power? Not unless one assumes that the actual universe had to be preceded by a possibility. If it had to be, why must there not first have been a possibility before there was a supposed primary decider?

Particular actualities come and go. As having futures, they are inseparable from relevant possibilities. But finalities always are. There is no antecedent possibility for them to realize. If there were, they wouldn't be there to realize them. But particular actualities still to come can have their possibilities assured by others now present.

Perhaps what is intended is to acknowledge just one finality, perhaps Existence, and to treat it as a primal decider? But this will not yet be enough to account for the independent presence, insistence, and resistance of actualities. Aristotle is right, I think, in holding that there always is some actuality or other.

32 To condition, control, affect is not to make or produce; we need not therefore suppose that finalities decide, act, or create. And if there is more than one way in which actualities are together, and these are distinct and independent, must they not be traced back to independent sources?

Let it be granted that one creative act could produce a plurality of independent conditions without itself being self-divided. Is there any way of getting back to the supposed common origin? We can see how the look, gestures, words, moves, and reactions of a man converge in and are sustained by him. Can one do something similar with cosmic space, values, and affiliations—to choose a few? A philosophic defense of the reality of a single primal finality would be radically advanced if this could be done.

33 When the finalities are envisaged as grandiose actualities existing in some remote universe, one rightly deals with them in terms of the categories that are appropriate to actualities. Seen to be operative, objective powers, no more remote from the particulars on which they intrude than one's organic unity and worth are from one's bodily parts, or the space and beauty of a painting are from its colors and shapes, there is no warrant for doing this. There is still a need to make evident how the finalities are together, but no need to have them subtended by some further finality. Just as the space and beauty of a painting are united by the painting, so the finalities are united by actualities. Apart from the painting, the space and beauty are not united, any more than the finalities, apart from all actualities, are one.

34 I grant at once that this, like every other account, is tinged with preconceptions, personal biases, and idiosyncratic judgments. The fact does not preclude its presenting steady truths that anyone can know. Logic, mathematics, and science are able to confront us all with neutral necessities to which we all must submit, no matter what our predilections. Philosophy does not have their rigor or persuasive force, but this does not prevent it from saying much that holds, apart from the saying.

35 The objections that have been raised, not once but a number of times in this section of the book, and elsewhere, make evident that something in my view or presentation is at fault. Even if it turns out that others have misread or misconstrued or just missed what was said and well-defended, I should have made it more evident.

It is my hope that the present discussion will make good some of the deficiencies of the work, or at least allow others to see what went wrong, where, and why. But it can do this only if there is no doubt that I am claiming that there are undeniable evidences, sound, controlled ways of using these, and unavoidable outcomes to which they lead. It would be easier to maintain that all that is being done is to exhibit the outcome of a private soliloquy. But were it that, there is no reason why it should interest anyone.

ANDREW J. RECK

OBJECTIONS TO SOME SUPPOSED

FIRST PRINCIPLES

AT PAUL WEISS'S INVITATION I raise the following objections to his first principles. In other places I have offered sympathetic expositions of his thought. Suffice it to say that I am permanently indebted to him for his theory of actualities, which restates the lasting truths of Aristotelian substantialism in the face of the recent excesses of process philosophy, and for his modal ontology, which presents a viable, speculative, systematic metaphysics in an age of analysis and postivism, and a flexible dialectic illustrative of the most comprehensive open-mindedness to be found in the entire history of philosophy. Here, however, I shall stress what I regard to be critical defects in the latest formulation of his philosophy. My objections are: 1) methodological 2) epistemological, 3) metaphysical, 4) cosmological, and 5) theological.

1. METHODOLOGICAL OBJECTIONS

Weiss's arguments are wholly dialectical. As such they often exhibit the offensive characteristics of what C. S. Peirce has called "the seminary habit of mind"—they are often verbal, interweaving puns, jargon, paradoxes, and commonplaces; they are dogmatic, expressing the author's intellectual preferences and prejudices; and they point to no method which, if adopted by different inquirers, would lead to the same cognitive results.

Weiss's discussion of evidence promises perhaps to secure his methodology. But the discussion is perplexing. At the least it might be thought that the inquirer moves from the evidence by means of rules to the evidenced, and that the evidence is what is given and the evidenced the ultimate principles explanatory of what is given. However, Weiss offers, as far as I can discern, no such theory. Rather he classifies his transcendents and qualifiers, which one would suppose are his ultimate principles and finalities, as "types of metaphysical evidences," and he takes these to point to some other sources which are evidenced. Hence it appears that he offers a procedure which moves from what is already remote as evidence to evidencing sources which forever retreat before any approaches toward them. A guide to the perplexed, Weiss leads us not out of perplexity but to greater and overwhelming perplexity. I assert that, unless the philosopher, who may himself have begun in perplexity, and whom we seek in our perplexity, leads us to a truth or truths which we may understand, he has done us little service.

Weiss's use of language obstructs rational inquiry. The obstructions stem not only from the ambiguity and vagueness which are constantly evident, but from the way noncognitive and even irrational factors intrude upon the course of argument. Weiss's theory of names makes explicit the erroneous way he has permitted emotion to dominate logic. Against Weiss I assert that proper names of actualities do not in most usages involve "an emotional act of acknowledgment, sustaining an acceptance or rejection"; if they did, roll call in class would be emotionally exhausting, rather than the mere routine it usually is. Nor can it be shown that, as Weiss says, naming a finality requires help given by the finality. Although an exalted name displays the high regard and intense feeling of the namer for the named, the namer may devise another name, a pure symbol without value or feeling, to name the named. Indeed, the technical terms of philosophic discourse have been invented and introduced, in many if not most cases, to shed emotional and valuational factors and to unfold the transparent conceptual meanings. Further, Weiss's theory of names, distinguishing sharply between adherent and exalted names, leads to a ridiculous quibble. Distinguishing the actual cosmos from the ideal cosmos, Weiss denies that there is a proper name for them when they are together. Since to invent a new name, which is always possible, would be inconsistent with the doctrine of names Weiss offers, he resorts instead to a naming. Of the physical and the ideal cosmoses together, he says, "there can be a naming of it."

2. EPISTEMOLOGICAL OBJECTIONS

Weiss's theory of knowledge is a form of critical realism. In my judgment the consummate expression of this theory is to be found in Santayana, whose remarkable formula is that "knowledge is faith mediated by symbols." Santayana's view has, of course, rather austere implications for the possibility of metaphysics, implications which Weiss explicitly rejects when he denies that metaphysics should be conceived merely "as a description of the pervasive features of experience or of language." But it is doubtful that Weiss's theory of knowledge can sustain the task of metaphysics as he defines it—namely, to reach realities (actualities and finalities). I raise the ensuing epistemological objections to render the personal doubt objectively forceful.

When Weiss describes the objects of knowledge as defying the subjects knowing them, he installs a barrier between the two which cognition can not leap. While it may be arresting to say that objects defy erroneous judgments about them, it is wrong to say, as Weiss does, that "when I correct the error, I continue to be defied." I assert that true judgment confirms an agreement, a correspondence, a coherence, between the knower and the known. Without pervasive, precognitional harmonious cooperation between objects and subjects there could be neither life nor knowledge.

Against Weiss I hold that a particular subject may know particular things without attending "to them as present to . . . [him] in a way they are not present to others." That knowledge in the ordinary sense is communicable supposes that in principle an object as known is the same for all subjects. Only knowledge in an extraordinary sense—mystical intuition, immersion in immediate experience—neglects the common features an object displays to all subjects; but such knowledge is ineffable, with the particular subject knowing particular things *in distinctive ways* which may be denied other subjects or may be accessible to them only by special noncognitional means.

Weiss's theory of the objects of knowledge leads inescapably to their identification with appearances. Appearances, moreover, are both subjective and objective. Thus when Weiss discusses the boundaries of objects, he notes that when the subject imposes boundaries on the object, it is a subjective appearance; and that when the object is considered in its own boundaries, it is an objective appearance. In the first place, of course, knowledge consists in establishing some sort of congruence between the boundaries manifest in the two sorts of appearances, with subjective appearance yielding to objective appearance. But knowledge must go beyond even objective appearances to the realities themselves. Against Weiss I object that, instead of removing the veil which philosophers have cast over realities, he has added another veil; he has succumbed to the philosophers' hypostatization of appearances and doubled it. I affirm that appearances are reducible to realities appearing.

Further objections may be raised against specific points Weiss makes concerning appearances. For example, he seems to contradict himself when he says that appearances are contemporaries and that they also have differing careers. But such points are minor when the commitment to appearances itself is challenged. If appearances can be brought together in a single "universe," then the line of reasoning which historically led from "wild data"—for example, errors, illusions, dreams and so forth—to the supposition of appearances is aborted; the acknowledgment of subjective appearances justifies no reification of them. If, furthermore, objective appearances can be brought together in a single universe, then the distinction between the universe of objective appearances and realities is not real, but verbal.

The incoherence which pervades Weiss's reified appearances spreads to his conception of realities. When he says that a reality is "a continuum of intensities with a maximum at the reality, and with a stretch of ever weaker intensities making up the constituents of an appearance," he proposes a conception with inconsistent implications, none of which is tenable. On the one hand, as *continuum* the reality is a set of appearances, including its subjective appearances; in which case, embracing properties which do not cohere, it lacks the unity requisite for being a nameable reality. On the other hand, as maximum intensity it has a core whose relation to its appearances is obscure. If, in fact, the intensities vary to such an extent that what is maximal at one point may be augmented or decreased at another point, then its core will vary. If, however, the core is always the same maximum intensity, then its relation to smaller intensitives, appearances, is such that they are necessarily excluded from it.

I agree with Weiss that the intelligibility of things depends upon their having intelligible natures and upon their entering into relations which constitute laws. But I deny that it is necessary to posit Possibility as a finality to account for such natures and laws. That things are intelligible requires instead a "fitness" between the human intellect and its objects. Such a fitness will find its explanation within Nature without appealing to some transcendent finality. Natures and their relations dwell and develop within Nature, as do human intellects which are, in large part, forms of natures within Nature, so that there is no mystery as to how these intellects may know.

3. METAPHYSICAL OBJECTIONS

Weiss proposes that there are two sorts of realities: actualities, and necessary realities; and he further distinguishes five kinds of necessary realities, or finalities: Substantiality, Being, Possibility, Existence, and Unity. For metaphysical objections I focus on actualities and the finalities in themselves. I term my objections centering on the finalities in relation to one another cosmological and those concentrating on Unity (or God) theological.

In regard to actualities, Weiss, whose pluralistic substantialism has always appealed to me, now seems to be stumbling in a direction which threatens their integrity. He invokes finalities as transcendents and qualifiers to do for them what they do for themselves, to compel and control them when they neither need nor want compulsion and control, and to intrude upon them and violate their natures. No wonder Weiss's actualities become defiant!

In acknowledging Substantiality as a finality which accounts for the fact that actualities are substances, Weiss denudes actualities of their own substantiality. I object that Weiss's view reduces actualities to modes of a single Substantiality.

A similar objection arises with regard to Being. Indeed, Weiss seems to be incoherent, as when he says, on the one hand, that every actuality has a being by itself, and, on the other hand, that the being of an actuality is an alien factor in it. Weiss invokes Being as "a power which overrides their [beings', actualities'] differences to make them coordinate with one another." But if actualities are together because of the relations which spring from their own natural needs for one another, Being as a finality is unnecessary. Here it is helpful to remember that in his modal ontology Weiss recognized actualities and put over against them: possibility (ideality), existence, and God (unity). Subsequently he admitted Actuality, which now in his late postmodal ontology multiplies by fission into Being and Substantiality. But since Actuality itself serves no function not already fulfilled in the modal ontology, Being and Substantiality are not only superfluous; they also endanger the metaphysical status of actualities.

In the modal ontology Existence served actualities in the ways which should have restrained Weiss from positing Actuality later. Even now Weiss claims that "Existence makes the actualities be extended severally and together; it makes each be present, spread out, and dynamic; and it makes them all be contemporaries, located, and effective." In supposing that actualities themselves lack the spatial, temporal, and causal characteristics from which Space, Time, and Causality are constructed, Weiss not only has too low an esteem of their natures; he also wrongly hypostatizes Existence at the risk of reducing existent actualities to mere modes of it. In retrospect I judge that Weiss would have improved his postmodal ontology if, instead of adding Actuality and of moving from it to Substantiality and Being, he had eliminated Existence.

Possibility is expendable, too. Earlier I objected that Possibility is not necessary to account for the intelligibility of things. Let me add that to appeal to Possibility is to appeal not merely to a principle less intelligible than the natures and the laws accessible to reason in nature; it is rather to appeal to an unintelligible principle. Possibility is Plato's mistake compounded. Having wrongly reified natures and laws, Plato sought to account for their curious ontological status by introducing Possibility—"the power to affect and be affected," as he said in the *Sophist*. Such power has its proper place within actualities. However, blown up in a separate and irreducible mode or domain of being, Possibility allows anything and its opposite and in any order. Possibility is anarchy; and as anarchy, it is no first principle.

Weiss's treatment of Unity provokes questions which constitute cosmological and theological objections to his first principles.

4. Cosmological Objections

The fundamental cosmological problem is whether actualities and finalities constitute a cosmos. Mention has already been made of Weiss's difficulty with the actual and ideal cosmoses; the difficulty, presented as a logical difficulty stemming from his theory of names, runs deeper. For Weiss there is a plurality of "worlds"—worlds which are shut off from one another when they should meet together, and which intrude upon one another when they are together.

Although it would be tempting to conclude that Unity accounts for the unities of realities and hence the unity of the world, Weiss rejects the temptation. It seems that all the finalities account for unities, in which case Unity qua unity is expendable. On the other hand, if, as I have suggested, the other finalities are demoted as finalities for the reasons I have set forth, then Unity remains alone as the sole finality.

5. Theological Objections

Weiss's conception of Unity (God) is problematic. For Weiss, God is the principle of unity and value. Yet God does not create; he is one among five finalities; and actualities, which need other finalities to be what they are, defy him. I object that this conception is incoherent. I submit that, if God is Unity, he is the sole finality, although to demonstrate that Unity exists requires more argument and evidence than I can offer. Further, if God is the principle of value, then he is a creator. Finally I suggest, as a simple and traditional alternative to Weiss's system of first principles, an ontology of actualities, among which is one supreme necessary Actuality (God).

Despite the sound of harshness in my tone, I address my objections as disciple to Master, to one who has taught me that it is better to be overcome in argument than to remain lost in error. I confess that I have not stated such objections before, mainly because I have not understood these matters, and, even when I thought I understood them, I did not have the confidence to say what I thought. Of course I am aware that what I accept as understanding now may later be recognized as confused. And I welcome Paul Weiss's replies, more confident that he will overcome my objections than that they will stand.

*

Further Thoughts on First Principles: A Reply

ALMOST EVERY CRUCIAL CONTENTION in the present work is here questioned with such directness and lack of qualification as to make it seem incompatible with the generous esteem which precedes them. I welcome both, the one because it points up the need to restate pivotal issues, the other because it respects the effort that has been made to arrive at truths about what is primary and forever.

One should remain alert to the fact that the universe is not as paltry or as narrow as one's preconceptions or experiences initially lead one to take it to be. Every philosophy should be backed by a constant effort to keep in mind that the universe is complex and richly nuanced, and therefore that one should probe, explore, adventure in every likely direction for cues and answers, and be ready to accept what is found, no matter how ill it comports with what had been maintained. The account should be subject to constant criticism and, when found wanting, be altered or replaced.

Important though these considerations are, they are not enough, even when bolstered by an avoidance of contemporary excesses and timidities, and grounded in a systematic metaphysics, at once careful and bold. A philosophy should also be fruitful, offering sound and illuminating conclusions. It must not only always be on the way; it should also have solid, justified, lasting resting points. Since it is the presence of these that are now being doubted or denied, it is to these that I will attend.

1 The method I pursue, it is said, would not lead others to the same cognitive results. How could that be? Is it because I have misused it? Is it because it is too broadly gauged? Is it because its beginning is not clear? Apparently it is the last that is being urged.

Evidences are of many kinds, and are found in many places. The most obvious are those involved with appearances since it is the appearances that we first confront and particularly those which have to do with the ways that the appearances are together in space and in time (since these are evidences that any one can note, and which anyone can see can not be accounted for by reference to the items that are in the space and time, or by a mind, unless it be cosmic and stretched out). Other evidences are not so conspicuous; still others

2 4 4

are available only after one has separated out the finalities and actualities to which the more obvious evidences lead.

Transcendents and qualifiers are not immediately evident or available. But once use has been properly made of the evidences which appearances sustain, one can focus on actualities and note how both must contribute to the presence of appearances and a cosmos.

Whatever the evidence, it makes possible the forging of claims. These articulate the nature of finalities and, accommodated by the finalities, become part of them. Because the finalities have a greater depth and density than is contained in the claims, they permit of further advances. To say that there is always more to reach is not the same thing as to say that the finalities "forever retreat before any approaches made toward them."

2 A symbol's functioning can be limited in many ways and for many purposes. It can be used as a mere sign; a proper name has this role when used just to distinguish one item from another. Its functioning, too, can be suspended, held up, well before it reaches the depth where it would otherwise be brought to a halt. A composer does not produce heard music, nor does he just put down black marks. He writes suspended interlocked symbols which performers complete by means of sounds.

A roll call can be used to count the number of students; here their proper names are used as mere signs. But the names of the students can also be used with some regard for the fact that they are human, that they are males or females, or that they have rights.

One can take names to be indifferent sounds and suppose that they are accompanied by various irrelevant dispositions on the part of the speaker. If only this could occur, it is hard to see why verbal insults, affronts, and expressions of contempt are produced when one deliberately misdirects a proper name. When a man gives the name of his mother to a hog, he makes evident to the rest of us that he is saying something about her. His mother may be ugly and fat, but her name is a symbol of a person; his use of it as the name of a hog is an abuse of it, her name misdirected. Those who called their animals "Adolf" in Nazi Germany were summarily killed. Why?

3 If a name is not accepted or acknowledged by the one addressed, the name may still serve to distinguish it. But, so far, the name will be distinct from the similar-sounding name that is used symbolically. We then must say that it is being abused, as in the foregoing example, or that it is not being used at all—which is the way the anti-Nazis would defend themselves.

In prayer, in fear, in love, symbolizing terms are used; these are involved with the realities toward which they are directed. The unpronounceable awesome name of a divine being was long ago replaced with others, such as Jehovah, Lord, and God, presumably not involved with that ultimate reality. But they were quickly transformed into proper names properly used so that their application to secular objects is now an act of blasphemy, not just error.

But perhaps the divine does not tolerate the use of any referent to him? He does not respond. To be religious is to address the divine; a religious man has faith that his God hears him, whatever is thereupon done.

An Aristotelian God, completely involved in a thinking on thinking, would not hear; he has no proper name, unless it be 'First' or 'Unity'. These are names that a philosopher might use. Are they accepted by that God? If not, that is one good reason for doubting that he exists. But an Aristotelian God can be loved and that love is acceptable; the utterances which accompany that love have a symbolic, penetrative role, terminating in a finality something like what I have called 'Being'.

But no finality known to a philosopher is the proper object of love. Why then should one suppose that his designations of finalities are genuine proper names, accepted by that to which they are addressed, pulled into them, made integral to them? There's a double reason: emotions are involved in using them; they are part of final claims accommodated by that of which they are claimed.

Evidences for the finalities are intruded, alien factors in appearances and actualities. To turn from what provides places for those evidences to the sources of those evidences is to open oneself to powers of which those detached evidences are attenuated limits. Designations of those sources are emotionally carried toward them and are, so far, proper names.

4 Not all philosophical terms are names. Those that are, though perhaps purely conceptual in import initially, and intended to remain so, accrete meaning, value, and function from their involvements with their objects. It was perhaps an awareness of this fact that led Peirce to speak of his primary categories and phenomena as First, Second, and Third. But now they have an import they did not have originally, since they have been affected by the very items to which they were directed and into which they lead.

Syntax is a matter of formal connections, coherence; semantics has a practical, emotionally toned dimension utilized by proper names. If we keep to syntax we will miss what semantics adds, and will then have to content ourselves with maintaining such oddities as that 'Socrates' could be replaced by 'Socratizing', or that a commitment is enough to put one in touch with what is objective.

5 I came most reluctantly to the conclusion that there were namings which did not end with the production of proper names. I would feel more at ease if I could get rid of the view. But, so far, it seems to be inescapable, tied as it is to the fact that the actual cosmos is necessarily incomplete.

It is of course possible to name anything, even a naming. But one does not then produce a proper name; this requires that there be an object with which it is involved. If there be no such object, one obviously never gets to the point of being able to forge a proper name for it. A religious man has faith that his naming ends with a name.

6 There is, I agree, a connection between knower and known. Subject and object are not wholly alien to one another; because I agree to that, I deny that I am a 'critical realist'. Still, subject and object are distinct and remain so even when the subject acts in perfect consonance with the object, or names it. This does not mean either that there is something surd which is never to be known, or that whatever there is will be exhaustively known. The known is two-faced, terminating knowing on the one side, and continuing into the object on the other. We know some things. But our knowledge never exhausts the things known; if it did, inquiry would be at an end, and things would have no other careers but those that the mind provides. Even the Hegelian identification of the two comes only at the end of his dialectically produced system; until then what is meant is always beyond what is said; what is known is here, too, recognized to be less than what is, and can be known.

It is not necessary, though, to maintain that there must be a "pervasive, precognitional harmonious cooperation between objects and subjects" if there is to be either "life or knowledge." Cooperation is rarely perfect. To accommodate that fact, it suffices to remark that the conditions governing what is do have subjectivized forms. Without these, the subjects might forever grope in abysmal darkness, never getting in touch with anything that is there; but those forms do not guarantee an absolutely precise or adequate union with what is beyond them.

One can know what others also know. Such knowledge is usually had, however, at the very same time that one faces what is present in a way that it is not present to the others. You and I see and know the same tree, though you face it from one place and I from another. Subjective and objective factors are to be found in all acts of knowing.

7 I agree that mystical intuition and immersion in the immediate yields what is then ineffable. That ineffable need not be different for different subjects. Any number, while involved in individualized aspects of an ineffable immediacy can lose themselves in it and thereby become subject to the same governances. Mystics, East and West, offer rather similar reports on what they encountered.

I, too, think that knowledge requires that subjective appearances yield to objective ones, and that from these one moves to realities. I, too, affirm that appearances are realities appearing. This does not require a denial of distinctions between them. Appearances are products, dependents, caught in contexts; actualities provide one of the essential constituents of those appearances in the form of attenuated continuations of what those actualities are in themselves.

8 I fail to see the contradiction between the contention that appearances are contemporaries and that they have differing careers. Contemporary entities do not all begin or end at the same time, nor do they have the same natures or ways of functioning. A flickering light and the crouch of a cat are contemporaries, but have different careers.

9 Subjective appearances, of course, are not to be reified, and objective appearances are to be distinguished from realities. I do not see that these observations are compromised when it is also said that there is a universe of objective appearances. The shape of this horse is different from the shape of that dog. Are not these shapes objective appearances, appearances which are present when no one is attending to them in an individualized way? Are they not together in one context? Are they not together with my shape? And with the shape of everything else? Must not similar things be said about sizes, colors, and other appearances?

10 A reality could be said to be a set of appearances, more and more intensive, more and more merged and centered. That entire set must, though, be credited with a base possessing every item in it. This is the core. It is not opposed to all the other distinguished facets, but is the most recessive and the most insistent of them, contrasted with what it in fact sustains.

11 It is desirable, I think, to try to understand the universe without making reference to any finality. But one is compelled to acknowledge a primal Possibility, indeterminate and omnipresent, in order to make sense of a common obligatory good, and the laws of nature, logic, and mathematics. It is necessary to acknowledge a transcendent, final Possibility, therefore, not simply to account for the ways in which humans know, but to make intelligible the connections between and the natures of independent actualities which can be predicted in principle and are in fact made determinate in the course of becoming present. Other facts, such as the equality of different actualities, their affiliations, their presence in the same space, and their comparable values, lead to the acknowledgment of still other finalities, with a consequent clarification and explanation of what had previously been dark and inexplicable.

12 A reference to finalities must not be taken to destroy the world from which one began. Speculation distinguishes constituents and sources in part in order to understand the outcome of the latter's insistence.

Actualities can not make themselves be related. They can not give themselves a single, common time, for example. Nor can they give themselves beings, to take another. A common time constrains actualities in their severalty and together; all also have beings which are on a footing. The actualities are not then denied reality or being in time—or substantiality, intelligibility, extension, or value. The actualities are not modes of the finalities, but distinct realities benefitting from the intrusive presence of those finalities. Set in contrast with the constraining, explanatory, omnipresent powers that enable them to be unified and together, they must, of course, be described in terms which contrast with those used to refer to the finalities.

13 A difficulty is said to be present in the acknowledgment of Being. The difficulty vanishes, I think, once it is seen that actualities all have the same degree of reality, despite differences in nature, function, and status, and that a being is possessed by each. Once it is recognized that their equality can not be accounted for except by making reference to an omnipresent power able to coordinate them, it also becomes evident that each actuality has present in it a specialized form of this.

An actuality is contrasted with and is to be characterized contrastively with Being just so far as it is not affected by it. But it is then characterizable in other ways, some of which reflect the presence of other finalities.

14 Were actualities "together [solely] because of the relations which spring from their own natural needs for one another" there would be no constraints, no compulsions, no conditionings imposed on all of them. Yet, despite the fact that a mouse and a man, a tree and an electron differ quite radically in nature, value, power, and act, all are equally real. Since they can not make themselves be equal to one another, they must be equal by accident and by accident be able to become unequal, or an omnipresent Being must equalize them.

15 The status and presence of actualities is not jeopardized by the finalities. Actualities stand apart from everyone of the finalities, thereby enabling these to be diversified and specified. Finalities stand apart from every actuality, thereby making it possible for these to give lodgement to substantiality, being, meaning, extension, and value, and to be related in ways no one or set of them is able to prescribe.

16 Might one be able to dispense with an acknowledgment of Existence? Not unless one can dispense with an acknowledgment of a single space, time, and dynamism. Not unless one can dispense with extensions, limited portions of which are occupied by independent actualities and their appearances.

17 Were Possibility a domain of eternal objects or Platonic forms, it could be well argued that anything and everything is allowed, and in no particular order. One will then be baffled by such questions as to how many imaginary toads are in an actual garden. It makes sense to say, I think (restricting ourselves to toads) that there is only one possible toad, specifiable in an indefinite number of alternative ways. Each of these specifications can in turn be specified as big and little, fat, young, male, and so on. Such specifications are themselves only possibles, never exhausting the initial possibility. An actuality, though, in making a possibility present, exhaustively determines it, sometimes in a number of concordant ways. Reproduction by actual toads dictates the appearance of quite a number of realizations of a possible toad in an actual garden. Similar considerations apply to the realization of Possibility itself at every moment and every place.

18 It may have been a mistake for me to designate one of the finalities as 'Unity', since this seems to make it difficult for some to understand how the other finalities could also provide unities of their own. I was trying to keep close to what I thought was a well-established use of the term. However it be termed, there is surely a finality which encompasses and reconciles various limited, partly diversified unities. That finality solidifies all those unities, altering each in accord with a need to reduce them to one. Alternatively, it internalizes them to the degree that they can be accommodated without alteration. I am not sure, at this moment, which is the better formulation. Perhaps both must be used to express the double fact that Unity and unities are both real.

Would it be enough to acknowledge no other finality but Unity? I have already given reasons why account must be taken of other finalities to explain the presence of a single occupied space, time, and causal process, a set of coordinate beings, affiliated substances, and a rational, mathematically, and logically comprehensible governing order.

19 Should one not accept the 'traditional' view that there are many actualities, one of which is supreme and necessary? It would be easier to answer that question if one could identify the supposed tradition. Plato and Aristotle's Gods are not actualities. Aquinas (and the tradition he epitomizes) sharply contrasts creature and creator; Hegel takes mind to be the source of all multiplicity. Only the last allows actualities and finalities to be dealt with in somewhat similar terms; but it loses the obstinate distinct reality of actualities.

Perhaps the suggested view is what these different thinkers intended or should have intended? But they could not have intended it without denying that there were appearances and actualities, and the fact that these are subject to a number of distinct, independent controls and governances.

Everywhere there are a number of insistent factors involved with, but still distinguishable from each particular. They are the evidences on which I have tried to fasten and to trace back to their sources. If there is warrant for holding that Unity is a finality, some such evidence was extricated from appearances or actualities and used to take us to that Unity. We are then left with such questions as:

was the task carried out well; is the outcome of the process of evidencing properly characterized; are there not other evidences which will take us to other finalities? If these questions are ignored, they erupt once again when one tries to understand how Unity is involved with actualities.

R. M. MARTIN

AN OPEN LETTER ON LOGIC AND GO[

Y OUR BOOK is of enormous range, containing many challenging views, comments, and arguments. It is worthy of a detailed and far-reaching commentary. On specific topics many philosophers will take issue with you, but all will be in agreement as to the breadth, subtlety, and integrity of your positions.

It is often said that the most important problem of metaphysics is the problem of God—his existence, his nature, his properties, his relations with the rest of the cosmos. The attempt to characterize these in a precise and adequate way would seem to be one of the main tasks of "first" philosophy. It is this that would give flesh and blood to the "principles presupposed by whatever is known" and God would emerge as "presupposed by whatever else there be." And indeed such a characterization can be both "rationalistic in temper and theological in orientation."

You contrast such a conception of first philosophy with another in which "a rationalism expresses only one of a number of legiti-mate, partial attitudes" and in which "God is but one of a number of finalities." But is there really a fundamental difference here? A rationalism, to be worth its salt, must embrace all partial attitudes. Indeed, these latter must find their proper place and *raison d'être* within the former. And no matter how many finalities we admit, that of God will surely be the fundamental one if he is truly given his proper place. In short, it seems to me that your conception of ratio-nalism is too narrow, and your conception of God, not sufficiently comprehensive.

Let us reflect a little first upon the notion of God and his role within the whole cosmos. To be clear concerning this latter we must of course have as clear a notion as we can of the former. One would not wish to say that you have not provided a viable characterization of God's nature in this book or elsewhere; but it is difficult to say what this characterization is in terms sufficiently precise for the kind of rationalism desired. You speak of an "ideal cosmos," a kingdom of heaven presumably, "embracing the possible unrealized ways in which actualities and finalities could have been together." You men-tion that "that ideal cosmos is a possibility which other possibilities specify" and that "it is the actualities and finalities as maximally together, together as they ought to be." These are suggestive comments worthy of a full elaboration. It is particularly interesting that you build the *ought-to-be* into the ideal cosmos, and presumably this ideal ought-to-be is the ground for ascribing ought-to-be's to the actualities in various ways. In this respect you join hands with both St. Thomas and Whitehead, the latter being much less explicit in this regard, however, than the former. One would have welcomed in your book a full topography of the ideal cosmos, but it is doubtful that you can provide this without a very considerable extension of your philosophical view.

The ideal cosmos is presumably unique—there is one and only one—so that it will not embrace *all* "the possible unrealized ways in which actualities and finalities could have been together," but only the one ideal one. You mention that the "other possibilities specify" the ideal cosmos, but is it not rather the other way around, as with Whitehead? The word 'specify' here is perhaps not a happy one. In any case, the primordial nature of God for Whitehead contains "valuations" of all actual occasions with respect to each and every eternal object, each possibility for actualities thus having its explicit place in the divine envisagement. It is not clear how this can be provided in your scheme, and if not, just how it is that the several possibilities for actualities specify the ideal one.

Before we know what the ideal cosmos is, we must have a close look at how the actualities and finalities can be said to be "together." What is togetherness? Is there only one kind, or are there several? If several, how are they interrelated? Some perhaps entailing others? If we can answer these questions satisfactorily, we will have answers as to how actualities and finalities are together in the *actual* world as well. In a forthcoming paper, I have made some effort to characterize these modes of togetherness in terms of a theory of primordial *determinations, obligations, permissions,* and *prohibitions.*[1] Although the word 'primordial' is borrowed from Whitehead, the full structure of the primordial valuations is never spelled out by him, nor even so much as hinted at. If we try to articulate this structure, we will end up with a classification not too remote from St. Thomas's "five signs of will," namely, *prohibition, precept, counsel, operation,* and *permission.*[2] For an articulate delineation of the ideal cosmos, some such characterization of the internal structure of the divine will would seem essential. In this way also we would gain a foundation for going on to discuss the *ought-to-be* as applied to actualities.

Especially important among the primordial acts are the determinations, which correspond roughly with St. Thomas's operations,

---

1. "On God and Primordiality," *The Review of Metaphysics* (March 1976).
2. *Summa Theologica,* q. 19, a. 12.

or at least with a species of them. Whatever is primordially determined does in fact obtain in the cosmos. (The determinations are a species of the obligations, which in turn are a species of the permissions.) Some of the determinations issue in *scientific law.* Strictly a determination is an act or fiat: let there be so and so. There would seem to be no other way of providing a rational ground for scientific law than by primordial fiat. Scientific law should be seen to enter into the "real internal constitution" of God's nature in a most fundamental way, and not as a mere appendage. On the Whitehead view, and on that of your ideal cosmos, no explicit provision is made for the reign of scientific law throughout the cosmos. Perhaps such laws govern the togetherness of actualities and finalities, both ideally and actually, but this is never said, nor are the consequences of saying it brought to light.

An important consequence of viewing scientific law as emerging from the primordial determinations is that science and theology are seen to be intertwined in the most intimate possible way. There are thus not two kinds of truth but only one. The very opposite is the view maintained by the eminent physicist Heisenberg, who thinks that there are two languages, that of science and that of religion, and that care should be taken "in keeping the two languages . . . apart from each other" and in avoiding "any weakening of their content by blending them."[3] Scientific theory, he maintains, "is unassailable in its own field" whereas the language of religion "is closer akin to that of poetry than to the precision-oriented language of natural science." The ideal-cosmos characterization of God's nature would seem to come dangerously close to this bifurcational view. In neither is there a sufficiently articulated analysis of the all-embracing, unified structure of the divine will, without which theoretical science is severed from the rest of knowledge and experience.

Of course there is all the difference in the world between the existence of a scientific law and our knowing it. The main activity of science may be thought to consist of that by means of which we come to know laws. We think no doubt to have come to know some and that these are "unassailable." We cannot be sure of this in advance, however, and future inquiry may show us to have been wrong at every point along the way. *A fortiori,* then, we cannot be sure of any specific characterization of the primordial determinations, but only of their general content "through a glass darkly." And similarly for the other primordial valuations. We merely do, in theology as in science, the best we can in the light of such speculative insight and improved logico-linguistic tools as we now have. Just as the language of natural science is "precision-oriented," that of theology is

3. W. Heisenberg, *Across the Frontiers* (New York: Harper and Row, 1974), pp. 213 ff.

nowadays undergoing critical improvement in the light of new developments in symbolic logic.

Just as the ideal-cosmos view can not give us an adequate ground for scientific law without a considerable extension, so likewise has it failed to enunciate a full scheme of moral and aesthetic values applicable to the actualities. To spell out in detail just how one goes from the ideal to the ought-to-be for each and every actuality would of course be an enormous undertaking and can not be expected in a general treatise. Nonetheless one would like to see how this can be done in principle. It is not clear in your account whether moral and aesthetic values are grounded in fact, or primordially, or in some other way. Although you try to do full justice to actual practice—and this is admirable—it would seem that not sufficient attention is paid to the place of values in the ideal vision. To draw out the full consequences for ethics and aesthetics of the view that values are primarily grounded primordially would help to bolster an objectivist view, it seems to me, and establish some semblance of order in an area otherwise chaotic and confused.

In the adequate characterization of the primordial God we find, then, the ground not only for both scientific law but for objective aesthetic and moral value as well. But what is an "adequate" characterization and how is it related to language? You are sensitive to logico-linguistic problems, and in some of your book you might even be said to have made "the linguistic turn" in philosophy. Logico-linguistics is under a continual, intensive development and almost anything said in this area is liable to be outdated very quickly, literally tomorrow. There can be no doubt but that one of the most significant developments in philosophy of our time is the increasing recognition of symbolic logic as a necessary and helpful tool of linguistic analysis. Whitehead predicted, you will recall, that an expanded symbolic logic would proceed to "conquer ethics and theology." He failed to note that it would conquer language first by providing a systematic theory of logical forms of sufficient breadth to accommodate all manner of sentences of a natural language. It is this latter, it would seem, that is of especial relevance for philosophy.

Just as Aristotle's metaphysics is based upon his logic, so is Peirce's based upon his. Our task now is to formulate a metaphysics on the basis of the broad theory of logical form now available. Some valuable steps are taken in this direction in your section "Names" and elsewhere. But more steps remain. In getting at the logical structure of the language of metaphysics we must be ruthless of all fictitious material at the beginning, making sure of course that nothing essential is being excised that we can not introduce by definition later. We can not do better than to start, as Henrich Scholz did, with the truth-functions, quantifiers, and identity.[4] We then

4. In his *Metaphysik als strenge Wissenschaft.*

add the calculus of individuals (Lésniewski's mereology) and an event-logic with event-descriptive predicates. And then a systematic semiotics on top of all this. Only on the basis of such a foundation, it would seem, can we hope to achieve a logical theory sufficiently sensitive to the delicacies of metaphysical insight to accommodate a theory of the primordial God, and therewith to provide a foundation for scientific law and a theory of value as well. It is to be regretted that you have not espoused this logical route more than you have. It seems to me that the very meaning of 'rational' as applied to metaphysics is to be found only in this way. No item need be left out, although the task of accommodating it may become more arduous.

My objections to your book are, then, to summarize, fourfold. There is no detailed characterization of the "real internal constitution" of God's nature. The reign of scientific law throughout the cosmos remains, on your view, an unarticulated mystery. Formulations for a theory of objective value are not provided. And your conception of rationality is too narrow and not sufficiently based upon recent developments in logic. Even so you have written a remarkable book of high quality, of genuine depth, and of tremendous scope. If these four objections could be adequately met, it seems to me, you would have gone far toward providing "a philosophical edifice that shall outlast the vicissitudes of time."

God and Logic: A Reply

ROOT QUESTIONS set within an appreciation of an entire enterprise have a distinctive value. They bring the parts and the whole into better focus, and make evident the limitations of other views which neglect what is being held, both in the large and in the small. Satisfactory answers to root questions, too, make possible joint explorations in new areas. I hope I can provide those answers or, at the very least, show why some of the offered alternatives will not do.

1 I do not think that "the most important problem of metaphysics is the problem of God," and this for three reasons:

a) The referent is not clear. The Gods of Aristotle, Aquinas, Spinoza, Kant, and Whitehead share little more than a name, and are quite different from the God which interests religious men—a God who attends to, loves, knows, and forgives them, and who can be persuaded to change his mind.

In the past I used the name in various connections, but eventually found that I so misled others about the nature and functioning of the reality to which I referred as to make necessary a constant disclaimer that I was referring to the supposed creator at the focus of Hebraic, Christian, and Muslim thought. I now speak of Unity in most of the places I once referred to a God.

b) The supposed primacy of God has been successfully challenged I think by those who have urged some other reality—Being, matter, nature, reason, will, creativity, duration, energy—as basic to all others. They were not offered as alternative ways of referring to God, but as nondivine final realities. Being is too imperfect, matter too brute, nature too variegated, reason too formal, will too arbitrary, creativity too blind, duration too contingent, and energy too this-worldly to permit identification with what even philosophers take to be God. An appreciation of what the challengers are urging makes evident that the major persistent features of the universe require references to sources independent of God.

c) There are evidences available in daily experience which direct us to finalities distinct from God. Partly alerted by others and by my own reflections, I discern in a flower a number of distinct factors which are not native to it—most evidently, its location and being. None of these requires a reference to the God of the philosophers or

2 5 7

of the religious. All, though, need to be accounted for. Whether or not one goes on to acknowledge other evidences, these suffice to raise grave doubts about the exclusive primacy of God, since they are traceable back to finalities distinct from him.

2 Since possibilities are pertinent to what can realize and specify them, an identification of possibilities with eternal objects, forever the same, intrinsically without bearing on the course of the world, forces one to make the *ad hoc* supposition that God emphasizes different eternal objects at different times. What is the warrant for supposing that there is a fixed set of eternal objects? I have been unable to find any. Let it, for the moment, be supposed that there is such a set. Is God free enough to impose any emphasis on this or that one of the eternal objects, or must he conform to what actualities have done, are, desire, and do? If he is free why does the universe remain more or less steadily on its course? If God is not free to decide any which way, will he not have only an instrumental role?

3 A determination which is the outcome of a fiat is arbitrary and inexplicable. If the result is the rational, the rational will be grounded in an irrational. Does one stop with this, or put behind it still another irrational fiat, and so on endlessly? If we do need a fiat to account for the rational it would seem that we would need it even more to account for the irrational, and thus for whatever fiat we already acknowledged.

4 A ball arrives at the base because it has been thrown so as to put the batter out. Must God constantly adjust his ordering of eternal objects so as to keep abreast of the ball game? I do think that a satisfactory religious view of God requires that he be taken to be attentive to what is happening, but this is far from requiring that God must be appealed to in order to make the next moment be pertinent to what is now occurring.

5 It may be correct to say that Whitehead makes no provision "for the reign of scientific law throughout the universe." That criticism does not apply to what I have been claiming. Scientific laws are intelligible and govern what takes place in space and time; their explanation takes us to an insistent Possibility operating within the limits set by Existence.

6 I agree that there are not two kinds of truth. But there are many ways in which truth can be achieved, articulated, and systematized. And there are many grades of universality, justification, and assurance.

7 If inquiry is carried on within the confines of interlocked ultimate realities, there is ground for hope that the outcomes of all major efforts will eventually dovetail. That ground is swept away when everything is made to depend on an "all-embracing, unified structure of the divine will." This is not known to anyone and, if it were, is not necessarily bound to keep within the confines of what we take to be the rational. Nor is it enough to offer a cosmology, no matter how subtle and arresting, for this depends on the presence of realities with integrities of their own, outside and apart from their cosmological roles. These can not be reached if one stays just with descriptions, makes only the distinctions that current science seems to require, or ignores what is daily known.

8 I am glad to see moral and aesthetic values insisted on. Prescriptive, and more or less realized by actualities, they set standards in terms of which what has been and can be achieved is to be measured. But why must they be grounded in God? Do they not, instead, express an Ideal, a Possibility, germane to what else there is? Does this not obligate because of what it is, and not because something alien makes it do so?

9 Treating a primordial God as the ground for scientific law, logic, aesthetic, and moral value, is to face oneself, once more, with the question of the independent roles that these play and, therefore, with the question of how they could be produced by one, indivisible reality.

10 I see no more warrant for the belief that symbolic logic or language will conquer ethics and theology than for the view that the reverse will occur. Why suppose that any one of them should or will ever be subordinated to the others? Their prescriptions are different, and they are grounded in different ways. Is there any reason for supposing that any or all of them are at the roots of history, art, technology, politics, or anthropology? Of course, the supposition that one of these is presupposed by the others is no less arbitrary. How can there be a gain in understanding if we make any of them yield place to the others, particularly since they are geared to the natures, rhythms, divisions, and powers of different realities or products?

Logic may offer a fine way to move expeditiously and clearly toward the goal we all seek. But it surely will at last come to a point where it makes little advance. It is not suited for an understanding of process, rights, responsibility, making. Because of its formal nature, it will necessarily leave untouched some of the characteristic features and achievements, the distinctive methods and assessments of every humanistic enterprise. I do not think we can look to it to teach us much about religion, love, war, or peace. It even falls short of the needs of science. Let it be pursued resolutely, but not in such a way as to preclude other ways of getting to what is and ought to be.

11 Yes, I have not attended sufficiently to the "real internal constitution" of God. It is not enough for me to have remarked on the completeness and purity of his unity and the fact that it grounds, encompasses, and harmonizes all others. What must still be done is to understand what Unity is in itself as well as how it is related to the Context in which all appearances are together, how it enables all

actualities to be together, and how it helps each actuality control its parts. Progress in that endeavor is promoted by trying to understand what the other finalities are in themselves and the kind of difference they make to one another. Guidance, clues, and tests are to be found in particular disciplines and in a metaphysics. Art yields insights into the depths of Existence which in some ways go deeper than, and in other ways fall short of, what religion seems to have learned about God. A speculative, systematic metaphysics, in turn, makes evident what neither knows, while failing to lay hold of what they can, vitally and concretely. The claims of all need correction; all require help and supplementation from logic—and other disciplines.

12 It is not entirely correct to say, I think, that I have left both the reign of scientific law and the presence of objective value unaccounted for. I grant, though, that much more needs to be said than I or anyone else has managed to say so far. I see, too, that a study of recent developments in logic might conceivably help me expand my conception of rationality. I hope it will.

INDEX OF NAMES

INDEX OF SUBJECTS

INDEX OF NAMES

INDEX OF SUBJECTS

Terms of respect, 73
Texture, 17, 33
Theology, 64, 243, 254–55
Theoretical judgment, 149
Theory: law and, 146
Thing, 59
Thinking, 7, 34, 97
Time: dialectic and, 13; evidencing, 91–96 passim; reality of, 154; pure time, 156; actualities, 178; distinctive, 194
Tractatus (Wittgenstein), 223
Traits: of actualities, 136
Transcendents: condition, 48; actuality, 50, 58, 102–3; power, 57; dominant, 59; evidence, 62, 63, 64, 65, 87; names, 71; Substance, 118
Truth, 8, 97, 147, 258

Ultimate: creation and, 236
Ultimate particle, 124–25, 178, 181
Ultimate realities: particulars, 13
Understanding, 88, 94
Undifferentiated experiencing, 5–6
Unification: of actualities, 38
Uniqueness, actuality, 48
Unities: imposed, 14; actuality, 37; evaluations, 160–61
Unit term, 44
Unity: actuality, 50, 52, 180; living beings, 60; judgments, 77; multiplicity, 81; ultimate, 123; Being, 130; plurality, 138; finalities, 161–62, 250; religious tonalities, 166; unknowable, 167; sentences and, 167–68; De George, 198; Neville on, 218, 219; Possibility

and, 204; substantial term, 233; Reck on, 243; God as, 257, 259
Universal distinctions, 8–9
Universality, 187, 195
Universals: evidence, 66; names, 70; actualities, 98–99; De George, 198; problem of, 205
Universe: cosmos and, 182; history and, 208; symbol, 211; Neville on, 216; finalities, 235; not paltry, 244; God and, 257
Unstructured philosophy, 25
Used evidence, 83, 90–91, 95–96, 103–4, 105, 109–12, 115, 128, 141, 168–69

Valuations: Martin on, 253
Value: variegated intelligible context, 42; appearance, 44; evidences, 64; men as source, 160; teleological argument, 165–66; pivotal items, 223; creation, 243; actualities, 254–55

Wanting: mysticism and, 7
Western thought, 87
Whole: parts as a, 53
"Why," 219, 220
Withdrawal: thinking and, 7; conditions, 21; mind and, 81; evidence, 83, 84, 85, 88–89; Substance, 112; actuality, 118–19; Being, 128; extension, 150
Wittgensteineans, 135
Words, 74–77
World, 34, 243
Worship, 166
Writing, 76, 206, 210